$\mathcal{S}$EXY THRILLS

EXY THRILLS

UNDRESSING
THE EROTIC THRILLER

NINA K. MARTIN

UNIVERSITY OF ILLINOIS PRESS

Urbana and Chicago

© 2007 by Nina K. Martin

All rights reserved

Manufactured in the United States
of America

1 2 3 4 5 C P 5 4 3 2 1

♾ This book is printed
on acid-free paper.

Library of Congress
Cataloging-in-Publication Data

Martin, Nina K., 1967–
Sexy thrills : undressing the erotic
thriller / Nina K. Martin.
p.   cm.
Includes bibliographical references
and index.
ISBN-13: 978-0-252-03195-3
(cloth : alk. paper)
ISBN-10: 0-252-03195-4
(cloth : alk. paper)
ISBN-13: 978-0-252-07437-0
(pbk. : alk. paper)
ISBN-10: 0-252-07437-8
(pbk. : alk. paper)
1. Erotic films—United States—
History and criticism. 2. Thrillers
(Motion pictures, television, etc.)—
United States—History and criticism.
I. Title.
PN1995.9.S45M33   2007
791.43 65380973—dc22   2006029376

CONTENTS

Acknowledgments   vii

INTRODUCTION   1

1 PLEASURES AND DANGERS
   The Erotic Thriller as a Women's Genre   13

2 HOW TO BE A GOOD FEMALE HETEROSEXUAL
   The Erotic Thriller's Instructional Discourses   57

3 THE SUBJECT OF PASSION, THE OBJECT OF MURDER
   Refashioning the Gothic and Film Noir Genres   79

4 VIEWING THE PROBLEM
   Therapeutic Discourses and Soft Core's "Talking Cure"   109

5 SURVEILLANCE, SUBJECTIVITY, AND SOFT CORE
   "You Like to Watch, Don't You?"   134

CONCLUSION
   Whose Porn Is It? The Case of *Women: Stories of Passion*   157

Notes   171
Works Cited   187
Index   197

ACKNOWLEDGMENTS

This feminist investigation of soft-core pornography and the erotic thriller has gone through a variety of stages, and there are many people I wish to thank for their insight and encouragement along the way. First, I must thank Laura Kipnis, Chuck Kleinhans, and Mimi White, who saw the earliest drafts of my ideas.

I was incredibly fortunate to meet some of the producers, directors, and writers of the television series *Women: Stories of Passion* at the 1996 conference of the University Film and Video Association in Orange, California. Meeting these talented, feminist women, and hearing of their struggles in trying to make women's erotica, raised for me countless new questions about the female authoring of sexual materials. Elisa Rothstein, the creator and producer of the series, graciously answered my questions and put me in touch with Richard Bencivengo at Playboy Entertainment, who also was very generous with his time. Nancy Rommelman, a series writer, was an outstanding and energetic source and also provided an excellent essay she had written on women's implicit goals, and disappointments, while producing the series.

I thank my colleagues at Emory University, Matthew Bernstein, David Cook, and Karla Oeler, for carefully reading one of my first major revisions and offering valuable and thoughtful advice. I also want to acknowledge the Feminism and Popular Culture graduate seminars that I taught in 2001 and 2005. The students in those classes, many of them self-described third-wave feminists, helped me to trace the changes feminism has wrought over the last twenty years. They also provided valuable insights toward the tyranny of sexiness infusing contemporary U.S. pop culture. Special thanks to Cary Jones, my research assistant, who found a "bachelor-pad coloring book" in an early 1960s *Playboy,* introduced me to Jenna Jameson's oeuvre, and helped me find evidence of a curious stripper-pole phenomenon sweeping the world.

I am grateful to R. Barton Palmer for championing my manuscript and contacting Joan Catapano, my editor at the University of Illinois Press. He and Joan have strongly supported this book's publication, and both have given me the confidence and encouragement I needed. I thank Peter Lehman for all his help and insight and for putting me in touch with Zalman King, the man who started it all for me with his *Red Shoe Diaries*. Also, thanks to Frank Tomasulo, who turned me onto film studies at the tender age of eighteen and has always wielded his red pen with skill and grace.

Many scholars have provided valuable examples and templates for my work, but none as inspiring as Linda Williams, who broke ground on the study of moving-image pornography in such an eloquent and intelligent way that she inspired a generation of film students to study sexual images as well.

Thank you to my friends and family: Elles, Tim, Priya, Brian, Angela, Scott, Steve, Diane, Chris, James, Louis, Tom, Julie, Karla, Elena, Valerie, Peter, Kent, Ana Sophia, Laura, Antje, John, Patty, Sarah, Michele, and Mom and Dad. Some of you were forced to watch all varieties of erotic entertainment, good and bad; others kept up a steady stream of support and encouragement, especially when I could not socialize and seemingly disappeared for months at a time. You have all done wonders to keep me sane.

Most of all I want to thank Michael. Your unending love, support, and encouragement are my daily fuel supply, and I would be so lost without you.

A woman dances slowly and seductively on a spotlit stage, moving her hips rhythmically to a throbbing bass beat. Her hands roam over her own body as she gazes at the crowd, gradually unbuttoning her shirt to reveal red lace lingerie. She feels the pull of eyes as she continues to undress, dancing closer to one audience member and then moving to the other end of the stage to undulate for another. Meanwhile, women in various stages of undress are scattered at tables around the floor, some rubbing their bodies on either men or women, who are seated and watching. Both performers and observers appear to be caught up in the sensual environment, erotic tension mingling with the pulsing music and light show.

This vivid scene exemplifies one of the erotic moments in *Lap Dancing* (Mike Sedan, 1995), a direct-to-video (DTV) erotic thriller about an innocent actress who takes a job at a strip club in order to "get in touch" with her sexuality; after her "education," she is finally experienced enough to land a mature and sensual role as a full-fledged screen actress. Similarly, 2002 DVD releases (or straight-to-video features) such as *Lady in Blue* (Michael Paul Girard, 1996), *Illicit Confessions* (Mike Sedan, 1997), *Two Shades of Blue* (James Deck, 1998), and *Kiss of Fire* (Antonio Tibaldi, 1998) all have significant scenes in strip clubs, where the art of exotic dancing represents a means to seduction and a path toward a woman's gaining sexual knowledge and empowerment.

Still, this specific description of an exotic dancer at work (or play) resonates well beyond the small screen, for it also describes a Cake "Striptease-a-thon," held periodically at a New York City hotspot by Club Cake, an organization devoted to fulfilling "the experiential part of women's sexual lives."[1] Cake (a euphemism for female genitalia) was founded in 2000 by two female (and one male) straight twenty-something New Yorkers. The club has subsequently taken off, currently attracting more than twenty-five thousand subscribers worldwide and sponsoring lap dancing gatherings, vibrator parties, and porn watching nights—all specifically geared toward straight female participants and the men they choose to invite.[2] As one of the founders, Melinda Gallagher, suggests, "The women participating are doing so not to fulfill a male fantasy but to fulfill an empowered vision of themselves not having anything to do with the male paradigm."[3] This same "empowered vision" can be witnessed in Los Angeles at Crunch Fitness, part of a nationwide fitness chain. There women participate in "Cardio Striptease" classes where they can learn to take off more than weight, but they're warned, "Careful, it may also improve your private life."[4] As Genevieve Field, copublisher of the "literary smut" Web site Nerve.com, explains, "Sex is chic right now."[5]

The connections drawn between the representations in the erotic thriller and these contemporary examples of female heterosexual culture are not accidental. They suggest a powerful intermingling of sexual consumerism, feminized niche marketing, and a postfeminist focus on sexual exploration as the means to female empowerment. All these themes circulate through, and are perpetuated by, the sexy and female-oriented erotic thriller genre. Part romance novel, part made-for-television movie, part noir thriller, these films are influenced by multiple genres and introduce a distinct, gendered formula for visual arousal. The scene from Mike Sedan's *Lap Dancing,* which highlights the experiences of a sexually frustrated and emotionally unsatisfied woman, typifies their narrative and subjective focus. Two primary components—erotic sex and suspenseful thrills—combine to create the erotic thriller genre, a contemporary form of soft-core pornography that, as opposed to hard-core, male-oriented porn, deals specifically with the sexual subjectivity of women and the social construction of gender.

The study of an erotic film genre geared toward women is inevitably an exploration of contemporary attitudes about femininity, for the sexual materials produced address larger cultural perspectives on sexual behavior and social gender roles. What popular culture deems "sexy" contributes to the commodification and construction of the contemporary sexual woman.[6] Representations in sexual entertainment products and the materials that make the experience of "sexiness" possible—lingerie, champagne, candles, soft lighting, mood music—evolve from a longstanding cultural imperative to differentiate gender roles, situating women's desire as "other" to men's.[7] All of these signifiers then contribute to the production of a "feminized" version of heterosexuality, as women are repeatedly linked in films and other cultural forms (magazines, novels, television) to certain standards of sexual behavior and to the products that contribute to maintaining femininity's status quo.

The DTV erotic thriller is a form of erotic entertainment that specifically addresses heterosexual female viewers, and the emergence of this genre coincides with a definitive cultural tension surrounding femininity, heterosexuality, and feminist discourses. "Feminism" remains a very contentious term and movement within contemporary culture, where the 1980s backlash outlined by Susan Faludi has continued to transform public opinion surrounding definitions of feminism and femininity.[8] Celebrity critics and authors, whose work circulates in the popular press and on network television, instigate many of the tensions surrounding the "correct" definition of feminism. This accessible, popular form of feminist-related writing and discourse I term "pop feminism," as distinguished from more academic and activist-oriented writing by its mass circulation and its predominant support of traditional representations of femininity.

The DTV erotic thriller intersects with pop feminist ideals about sexuality. In the last decade, the popular press has been glorifying the "bad girl," and sexual experiences are seen as intrinsic to the construction of heterosexuality, evidenced in articles written for *Cosmopolitan, Marie Claire, Glamour, Redbook,* and other traditional women's magazines. The narratives and structural characteristics of the erotic thriller are similar to the rhetoric of sexual self-help articles that claim sexual experience and experimentation as a quick way to liberation and empowerment. Both forms of popular culture posit a hyperidealism toward the possibilities of sexual exploration, without considering the sociopolitical power dynamics that influence sexual practices. The erotic thriller's system of contradictions maintains an either/or structure regarding femininity, similar to the madonna/whore binary circulating throughout representations of women in all forms of culture. While the heroines of the films explore various sexual practices, an underlying threat of danger and destruction relating to this exploration always exists. On a superficial level, these films offer a kind of how-to scheme for creating desire and romance in the bedroom, and a safe way for spectators to experience "bad girl" sexiness—stripping, exotic dancing, and prostitution. Yet the films simultaneously limit sexual exploration through a system of dangers and punishments, where the heroine's "freedom" to explore is allowed within the constraints of marriage, compulsory heterosexuality, and romantic idealism. The feminist values of economic and emotional independence are always accompanied by danger and murder, so while heroines may experience the majority of their sexual interludes outside of marriage, through infidelity, the murders and threatening situations that ensue within the narrative reinforce the importance of certain standards of femininity.

The predominating syntax that shapes these films combines a romanticized, "erotic" appeal with a dangerous "thriller" narrative—a "pleasure/danger" principle. In the erotic thriller, the narrative thrust of infidelity provides pleasure for the film's heroine while simultaneously containing that desire with threat, often in the form of a murderous husband or a psychotic lover. Inevitably, someone ends up dead, and the heroine is either blamed or positioned as the next victim, suggesting that her desires elicit some form of punishment. The structure of the film perpetuates discourses surrounding active female sexuality within other pop culture forms, especially in the wake of the 1980s porn debates that coined the phrase "pleasure and danger."[9] Contemporary women's magazines, talk shows, and soap operas utilize both instructional and therapeutic discourses in an attempt to fix heterosexual female identity, focusing on women's responsibility for their own sexual pleasures (with articles and stories such as "Seven Days to Even Better Sex," "Are You Having All the Orgasms You Can?" "8 Pleasure Maxing Positions" and "The Better-Orgasm Diet!").[10] The erotic thriller replicates these issues, focusing upon the heroine's pursuit of sexual pleasure, yet regulating these desires through the danger these pursuits appear to entail. These films verify the instability of female heterosexuality within modern culture: a sexuality that exists in an active, mutating form that requires containment and suppression.

While this book can be seen as feminist film criticism, I do not see these films as feminist films; rather, I recognize that the erotic thriller emerged within a period influenced by the women's movement and its public media backlash. The tensions surrounding definitions of feminism and female heterosexuality structure the ideological meanings implied in these texts. In providing a context for these films, I look closely at two forms of popular culture associated with female consumers: the women's magazine and the erotic romance novel. Neither of these media forms proposes to be feminist in idea or goal, but each still contains discourses important to women, feminist and otherwise. In looking at women's culture, I also explore the way the media currently defines "feminism," and the interest within pop feminism in how "sexual women" relate to power and pleasure. Still, throughout this text, I suggest that the term "feminism" is slippery and elusive, a historically specific term that evolves and mutates.[11]

The foundations of this research on the DTV erotic thriller were laid years ago amidst a deluge of theoretical work on pornography. Hard-core porn resonates with controversy, dividing both feminists and film theorists regarding the interpretation of its meanings and function within popular culture. Hard-core pornography is generically unique in revealing the evidence of sexual pleasure and the construction of heterosexual male subjectivity through its conventions. However, soft-core porn dwells between two realms: the explicit sex of hard core and the rather mundane world of mainstream narrative cinema. In a way, soft core would appear complicitous with the worst of both realms, pandering in the blatant sexual exploitation of women's bodies while forming a universe around a male character's actions and voyeuristic gaze. Yet, beginning in the 1990s, soft core emerged in another incarnation that complicated any tidy definitions of its purpose: as the erotic thriller.

The direct-to-video market labels these soft-core films "erotic thrillers," the designation clearly readable on the display cases at the local video store or after a Netflix description, accompanying titles such as *Illicit Dreams* (Andrew Stevens, 1995), *Two Shades of Blue* (James Deck, 2000), *Sexual Malice* (Jag Mundhra, 1994), *Dead Sexy* (Robert Angelo, 2001), and *Bare Deception* (Eric Gibson, 2000). What distinguishes these films from mainstream fare such as *Fatal Attraction* (Adrian Lyne, 1987), *Basic Instinct* (Paul Verhoeven, 1992), or *Killing Me Softly* (Chen Kaige, 2002)—besides lower budgets, more sex, and "B" movie stars—is that they never play the big screen. These films are strictly straight-to-video or cable broadcast films, which displaces their reception from the public experience of a darkened theater to the private experience of the home. Their proliferation in video stores and on Netflix also coincides with the porn industry's interest in garnering a female audience, trying to attract couples (instead of just heterosexual men) to sexually explicit viewing. While hard core throughout the last twenty years became more episodic in structure, the erotic thriller combined both narrative and sexual spectacle, attaching a story to the interplay of bodies. Furthermore, erotic films geared toward women appear to require richly detailed, feminized mise-en-scène to appeal to their target audience. According to the way the films are marketed, with box covers displaying half-naked men and women in a romance-novel clinch, female-oriented sex and the trappings of romance are interdependent and indistinguishable.

This project focuses upon how the erotic thriller engages with female het-erosexual spectatorship and desire, for the genre does maintain certain seman-tic and syntactic elements that link it to other women's genres: the "woman's film" of the 1940s, the bodice ripper or erotic romance novel, the female gothic, the made-for-television movie, talk shows, and soap operas. Like most genres, the erotic thriller repeats a formulaic system that provides certain pleasures and fulfills expectations; this formula becomes apparent in terms of the nu-merous sequels involved (*Body Chemistry 1–4*, *Indecent Behavior 1–3*, *Night Eyes 1–4*, *Animal Instincts 1–3*). Each film focuses upon a heterosexual female protagonist who is actively negotiating her sexuality, the narrative usually fol-lowing the trajectory of her sexual frustration to her sexual fulfillment. Fur-thermore, male bodies are also objectified (within the parameters of R-rated film) and women are positioned as looking, watching, gazing, and acting on their desires. Frequently, flashbacks and fantasies are shown on screen to indi-cate the heroine's subjectivity, and sex scenes are very romanticized, focusing upon the mise-en-scène of desire rather than the explicit display of bodies. Sex scenes are candle-lit, soft focus, with billowing curtains and luxurious bedding, designer lingerie, champagne, strawberries, bubble baths, and much kissing and caressing. This emphasis on material objects indicates the connec-tion the genre has to popular cultural products and consumption.

Yet, a tension exists between the accumulation of material wealth and the lack of emotional and sexual satisfaction in the heroine's life. The heroine is usually a high-powered career woman, frequently married, who emasculates her husband by making more money than he does. The husband denies the heroine sexual pleasure, so she must move outside of the marriage in order to achieve fulfillment; this move toward infidelity contradicts many Hollywood narratives, past and present, where marriage is the goal.[12] Here, marriage is dreadful and often deadly. Still, infidelity, in the end, is never completely encouraged, as the heroine's experience of life-threatening danger indicates the narrative tensions such generic disruption causes. In an erotic realm of seemingly "both/and" sexual experiences, where a woman is "free" to explore her sexual appetites, the "either/or" structure of contemporary femininity maintains a firm hold. The madonna/whore binary means you can't have your cake (sexual pleasure) and eat it too (romantic commitment).

My research does not include demographic statistics or ethnographic sur-veys that would suggest who the "actual" viewers of the erotic thriller might be. As Chuck Kleinhans stipulates, there is very little reliable demographic information as to who is watching and buying certain types of sexual materials.[13] Furthermore, since sexual entertainment viewing is linked to issues of privacy, and in some cases, secrecy, the trail of "actual" viewers becomes hard to trace. While I think this area of film studies is underdeveloped in the examination of both hard- and soft-core porn, to constitute the exact audience for the erotic thriller would have to take into account the industrial and marketing concerns that construct that audience (and therefore have a stake in creating a certain demographic). Instead, I am interested in how the genre's specific formal, narrative, and textual operations position certain types of engagements and forms of subjectivity. The erotic thriller's relationship to other women's genres, as well as its narrative concern with active female protagonists, suggests its worthiness as an object of study for critical feminist inquiry.

Academic feminists and feminist film theorists throughout the 1980s and 1990s (and continuing today) critically explored the ramifications of hard-core porn as a visual medium and a male genre, interrogating the visual strategies used and resituating power within shifting constructions of sexuality.[14] By contrast, soft-core films, particularly erotic thrillers, have remained critically unexplored, perhaps because their structures resemble sexualized narrative cinema rather than the explicit sexual subjects of hard core. Their direct-to-cable or video/DVD status also removes these films from the mass-marketed ad campaigns common to the Hollywood mainstream cinema. Video and film critics often consider these texts as "low culture" or "trash," but many mass-consumed popular products (for example, soap operas) endure similar criticisms. An analysis of the erotic thriller allows an investigation into how pop culture manifests itself within certain forms of media, as well as the derogatory way "women's culture" is dealt with in contemporary media. Negative or dismissive attitudes toward the erotic film genre indicate fears and anxieties surrounding female-driven sexual representations and the depiction of women's active sexuality and desire.

The critical investigation of the DTV erotic thriller is important to contemporary feminist cultural analysis because of the genre's prominence as a consumer product addressed to women and its emergence within a cultural redefinition of feminist ideals. Sexuality and sexual representations continue to evolve, and the erotic thriller suggests ways in which younger sexually active women are negotiating gender roles and sexual desire through the use of popular culture—these negotiations frequently expressed in the writings of third-wave feminists.[15] Analyzing these films uncovers concerns about femininity and heterosexuality. Even though these films display a sanitized version of "deviant" eroticism, their repeated fascination with these practices signifies the way sexual ideologies are circulated and reproduced within popular culture.[16] Pop culture hype and products deemed "feminine" interconnect to define femininity and feminism's ever-changing parameters. The changing contemporary vision of "feminism" can be traced through exploring this new media expression of female heterosexuality and desire.

The scope of the erotic thriller's sexual images is largely limited to heterosexual representations (most frequently of white men and women, with few exceptions), which further points to the marketing conception of very specific spectators. Yet, the prevalence of these films within numerous venues—video stores, Netflix subscriptions, cable, satellite projection—produces a need to assess their historical and cultural placement within the entertainment industry, as well as their role in the construction of a popular women's culture. Ultimately, examining the presence of the erotic thriller within contemporary sexual discourse also takes a closer look at the way female heterosexuality is produced and regulated within contemporary popular culture, and how these discourses intersect with the construction of "feminist" thought.

This analysis is primarily a genre study, an attempt to posit the DTV erotic thriller as an example of a "women's genre." Chapter 1 situates the defining elements that make up the erotic thriller, established through textual analysis and a comparison to hard-core pornography, a genre with similar goals (to arouse and stimulate) but very different aesthetic practices. The erotic thriller establishes its connections to fantasy specifically through various mise-en-scène elements, focusing upon the setting of desire and an accumulation of sensual details. This chapter looks specifically at the work of the filmmaker Zalman King, an auteur who, over the last twenty years, has shaped and defined the aesthetics and parameters of soft-core/erotic films, creating a template or brand image especially attuned to cultural understandings of heterosexual female desire.

The combination of pleasure and danger present in the erotic thriller reiterates some of the discourses surrounding female heterosexuality, in which the pleasures of sex can coincide with the dangers of public censure and inappropriate or deviant behavior. These films often utilize socially derided sexual professions—prostitution, exotic dancing, stripping—as ways to explore female sexuality, and they give spectators subjective and vicarious access to the world of "bad girls." The way popular culture defines "bad" reflects changing views on female heterosexuality in the popular press and within contemporary feminist writings. Chapter 2 therefore looks at how "bad girls" are constructed and defined within the erotic thriller, and within pop feminism, and how both participate in the regulation of female sexual behavior. Likewise, some recent third-wave feminist writings on sexuality reflect an infatuation with "bad girl" allure, illustrating how certain popular cultural representations and images can affect discourses on feminism and femininity. This chapter also examines the way self-help and instructional discourses work to construct a normative female sexuality. The erotic thriller's recurring need to educate women on how to be "sexy" or "sexual" points to the instability of heterosexuality as a construct, and to the terms of femininity (and masculinity) that define and control contemporary sexual ideologies.

Chapter 3 investigates how a contemporary genre such as the erotic thriller borrows from, and in some ways transforms, genres from different social and historical contexts. In postmodern culture, new generic forms often borrow from and rearticulate older ones, creating hybrid genres that give new meaning to the genres they quote and parody. The erotic thriller especially borrows from the "female gothic," a genre known for its exploration of female subjectivity through actively investigating heroines, and its suspicious relationship to the institution of marriage, which is often directly connected to murder. The flip side of this genre is film noir, where, in the traditional 1940s form of the genre, the male character acts as the chief investigator and subjective point of view for the narrative. The erotic thriller also borrows from this genre, utilizing female investigators and "fatal men," or allowing femme fatales increased subjectivity and the ability to get away with murder. The erotic thriller notably puts a sexual spin on both of these older genres by incorporating explicit sex scenes into their narratives.

The erotic thriller replicates its "either/or" structure through the representation of the successful female career professional who is unsuccessful in love and relationships and, therefore, often unsuccessful at sex as well. This tension between the heroine's private and public lives is especially pronounced in examples of the genre that deal with therapeutic discourses and the doctor/patient relationship. In chapter 4, I look at three different therapeutic strands of the erotic thriller genre: the sex therapy thriller, the countertransference thriller, and the talk show thriller.[17] Each type of erotic thriller utilizes popular understandings of psychology and therapy within contemporary American culture to situate the "problems" of female sexual identity, and each type works these dysfunctions out through a kind of visual "talking cure." The therapeutic thriller also establishes heroines as experts in sex and relationships, only to undermine their positions of authority through both narrative and visual techniques. The heroine often struggles to maintain the subjective point of view of the narrative, and she is frequently deceived within the narrative by her patients, a situation that undermines the power relations involved in the therapeutic relationship. This chapter combines both Freudian and Foucauldian methodologies to explore the gender dynamics that are involved in sexual therapeutic interactions. As in other examples of the genre, the pressure within the narratives to normalize heterosexuality and female sexual behavior indicates their changeable and unnatural character.

The structuring of gender relations in the erotic thriller also translates into the way women are positioned in relation to surveillance technology and constructions of voyeurism. Earlier feminist film theory, from the 1970s and early 1980s, suggested that gender imbalances within the cinema were demonstrated through the male possession of a voyeuristic gaze. The erotic thriller, through its construction of female protagonists with agency and social subjectivity, also positions *women* as participating in voyeurism and gazing at male and female sexual objects. Still, the use of cameras and virtual reality (VR) equipment, to both survey and instruct, contributes to the pleasure/danger aspect of the thriller's structure.

The genre's many different ways of handling sexual discourses, and its specific focus on the trials and tribulations of heroines, suggest that the erotic thriller is addressed to a female audience. Yet, what the market and the (soft- and hard-core) porn industry offer to women may not actually be what women *want*. Since the adult film industry is male-oriented and male-driven, some feminists have dismissed the sexual materials available as created for heterosexual men, and they have posited the idea of sexual materials created exclusively by women, for women. While the question of female authorship seems relevant in exploring the construction of sexual materials and their relation to gender identity, this book's conclusion suggests that sexual pleasure cannot be easily defined by feminist politics or normative gender identity. While the erotic thriller stands as a sexually explicit genre unique in structure and style, its differentiation from other sexual entertainment stems from social preconceptions of female sexual desire. The attempt to make a form of sexual entertainment different from an already established set of aesthetics and characteristics further solidifies the ideological strength of male-driven and addressed pornography. I do not overtly dismiss women-produced-and-directed sexual entertainment as unimportant (as that form of entertainment contributes to the wide array of sexual materials available to women); instead, in looking at the erotic thriller and female-oriented sexual representations and materials, I shift my focus from whether women have a more "authentic" relationship to their sexual desires, to how those desires are produced and constructed through different circulating ideas about sexuality, femininity, and feminism. Through the tracing of patterns within a variety of cultural products geared toward female consumers (films, television, magazines, novels, clothes, luxury goods), one can eventually uncover the persistent representations and ideologies that construct gendered power relations within contemporary culture.

The emergence and continued existence of a sexually explicit genre that specifically addresses female spectators raises pertinent questions about current constructions of femininity and heterosexual female desire. While certain advances due to feminist activism and progress can be seen within the narratives of the erotic thriller, the threat and danger to the heroine within the films, however titillating, translates into a proscriptive understanding of female sexuality. Active sexual heroines enact elaborate cultural fantasies about sexual women, fantasies that are not ultimately empowering, but regulatory in their need to construct a particular view of sexual exploration and power. The erotic thriller, then, is a cultural product, a marketing niche, an educational tool, and a vehicle for sexual entertainment and arousal—a form that articulates contemporary ideologies surrounding feminism, sexual desire, and femininity within American popular culture.

1

PLEASURES AND DANGERS:
THE EROTIC THRILLER AS A WOMEN'S
GENRE

The narrative structure intrinsic to the erotic thriller is comparable to the conflicting discourses surrounding sexual women
within contemporary popular feminism. The celebration
of the sexual is accompanied by a corresponding anxiety surrounding
the construction of gender. Thus, the heroine's narrative trajectory in the
erotic thriller follows her growth toward sexual fulfillment and knowledge, a
theme that has increasingly become a crucial component of feminine identity in contemporary culture. Yet, these narratives reinforce tensions regarding women's role within contemporary American culture. In these films,
while women have become more economically independent and forceful
within the public sphere, their private lives subsequently falter. This generic
phenomenon within the erotic thriller cannot be explained by a simplistic
"backlash" mentality, whereby women are again being pushed back toward
marriage and motherhood. On the contrary, the narrative of the soft-core
erotic thriller celebrates the dissolution of marriage and heterosexual romance by relating these institutions to danger and murder. Infidelity is revealed as the path toward sexual fulfillment, the heroine's primary goal.
Within these films the tensions between the pleasure of sexual fulfillment
and the danger in attempting to maintain heterosexual normativity become
palpable, emphasizing the changing role of women's current sexual and
social circumstances.

The conflict necessary for the "thriller" part of the narrative creates limits
for the utopian "erotic" moments of soft-core porn. As Linda Williams has
suggested in her analysis of cinematic hard-core porn, "we encounter a profoundly 'escapist' genre that distracts audiences from the deeper social or po-

litical causes of the disturbed relations between the sexes."[1] In contrast, erotic thrillers deal pointedly with gender differences, their narratives continually testing the limits of what is "gender appropriate." These films systematically approach sex as an essential construct of identity, displaying it in detail. Still, the anxieties accompanying the representation of sex leave the construction of heterosexuality unstable, dissolving comfortable boundaries. The fear inherent in the erotic thriller, along with a conflicting mixture of generic conventions, mirrors the structural problems in creating new sexually oriented dramas for female viewers (or even aligning sexual entertainment with specific genders). These thrillers emerged amidst the "postfeminist" 1990s, a period in feminist theory and thought when popular understandings of feminism could not (and still cannot) be clearly defined. Within these struggles (past and present), sexual representations perpetuate contradictory discourses, simultaneously glorifying and deploring women as active sexual subjects.

Direct-to-video/DVD (DTV) movies currently saturate the market, filling in the spaces on video store shelves next to Hollywood blockbusters and fleshing out Netflix's online catalog. These films fall chiefly into three major production categories: films that are green-lighted by major studios and niche production companies as "B" products that feature their own cadre of lower-level stars; films produced for cable that never achieve a theatrical release (although there have been some exceptions, such as John Dahl's two films, *Red Rock West* [1992] and *The Last Seduction* [1994]); and independent, underground films that cannot find distributors. The soft-core direct-to-video/DVD erotic thriller and the episodic soft-core series on late night cable and DVD release fall primarily into the first and second categories, producing a genre of films that deal with explicit narrativized sex.

Structurally, the films exhibit characteristics of both hard-core pornography and R-rated thriller narratives, melding the two to produce a class of films that evades the stigma of hard core, while never reaching the level of "quality" associated with theatrical Hollywood narratives (especially in terms of budgets and stars). Direct-to-video/DVD erotic thrillers employ a different caliber of stars than those in the Hollywood mainstream, with very specific qualifications. While some A-list stars have nudity clauses and shy away from explicit sexuality, DTV actresses in particular—such as Shannon Tweed, Shannon Whirry, Angie Everhart, Rachel Hunter, and Joan Severance—are incredibly adept at infusing highly choreographed sex scenes with authentic desire, and they spend a great deal of time partly clothed or nude. Male actors cast in DTV erotic thrillers (for example, Andrew Stevens, Doug

Jeffery, and Richard Greico) must be prepared to bare all as well, for their bodies are visually important to the narratives.

Direct-to-video erotic thrillers significantly lack the marketing and promotional campaigns that accompany big-budget theatrically released erotic thrillers, and they are mostly advertised through video/DVD cover art and recommendations on Netflix lists. These low-budget thrillers have proved very lucrative and undoubtedly have inspired some big-budget versions. As James Naremore explains,

> Like the B movies of yesteryear, DTVs sometimes imitate the plots of more lavishly produced pictures. But in an era when videotape [and DVD] has become the dominant form through which people see feature films, it is difficult to say whether the big-budget theatrical market actually determines the important stylistic or generic trends. Major-studio films such as *Basic Instinct* (1992), *The Color of Night* (1994), *Showgirls* (1995), and *Striptease* (1996) were almost certainly made in imitation of DTVs, hoping to capture their particular section of the home-video market. The difference, as Lance Robbins explains, is that DTV producers "are doing *Sliver* without the $10–million actress attached."[2]

Soft-core sexuality also rides the fine line between porn and R-rated conventions. The films are often as explicit as R-rated narratives (and slightly more so if labeled "unrated"), yet they exhibit a frequency of sex "numbers," or scenarios, comparable to hard core.[3]

Still, the definition of what is considered explicit and acceptable sex within the mainstream is constantly fluctuating. Explicit sex and violence are often permitted on cable television (with network television indicating an "M," or mature rating, for made-for-TV movies and other programs), yet they are also decried (as in the infamous exposure of Janet Jackson's nipple during the 2004 Superbowl's halftime show), suggesting that the boundaries of permissible sex can be malleable. Sex as a topic of discussion and confession already exists in explicit detail on daytime talk shows, and daytime and nighttime soap operas push the limits of nudity, leaving little to suggestion. The home has become an arena for sexual stimulation through visual narrative entertainment, for video and DVD has allowed porn spectators (hard and soft) to view these films in the privacy of their living rooms (as opposed to the peep-shows and "XXX" theaters of the past). During this period of evolving sexual discourses, the erotic thriller genre emerged, specifically exploring and producing discourses of female heterosexuality and the construction of sexual identities.

The difficulties in defining a contemporary, emerging genre are numerous. As Andrew Tudor has outlined in his study of the western, "the crucial factors that distinguish a genre are not only the characteristics inherent in the films themselves; they also depend on the particular culture within which they are operating."[4] Genre criticism often also entails the exploration of the industrial practices regarding exhibition space, budgetary concerns, and distribution channels. The DTV erotic thriller genre includes films that are labeled as such by the industry on the video and DVD packaging, as well as films that exhibit formal and stylistic conventions that are similar to those of films called "erotic thrillers" by the popular press. Mainstream Hollywood films such as *Fatal Attraction* (Adrian Lyne, 1987), *Basic Instinct* (Paul Voerhoven, 1992), *Body of Evidence* (Ulrich Edel, 1993), *Killing Me Softly* (Chen Kaige, 2002), and *In the Cut* (Jane Campion, 2003) exhibit many characteristics of the erotic thriller genre, but they are still distinct from the direct-to-video, low-budget market that produces the lower-status product. The DTV erotic thriller is defined not only through its particular elements, but also in opposition to other genres and other formats. In this sense, soft-core aesthetics and narrative are compared and contrasted to hard-core porn and Hollywood R-rated thrillers, respectively.

A combination of "ritual" and "ideological" approaches will be used to explain genre, with "ritual" referring to the audience's participation in constructing genre, and the "ideological" approach relating to the business and political interests of the filmmaking industry that produces the genre.[5] While consumers (in the process of consumption) do constitute a market and contribute to the production of culture and its artifacts, the market, in turn, ideologically produces its consumers. Soft-core erotic thrillers may fill a need for consumers (primarily female) for sexually explicit, narrativized representations; yet, the industry, through demographic successes with the films and thereby an increasing exposure of the product, also constructs the need within the consumer. This interdependent relationship between the audience and the product (understood here as soft-core porn) depends upon a certain amount of repetition as well. As Edward Buscombe points out, genres depend upon "a combination of novelty and familiarity. The conventions of the genre are known and recognized by the audience, and such recognition is in itself a pleasure."[6] Genre films are well known for containing formulaic elements particular to their genre, and the proliferation of sequels adds to the recognition of the film's existence within certain generic categories. In the early 1990s, as the erotic thriller first became a recognizable genre, and a successful one, the structures of the genre evolved through the films' reproduction, producing numerous sequels. The films maintained ambiguous, inconclusive endings to leave room for the next generic installment (for example, *Night Eyes 1–4, Body Chemistry 1–4, Animal Instincts 1–3,* and *Indecent Behavior 1–3*).

Formally, the DTV erotic thriller's structure combines "semantic" and "syntactic" genre elements, these terms derived from a model originally formulated by the film theorist Rick Altman. He states that

> we can distinguish between generic definitions that depend on a list of common traits, attitudes, characters, shots, locations, sets, and the like— thus stressing the semantic elements that make up a genre—and definitions that play up instead certain constitutive relationships between undesignated and variable placeholders—relationships that might be called the genre's fundamental syntax. The semantic approach thus stresses the genre's building blocks, while the syntactic view privileges the structures into which they are arranged.[7]

The semantic "building blocks" of soft core provide a representation of sexuality specific to the genre. Direct-to-video erotic thrillers contain heroines who encounter sexual scenarios within romanticized narratives, so the requisite lighting (often apparently candle-lit), soft-focus cinematography, and attention to setting and costume elaborate on the trappings of romance within a sexualized context. Before investigating the aesthetic and narrative semantics of the genre further, one must explore the syntactic form that produces and maintains these elements.

The DTV erotic thriller emerges through the film industry's appeal to female viewers and consumers of sexual materials. These industrial circumstances interconnect with popular discourses on women, sexuality, and power within pop feminism, creating representations that sustain extensive contradictions and anxieties surrounding contemporary femininity and female heterosexuality. These same societal tensions produce the syntactical structure of the erotic thriller, building an inherent level of contradiction into the film's construction of female subjectivity (both onscreen and in the viewer). The soft-core or erotic nature of the films focuses on the pleasures of sexual expression and stimulation; each sexual scenario portrays the growing pleasure and knowledge of the film's heroine, often accompanied by the progressive building of a heterosexual bond, a commonly required component of Hollywood narrative resolution. These DTV films frequently attempt to equate sex with love within their narrative structures, but this narrative approach is foiled by the contradictory nature of the erotic thriller's syntactical structure. The films display sexual scenarios, while joining these representations with a thriller narrative, thus creating anxiety within every sexual situation. For example, the film *Sexual Response* (Yaki Yosha, 1992) tells the story of Eve (Shannon Tweed), a woman unhappy in her marriage, who finds a new and fulfilling lover. The heroine appears to experience pleasure and new knowledge regarding her sexuality through the sex numbers with this lover. Simultaneously, she is somehow threatened within the narrative, in this case by a sexually indifferent husband who turns out to be homicidal. Thus, the heroine is allowed to explore the "pleasures" that the narrative offers only if she faces the danger these pleasures afford—simultaneous punishment and reward (figure 1). The celebration of the sexual is always accompanied by a pervasive anxiety surrounding the construction of gender.

The erotic thriller also exhibits similarities to other genres, manipulating the syntactical elements of melodrama, the gothic, the woman's film, and others in order to formulate its syntactic/semantic generic imperatives. Semantically, the erotic thriller utilizes stylistic elements from these same genres (and also film noir and hard-core porn) to create a visual universe unique to its specific generic form. In a postmodern milieu noted for the appropriation and reintegration of past cultural artifacts, genres are no longer "original," for any new genre invariably contains elements of other media forms. New film genres are therefore hybrids, often parodying and reinterpreting the concerns of other film genres, placing contemporary contextualization onto previously raised issues and concerns. Contemporary soft core, particularly the erotic thriller, exemplifies this hybrid quality of genre. The form utilizes the affectivity and focus upon human relationships common to melodrama and the soap opera; it also contains elements of mystery, with an investigating heroine, and peril, with a heroine in danger, reminiscent of the female gothic and suspense thriller (further seen in the "movie-of-the-week" or made-for-TV thriller). The films often contain a softened, romanticized (but still explicit) sexuality similar to that found in romance novels or "bodice rippers," and they exhibit the alternation of narrative and "number" common to both the musical and hard-core porn.[8] The erotic thriller steals from all these genres to create an environment that simultaneously imparts pleasure and incurs danger for the heroine.

Figure 1. Pleasure and danger are entwined in *Sexual Predator* (2001). All photographs are frame grabs from the films.

The reintegration of generic forms into "new" forms has been interpreted and criticized by several scholars. Fredric Jameson examines postmodern painting, architecture, and film in particular, claiming that "real" history is lost or displaced by these "new" artistic forms, where "the past as 'referent' finds itself gradually bracketed, and then effaced altogether, leaving us with nothing but texts."[9] Jameson believes that the ideology of "style" has shifted, and that "nostalgia films" reuse elements with a "formal inventiveness" but strip these forms of their political magnitude through the irretrievable loss of history.[10] Taken out of context, the elements of film noir in a film such as *Body Heat* (Lawrence Kasdan, 1980) connote "pastness," but they do not resonate with the particular post–World War II politics of the "original" genre.[11]

In opposition to Jameson, Linda Hutcheon explicitly theorizes the political ramifications of reappropriation, suggesting that new genres perform a "cultural critique" through their relation to the past.[12] She states, "Parody also implies, though, another kind of 'worldly' connection. Its appropriating of the past, of history, its questioning of the contemporary by 'referencing' it to a different set of codes, is a way of establishing continuity that may, in itself, have ideological implications."[13] Hutcheon explains that the borrowing or quotation of other forms represents a "stylistic confrontation," where the meaning of the referent is significantly "altered" by its reappropriation.[14] The "continuity" or the process of a text's referencing and use of quotation thereby lends a political history to that specific text.

The erotic thriller does appropriate past genres (many of them "women's genres"), and the process by which it appropriates, as well as the context that allows these recombinations, contributes to the ideological charge in using these old forms. The erotic thriller purposefully uses certain semantic elements in an attempt to comment on female representation and subjectivity, recontextualizing the semantic elements of these genres into a contemporary syntax that heightens the film's pleasure/danger formula. For instance, if a film such as *Illicit Dreams* mimics the female gothic's narrative while applying stylistic qualities from romance novels and the film melodrama, this thriller then ideologically reconstructs these previous genres by referring to their history and simultaneously creating a new, contemporary form.[15]

Furthermore, as Hutcheon also suggests, the pleasure from these films comes from the viewer's familiarity with these forms and from the spectator's knowledge of generic reappropriation; the hybridity of the genre requires some recognition by the viewer in order to understand the work's intentions.[16] Direct-to-video erotic thrillers address and appeal to a female spectator through their reuse of familiar women's genres, creating a formula that genders the soft-core erotic thriller and creates pleasure for the "in-the-know" spectator, while systematically creating "unpleasure" or lack of recognition for the spectator unfamiliar with its various forms.

Film genres have always been constructed to appeal to different genders. In defining soft core as a women's genre, one must first distinguish the aesthetic and narrative principles that mark the erotic thriller as feminine as opposed to masculine. This type of genre exploration is part of a history (however short) of feminist interventions in film genre study—specifically the work of Mary Ann Doane, E. Ann Kaplan, Linda Williams, and Tania Modleski.[17] References to the masculine and the feminine stem from interpretations of the social constructions of sex roles—distinctions that are always malleable and fluctuating, yet solidified through performative acts of repetition.[18] The preponderance of female protagonists, and narratives that follow a trajectory of female subjectivity in the DTV erotic thriller, indicates a purposeful address to a female spectator through strategies of identification.

Because of ingrained binary divisions, social subjects are perceived by the market along a gendered axis. Mary Ann Doane's theory regarding the proximity of the female spectator to the cinematic image becomes translated into what the market perceives as certain "feminine" genres. She indicates that there is "a peculiar susceptibility to the image—to the cinematic spectacle in general—attributed to the woman in American culture. Her pleasure in viewing is somehow more *intense.* The woman's spectatorship is yet another clearly delineated mark of her excess."[19] According to Doane's interpretation of Freudian and Lacanian theory, because of the female spectator's proximity and overidentification with her onscreen representation, she is less likely than a male viewer to separate fantasy from reality. The erotic thriller speaks to (and assumes) this theoretical susceptibility by utilizing genres that are associated with the emotional and sentimental—the melodrama, the soap opera, and the romance. Yet this overidentification with "weepies" and "tear-jerkers"—body genres that the spectator feels through bodily affect—does not seem to translate to more "masculine" genres such as action films or hard-core pornography.[20]

DISTINGUISHING HARD CORE FROM SOFT CORE

The April 18, 1995, issue of *Newsday* contained the following exchange in the Personal File column:

> Q: I read with interest your answer to a man who caught his wife watching dirty videos. You assured him there was nothing wrong with her. I'm considering watching some with my husband. Do you have recommendations?
>
> Dr. Judy: It is useful to distinguish among three types of sex videos: "Hard core" tapes concentrate on sexual acts with barely any story or relationship. . . . Educational films (even with graphic nudity) spell out specific therapeutic steps to enhance sexual performance or enjoyment, while "erotic entertainment" is meant to be stimulating rather than educational, by presenting explicit sex in the context of sensual or romantic story lines.[21]

Hard-core heterosexual pornography has been theorized as a male-oriented genre, dealing with male spectators and female objects. Linda Williams in *Hard Core* has detailed the specific aesthetic and narrative strategies that distinguish hard core from other film genres. She surpasses stereotypical understandings of the hard-core porn genre and bases her analyses on questions regarding the genre's history and construction. Looking specifically at how conventional understandings of masculinity are maintained within the genre, Williams explains, "According to [the] stereotype, pornography is deviant and abnormal, but at the same time these qualities are seen as emanating from what has traditionally been defined as typical or 'normal' in heterosexual male sexuality: its phallic 'hardness' and aggression."[22] Sexual practices considered either "deviant" or "normal" are determined through shifting hierarchies, where those practices on the margins restate and redefine those in the center. As Williams implies, heterosexual pornography maintains a unique position within these discourses. In relation to class distinctions and acceptability, hard core proves less acceptable than "erotica" (or soft-core porn), which maintains a veneer of high culture; the word "porn," even within contemporary discussions of sexuality, connotes obscenity. Yet the aggressive sexual masculinity and objectification of women represented within the hard-core genre serves to perpetuate and produce "normal" male heterosexuality (a biologically determined sexuality that situates males as sexual predators ruled by a biological need for sex). Hard core is simultaneously "deviant" and "normal," accepted and derided.

Williams examines the characteristics of hard core that produce pleasure for a heterosexual male spectator, using a combination of psychoanalytic, Marxist, Foucauldian, feminist, and historical approaches. Like other male-oriented genres, heterosexual hard core maintains gender differences based on narrative strategies and processes of identification directed toward heterosexual men. In interrogating the gender distinctions that structure a genre closely associated with sexuality, inferences can be drawn about the relations between gender and sexual roles and representations. Hard-core porn is a genre associated with explicit sex, and its goals are sexual arousal; soft-core porn exhibits similar structures and goals.

During the late 1980s and early 1990s, soft-core pornography reemerged into the mainstream as an alternative to the episodic structure of hard-core video. In the 1970s, films such as *Emmanuelle* (Just Jaeckin, 1974) or *The Story of "O"* (Just Jaeckin, 1975) represented high-culture alternatives to hard core, with exotic locales and attractive actors. Yet, these films shared more similarities with hard core than with contemporary soft core, for, in the 1970s, hard core was explicit but maintained a greater emphasis on narrative. In the 1980s, soft core became prominent on the Playboy channel, but Playboy, as a popular icon of male sexuality, addressed these sexual discourses to a predominantly male audience; back then, the channel still represented impropriety for women. Then, in the early 1990s, Zalman King emphasized the female leads in films such as *Wild Orchid 2: Two Shades of Blue* (1992) and in the *Red Shoe Diaries* cable series, exploring women's desires through point-of-view camera work and fantasy structures. He thus provided the impetus for an array of straight-to-video soft-core films and thrillers.[23] Throughout the 1990s, as hard core became less narrativized, the erotic thriller emerged as a prominent strand of soft core that explicitly addressed sexual women, combining melodrama with the thriller to tell their stories.

Soft-core porn differs from hard core primarily through its visual and narrative portrayal of the sex act. Hard core is graphic and well-lit with close-ups of the sexualized parts of the female body and male erections. The emphasis in hard core is on the visual evidence of the man's sexual pleasure, encapsulated in ejaculation, or the "money shot."[24] Since the evidence of female sexual pleasure is never visible on camera (except through female ejaculation, which remains controversial), the visual representations of hard core compensate through focusing upon organs and orifices. This clinical quality to the shots and compositions in hard core contributes to its role as a body genre, through both representation and function (for arousal). Close-ups bring the spectator into the depths of the female body, closely examining the site of sexual difference. Because of these mandatory explorations or displays, narratives were simplified, and storylines were incorporated less and less frequently as hard-core exhibition moved from public theaters to private bedrooms on video/DVD. As Linda Williams explains, "Since the genre must keep close to the documentary evidence of this truth [of sexual pleasure], it has habitually resisted narrative elaboration, complex plots, character development, and so forth."[25]

By contrast, soft-core porn is similar to R-rated narrative, where sex is less explicit. Lighting is softer and more shadowy and closeups show indistinct expanses of skin rather than genitalia. The images focus on the surfaces and textures of the sex act, rather than the depths, usually maintaining a distance from the sex act for the soft-core spectator. These visual qualifications distinguish the softer, more subtle genre as "erotic." Sexual explicitness in soft core borders more on the norms of narrative film; penises and penetration remain largely invisible, female frontal nudity is discreet, intercourse and oral sex are implied. This limitation of visual evidence within the genre's sex numbers already stipulates a certain kind of relationship of the spectatorial body to the bodies on screen. Sexual representations are about surfaces, not inner depths. Lighting and soft focus create shadows and contours on bodies that meld them together as skin and flesh, a conglomeration of surface textures.

Soft core's focus on surfaces contributes to ambiguity during the sex numbers, lessening the rigid presumption that women are mere passive sexual objects without possible subjectivity. As Elizabeth Grosz suggests, the skin elicits a "double sensation" that dissolves the dichotomy aligning gender with passivity and activity. She states, "Double sensations are those in which the subject utilizes one part of the body to touch another, thus exhibiting the interchangeability of active and passive sensations, of those positions of subject and object, mind and body."[26] The skin and its cinematic representation signify this dissolution of boundaries, for "the surface of the body is in a particularly privileged position to receive information and excitations from both the interior and the exterior of the organism."[27] Soft-core film uses a variety of camera techniques to linger over body surfaces, both male and female, relating sensory experiences to the outer body while discussing, often through voice-over, the effects on the inner body; the two modes are seen as indivisible, even though the visual representations of the body rely on images of the outer body for information/stimulation.

Erotic thrillers maintain standard R-rating codes by providing more images of female frontal nudity than male, but the male body is also presented as an *object* of desire, gazed upon by a female subject. Male chests, stomachs, and buttocks are highlighted; female genitals are rarely openly displayed, but discreetly suggested through glimpses of pubic hair.

While soft core maintains gendered narration and address by focusing explicitly on heterosexual heroines and "women's genres," the shifting images of male and female bodies being represented open possibilities for a splintering of identifications over both gendered and sexual orientation lines. The focus upon body surfaces dissolves boundaries, suggested in the shadowy, high-contrast lighting that continuously brings different body parts, both male and female, in and out of the darkness—highlighting lips, a leg, a stomach, a breast, or the caress of fingertips. In many of Zalman King's films and television episodes, the camera circles the bodies again and again or cuts to a music rhythm, never revealing a hierarchy that would position the female body as the sole object of the camera's gaze. Doubled sensations become prevalent as shots encompass a man's lips and tongue descending and licking a woman's bare skin. At this point, the bodies are highly fragmented and represented in extreme closeup; anatomical difference is lost in the representation of lips and tongue touching skin. The fragmentation of the body, the turning of the woman into a fetish object that Laura Mulvey argues is a primary component of narrative cinema, becomes altered by the spectacular quality of the sex scene.[28] Narrative becomes halted by the spectacle, but the extreme closeups create an ambiguous sexual object. Does a female viewer identify with the lips and tongue, touching and licking, or the skin that is being touched? How is possessing the sensation of breasts related to the sensations involved in watching breasts being touched? Same-sex desires may be encouraged when a man's hands caress in closeup the skin on a woman's arms or thighs. Whether the female spectator identifies with the actor or recipient of the touch, the active or passive participant (or possibly both at the same time) remains uncertain. These questions become imperative in the sex numbers of the erotic thriller, for, in comparison with hard-core porn, soft core also separates "narrative" from "number." While narrative constructs female subjectivity within its parameters, the soft-core sex number, which is primarily spectacle, presents more diffuse possibilities.

SOFT CORE'S SETTING OF DESIRE

While the soft-core film represents bodies as soft-focus, romanticized surfaces, the surroundings of these sex numbers are equally important semantic elements to the genre. Furniture, clothing, and lavish homes and offices connote glamour and status for the heroines. An erotic thriller such as *Night Eyes 3* (Andrew Stevens, 1994) represents a successful woman who has a high-powered job (she is a television actress) and a wealthy lifestyle (she owns a multi-million-dollar home, beautifully decorated, which ends up requiring an expensive security system). The heroine, Zoë Clairmont (Shannon Tweed), repeatedly changes designer clothing, and the film highlights her evening wear and lingerie. In opposition, hard-core aesthetics geared toward men are much less concerned with the romanticized accoutrements of sex, for hard core is more concerned with unclothed bodies and their depths; hard core's visual focus revolves around the body, its actions and orifices.[29] Furthermore, the setting of hard core is often unimportant and barely distinguishable (even though there are some distinctive exceptions).[30] A director will frequently use the same room and bed for all of the film's sex numbers.[31] This lack of attention to detail is most apparent in extremely episodic versions of hard core.

The elaborate settings and costumes in soft core explicitly address issues of class and high/low culture. High production values and lavish settings give soft core the veneer of art or "erotica." These characteristics were also distinguishable within the soft-core fare available in the 1970s. Films such as *Emmanuelle* and its sequels or *The Story of "O"* were examples of a foreign film product (specifically, French) seen as artistic and sensual in tone. European soft core put beautiful women in exotic settings, yet these women were treated largely as objects of a camera's, and spectator's, gaze. The production values of these films differentiated them from the "lewd" Russ Meyer soft-core vehicles produced in the United States during the 1970s, shot on a shoestring budget. Films such as *Vixen!* (1968, distributed by Meyer's own company, Bosomania) featured extremely large-breasted women flouncing around in various degrees of undress with randy men chasing them. Like the women of hard core, Meyer's soft-core female characters were often nymphomaniacs, the male fantasy of the sexually aggressive and insatiable female. Still, both of these types of soft core were released theatrically, either to art houses or drive-ins, which provide very different exhibition experiences from those of current DTV erotic films.

Contemporary soft core maintains high production values, with budgets often two hundred times that of a hard-core film; yet, their budgets still distinguish them as B-grade films, for they are a fraction of those of mainstream theatrical thrillers with highly paid stars such as *Basic Instinct.*[32] The lavish sets of these DTV soft-core films do not connote the dirty raunchiness associated with hard core and the masculine. Beds are draped in gauze and covered in lace, candles softly light the rooms, and a fire often burns in the hearth. The wealth of the environment becomes part of the escapist fantasy, as in so many classical genres. The class distinctions between hard core and soft core produce and maintain the stereotypes of purity and goodness associated with women as social subjects and consumers. The influx of feminized porn serves to sanitize the sex industry; "erotica" is an acceptable outlet for women, while "porn" reverberates with a stigmatized, perverse echo.

As Naomi Schor suggests, femininity is commonly associated with ornamentation, a fascination with and overinvestment in objects.[33] Melodrama, a "women's genre," is also linked to a stylistic focus on setting. The film historian Thomas Elsaesser describes melodrama as "iconographically fixed by the claustrophobic atmosphere of the bourgeois home . . . reinforced stylistically by a complex handling of space in interiors."[34] Soft core also focuses on a "complex handling of space in interiors," yet its claustrophobia reveals the threat of sexual danger, simultaneously existing with the diffused light and draped fabrics of romance. Often, the DTV erotic thriller exhibits more similarities with the female gothic, a genre that combines melodrama, sustained suspense, and danger to the heroine. Likewise, the gothic genre, represented by classical Hollywood films such as *Rebecca* (Alfred Hitchcock, 1940), *Gaslight* (George Cukor, 1944), or *The Secret beyond the Door* (Fritz Lang, 1948), also creates emotion by its handling of setting, expressing fear through the presence of a threatening house. In erotic thrillers such as *Illicit Dreams, Night Fire* (Mike Sedan, 1994) and *Sexual Malice* (Jag Mundhra, 1994), or any of the *Night Eyes* films (1990–95), the heroine's danger and desire are elaborated through the space she inhabits. In fact, the entire premise of *Night Eyes 1–4* relies upon a heroine threatened within her home, who then must have security equipment, including video cameras, installed.

The emphasis on emotion through setting and its feminine associations connects to the female spectator's theoretical overinvestment of the image in the cinema. As Mary Ann Doane suggests, an emphasis on spectacle and excesses of femininity creates the requisite distance needed for the female spectator to experience visual pleasure.[35] Doane finds Von Sternberg's use of veils, feathers, and lace in Marlene Dietrich's films indicative of a manipulation of mise-en-scène that creates excess, femininity as "disguise."[36] The erotic thriller also manipulates mise-en-scène through the use of "feminine accoutrements," especially lingerie and lavishly outfitted bedrooms. Such an investment in objects and ornamentation implies a study of surfaces; similarly it is the mask or disguise that allows the female subject to experience voyeuristic pleasure. The erotic thriller, with its focus on both sexual body surface and the glamour and luxury of mise-en-scène, appears to specifically address itself to women. Soft core stresses setting, costume, and exotic locale to establish distance for the female spectator while maintaining emotional investment.

EROTIC ROMANCE NARRATIVE AND SOFT-CORE FANTASY

A number of mainstream critics have written dismissively about films in the soft-core erotic genre. Roger Ebert commented, "Zalman King's writing and direction are unashamedly sentimental, melodramatic and sensational. He has no greater mission on his mind. *Wild Orchid II* is the R-rated, spiced-up equivalent of those trashy romance novels with heaving bosoms and narrow-eyed rakes on their covers, and if you like that sort of thing, as the saying goes, then this is the sort of thing for you. It's preposterous, but after its own fashion, it's sincere."[37] Writing in the *Chicago Tribune,* David Kehr also took on King and *White Orchid 2,* pointing out that the filmmaker "has identified a market somewhere between genuine pornography and Harlequin romances. He provides titillation without intimidation, a sense of transgression without real risk.[38] And in the *San Francisco Chronicle,* Edward Guthmann wrote, "It's Paris in the late '20s, times are tough, and a girl has to make a buck somehow. That's why Elena, a sexy American writer, agrees to lower her standards and write steamy erotica at 200 francs per page. Of course, since this is the movies, Elena has to walk the walk before she can write the words. Research is in order—the kind that's conducted with champagne, candles and legs akimbo. So goes *Delta of Venus,* a dopey bodice ripper that Zalman King, director of *Wild Orchid* and *Two Moon Junction,* has freely adapted from Anaïs Nin's posthumously published erotic novel."[39]

All of these critics, in a rather derogatory way, deftly describe a primary focus of the soft-core erotic film genre—romanticized sex. While Kehr and Ebert refer specifically to Zalman King's *Wild Orchid 2* (1992), and Guthmann to *Delta of Venus* (1995), the semantic and syntactic elements of contemporary soft core, including erotic thrillers, remain widely predictable across a large body of films (as do most genre films). Feminist film theory and cultural studies have already had a hand in re-visioning various derided or ignored "feminized" genres—soap operas, talk shows, home shopping networks, and movies of the week.[40] Whereas hard core has been rigorously explored by Linda Williams, and romance novels have been critiqued by Tania Modleski, the relationship between the two—present within most soft-core erotic thrillers—has yet to be explored.[41] These films contain elements unique to hard-core porn and the romance novel, where erotic fantasy intertwines with a romantic suspense narrative to form an escapist haven addressed to heterosexual women.

As mentioned earlier, hard core differs significantly from the erotic thriller in its sexual explicitness. Soft core deals with the peek-a-boo quality of what is invisible, nonthreatening, and titillating. Where erotic romance novels can explicitly describe the act of penetration in a myriad of different ways (albeit with flowery language), soft-core cinema must try to maintain an R rating, making the depiction of intercourse a fantasy of smoke and mirrors, where the act itself must be left *to the imagination.*[42] This subtlety is the key appeal to the viewers of the erotic thriller, since it presents a sanitized version of the explicit sexuality of hard-core pornography. The ambiguous shadows that dance across the screen of many erotic thrillers, created through soft-focus cinematography and chiaroscuro lighting, trigger the use of fantasy, and the most fleshed-out fantasies depicted in these narratives are those of the heroines.

This distinctive combination of romance and suspense conventions and explicit sex creates a foundation of fantasy in the soft-core fantasy film and the erotic thriller. There is a profound lack of extraneous material that would tie the narrative to an overly realistic logic and coherence. The wealth and luxury displayed, and thus experienced through lavish setting (also a trait of the erotic romance novel), contributes to the films' escapist tendencies. Richard Dyer succinctly explains the purposes of escapist entertainment: "Two of the taken-for-granted descriptions of entertainment, as 'escape' and as 'wish-fulfillment,' point to its central thrust, namely, utopianism. Entertainment offers the image of 'something better' to escape into, or something we want deeply that our day-to-day lives don't provide. Alternatives, hopes, wishes—these are the stuff of utopia, the sense that things could be better, that something other than what is can be imagined and maybe realised."[43]

Although the filmic utopia represented within the erotic thriller is sullied by the threatening aspects of its suspense thriller narrative, the romantic qualities of the genre still exhibit escapist characteristics. This utopian outlook is also prevalent in the escapist fiction of erotic romances, the genre most critics compare to the soft-core film. These novels, full of kidnappings, pirates, dangerous highwaymen, heiresses, and torrid adventures, diverge greatly from the gritty realities of minimum wage jobs, five kids, a not-so-exciting sex life with a husband of twenty years, or a quiet night with the cat. As one romance writer has said, "I'm always amused when such critics accuse romances of being unrealistic—talk about missing the point! Of course they're unrealistic, that's *why* we like them. Anybody who wants realism can find it in the nonfiction section of the bookstore or on the news."[44] What is profoundly appealing about these genres is their *lack* of reality, leaving room into which slips the force of fantasy.

Even though some similarities can be drawn between the hard-core genre and these soft-core erotic films, the narrative structures of the latter, with their romantic influences, are invested in maintaining a certain lack of gratification that is not available to the hard-core viewer. This suspension of gratification is intrinsic to the romance heroine (who usually does not achieve her goal—the love of the hero—until the end of the novel) and to the narrative film in itself (where, without the maintenance of an enigma, resolved at the film's conclusion, there is no film).[45] As Ann Barr Snitow states in her analysis of mass market romances, "In romanticized sexuality, the pleasure lies in the distance itself. Waiting, anticipation, anxiety—those represent the high points of sexual experience."[46] The anxiety that heightens sensual experience in romantic fiction is also incorporated into the suspense plot of the erotic thriller, where the pleasure and danger of sex are hopelessly interdependent upon each other for titillation. This conventional use of both romantic and suspense elements (also common to made-for-TV movies) is what creates familiarity for the female spectator.

As the film theorist Elizabeth Cowie states, "Conventions are thus the means by which the structuring of desire is represented in public forms. . . . What is necessary for any public forms of fantasy, for their collective consumption, is not universal objects of desire, but a setting of desiring in which we can find our place(s)."[47] Although the conventions in contemporary soft core may be derided by some critics, repeated aesthetic qualities are highly recognizable and accessible to certain audiences; for those conversant with erotic romances and their specific appeal to heterosexual women, soft-core film conventions will seem very familiar.

Films of the soft-core genre are lush with "feminized" touches, focusing always on the clothing and living spaces of the characters and the requisite romance and glamour conveyed through their possessions; these are characteristics specific to romance novels and "feminine" fictions. As Kathleen Gilles Seidel explains, "The appearance and wardrobe of the male hard-boiled detective don't matter to him or to the people he encounters. Mystery readers don't expect much description of hairstyles and sleeve length. Romance readers do. They are interested in the physical detail of the fantasy world. They want to know what the characters look like: they want clothes and rooms described."[48]

Physical appearance and setting are articulated through the wisps of a curtain and the lace on lingerie; fashion always makes an important statement. In the film *Red Shoe Diaries* (Zalman King, 1990), the instigation for desire is the high-heeled red shoes designed by Kenneth Cole that the heroine purchases from her seducer. The protagonist is also shown in numerous combinations of lingerie that subtly peek out from between the folds of her designer clothes (the film credits the costumes to the fashion designer Randolph Duke). King eventually developed Web sites for both the *Red Shoe Diaries* and *Chromiumblue.com* erotic series that would help connect viewers/consumers to the luxury products that they saw on screen (although the site for *Chromiumblue.com* would never come to fruition due to Showtime's premature cancellation of the series).

In the erotic thriller *The Dark Dancer* (Robert Burge, 1995), Margaret (Shannon Tweed) is a college professor by day but wears glamorous costumes when she masquerades as an exotic dancer at night. The camera explores the palatial house owned by Grace, an executive financial adviser in *Smooth Operator* (Kelley Cauthen, 1995), focusing on the shimmering blue water of her swimming pool and on the rows of luxurious clothing lining her walk-in closet. Similarly, each house in the *Night Eyes* erotic thriller series exhibits material signs of wealth and luxury, a visual display of elegance emphasized throughout the requisite installation of high-tech video surveillance equipment. In Robert Angelo's *Sexual Predator* (2001), a great deal of screen time is spent on Beth's (Angie Everhart) slinky black gown as she visits an underground sex club with J.C. (Richard Greico). Likewise, when Amanda (Rachel Hunter) visits the home of two wealthy Welland University law students in James Deck's *Pendulum* (2001), she admires not only their beautifully decorated loft space, but also the designer clothes they wear.

Every scene focuses upon the heroine's or other characters' luxuries, and the incongruity of these goods within the scene reinforces the notable lack of "reality" in these films, not the fantasies of desire they stimulate. Both the erotic anthology series and the erotic thriller create a "fore-pleasure" through aesthetic objects, which sets up the spectator to experience the fantasy. This arranging of desire is what Elizabeth Cowie defines as "a veritable *mise-en-scène* of desire."[49] The appearance of "all that glamour and style" is typical of many female genres and is important to fantasy, which allows the fantasizer to escape her own life and settle into a more glamorous environment.[50]

If fantasy is about the mise-en-scène of desire, where a spectator can observe the scene and shift identification with many of the characters, then soft core's fantasy structure provides another opportunity for a more varied, malleable form of spectatorship (focusing again on surfaces rather than depths).[51] As Elizabeth Cowie explains, "The audience is opened to the 'greater pleasure' of the fantasy by a fore-pleasure produced through the aesthetic or formal presentation rather than by an *a priori* identification with the fantasy as such. The aesthetic is then another level on which conventions of representation are brought to bear, but in this case it does not extend the workings of censorship, but enables it to be undermined."[52] With the explicit focus on setting and a romanticized aesthetic, the "fore-pleasure" set up by the erotic thriller perpetuates and reinterprets conventions from other women's genres, especially the erotic romance novel.

The one area that proves most elusive to the influence of censorship, despite the belief that "the personal is the political," is the realm of fantasy.[53] When discussing fantasy, there is a difference between "phantasy," as a working of the unconscious mind, and "fantasy," as a working of the conscious mind. Leslie Stern best states this distinction in terms of Freud's work on fantasy.

> Much psychoanalytically-oriented work on the cinema has dealt with phantasy. . . . The understanding of "phantasy" used in this theoretical work is fairly broad, and indeed capitalises on a lack of clarity in Freud's own work. Freud uses the term in three ways: firstly, to denote conscious imaginings or day dreams (in less specialised writings this is often spelt "fantasy"); secondly, to denote unconscious phantasies which have a similar structure to dreams in that their origin lies in repressed material . . . and thirdly, to denote primal phantasies, fundamental unconscious structures which transcend individual experience.[54]

This distinction between conscious fantasy construction and unconscious phantasy is important to the argument over sexual and pornographic representation. In the stereotype of female overidentification with image and narrative, women are thought not to be able to distinguish between the stories they are reading and the lives they are living, even when romance novels are well known as "escapist" fiction. As Daphne Clair, an erotic romance author, states, "Kathleen Woodiwiss's *The Flame and the Flower* and Rosemary Rogers's *Sweet Savage Love* generated a flood of immensely successful rape-romances that enraged feminists, created guilt in many avid readers, and were cited as perpetuating the notion that women really do like to be forced. (We might assume then that men, major consumers of thrillers, westerns, and detective fiction, enjoy being beaten up, tortured, shot, stabbed, dragged by galloping horses, and thrown out of moving vehicles.)"[55]

The notion that women (and men) are ruled or controlled by images and sexual representations places an overwhelming emphasis on the effect of fantasy on the unconscious; this diminishes the conscious agency involved in creating sexual fantasy for one's own pleasure, and it supports the belief that women identify too closely with their fantasies and cannot distinguish fantasy from reality.

Bodice rippers and erotic romance novels employ familiar conventions for their fans, and the utilization of escapism and fantasy is central to their enjoyment. There is no prescribed way to identify with the characters, although the books are often structured in the heroine's voice and point of view. Identification can shift throughout the narrative, contradicting the idea that the female reader is enthralled only in the fantasies of submission.

As the romance novelist Jayne Ann Krentz states, "There are also occasions in the books when the reader identifies with both hero and heroine simultaneously. This simultaneous identification is very common during love scenes. Seductions in well-written romance novels are especially powerful because the reader experiences them as both seducer and seduced."[56] These shifting identifications allow for the fluctuation of subject positions in the novel as well as in soft-core and erotic thriller films; this flexibility can be attached to the experience of fantasies in other public forms in presenting "a setting of desiring in which we can find our place(s)."[57]

Fantasy and romanticized sexuality are intrinsic to both the erotic romance novel and the erotic thriller. Bodice rippers are a literary version of soft core. Both types of texts maintain a distance from the sexual act, either through the use of language or through unfocused and softly lit visuals. The narratives of romance novels reflect soft core in their ability to delay the gratification of sexual pleasure. Delayed gratification is one of the primary traits of the soft-core genre, and it works on several different levels. For one, hard-core porn is about sexual gratification and the overt signs of pleasure (visual for men, aural for women). The episodic nature of heterosexual hard core allows gratification to be experienced by the spectator (addressed as male) again and again. Soft core's allure is cumulative; the heroine of soft core often experiences a great deal of erotic tension. Sexual gratification occurs, albeit less graphically, but *true* gratification occurs only once the love relationship is formed. This narrative structure of increased erotic tension can be seen especially in films such as *Poison Ivy 2: Lily* (Anne Goursand, 1996) or *Personals 2: Casualsex.com* (Kelley Cauthen, 2002), where the heroine has sexual experiences but they are not as meaningful as the love relationship she develops at the end of the film.

This particular narrative structure is repeated again and again in the erotic romance novel. As Carol Thurston explains in her analysis of that genre, "Women romance readers seem to derive a sustained level of sexual awareness and pleasure from the tension built into the development of this loving relationship *over time*."[58] The narrative of the erotic thriller sustains a level of anticipation on both a romantic level (will the man and woman form a couple?) as well as the suspense level (will the murderer be caught, will the danger end?). What remains crucial is the prolonged (and simultaneous) experience of these two narrative strains in order to maintain the DTV erotic thriller's titillation; in fact, many erotic thrillers end uncertainly, or with narrative gaps, so that sequels can exist, such as the films in the *Body*

Chemistry series. In contrast to the erotic thriller, hard core forgoes anticipation for frequent and prolonged gratification both visually and narratively. A sequel in either genre would suggest "more of the same," but expectations for hard core and soft core are structured very differently.

Delayed gratification in soft core is played out on a visual register and on an aural register as well. Visually, the spectator is not allowed to see penetration, erections, or graphic oral sex; instead, the aesthetic properties of soft core keep sexuality suggestive. Similarly, the erotic romance novel uses vivid metaphors and analogies to describe the sex act, but it never clinically discusses body parts or acts. Titillation comes in the form of verbal explanations and descriptions in both genres, and it frequently occurs in erotic thrillers that deal with therapeutic discourse and sexual confession.[59] While the spectator of such films may not be able to witness explicit sex (in order to maintain the film's R rating), the film's characters can verbally describe their sexual encounters. The telling of the erotic story becomes a form of oral foreplay, existing for the character and the spectator simultaneously; this narrative technique contributes to the delayed gratification of the genre and connects the erotic thriller to the romance novel. Carol Thurston describes the allure of the "twice-told tale" in the romance novel, as contributing to anticipation and delaying gratification.

> First [the hero] tells the heroine exactly how he wants to and is going to make love to her (verbal foreplay), thereby putting the reader in a state of anticipation and heightening the intensity of every encounter between the two characters thereafter until the event actually takes place, fifty or more pages further along, when it is described again. This time factor is not only crucial to the erotic romance, but also speaks to what many women believe to be a fundamental difference between pornography and erotica—the encounter versus the relationship—and ultimately to why one is sexually stimulating to most women while the other usually is not.[60]

Thurston distinguishes between pornography and erotica by focusing on the reliance on narrative tension for arousal, thus validating the connection between narrative and the feminine (men are stimulated visually, women cerebrally). While this belief is commonly asserted in relation to sexual materials and representations (perhaps due to the preponderance of female objectification within our culture), this gender distinction is difficult (if not impossible) to prove. The marketing of erotic materials supports these social conventions, producing a desire in the female consumer for "narrative," but the need for narrative is not an inherent characteristic of gender difference. Still, both soft-core film and erotic romance novels support these distinctions; in both media, the sex act is often a culmination of the narrative and is laden with emotional investment. Narrative encourages identification with characters through their psyches as well as their bodies; it also prolongs sexual gratification. Through strategies such as the "twice-told tale," the explicit use of anticipation for a "women's genre" is reiterated in the erotic thriller. Creating certain expectations in the spectator through delayed gratification is essential to the soft-core narrative.

THE WORKINGS OF NARRATIVE WITHIN THE EROTIC THRILLER

One of the most distinctive differences between hard-core and soft-core porn is the quality and quantity of their respective narratives. Although both genres are structured somewhat episodically, with narratives that revolve around sex numbers, the sustained narrative of soft core deals specifically with romance and love relationships; this narrative focus is a common trait of most women's genres, and the woman's film in particular. Typically, the "woman's film" denotes a certain type of film, primarily from 1940s Hollywood, that explores "women's issues" through the point of view of the female lead. These films appear to address female spectators through their narrative concerns (often melodramatic, regarding love, family, emotion) and their visual strategies (narrational devices, point-of-view shots and/or voice-over).[61] Molly Haskell points out that "the woman's film" maintains four fundamental themes, "often found overlapping or in combination: sacrifice, affliction, choice, and competition."[62] According to Haskell, heroines often experience some sort of conflict surrounding love within the course of the narrative.[63] Erotic thrillers deal with conflicts similar to those of the woman's film, but these conflicts are situated precisely within sexual situations; love is always a *factor* within a *sexual* relationship. Common themes of the erotic thriller are sexual frigidity or inexperience (affliction); split affections for husband and lover or infidelities (choice); sexual dissatisfaction within marriage (sacrifice); and vying with other women for sex and love (competition). Sacrifice is a common denominator of the erotic thriller, as female protagonists continually struggle with unsuccessful personal lives.

Molly Haskell describes the morality of the woman's film as "you can't have your cake and eat it too."[64] This morality translates into the erotic thriller through the genre's strategic use of sexual danger; even as the heroine experiences sexual pleasure or fulfillment, the thriller narrative provides danger and threat to circumvent her sexual experiences. For example, the erotic thriller *Night Eyes 3* reveals a successful television star (Shannon Tweed) whose burgeoning relationship with her security guard (Andrew Stevens) can exist only simultaneously with the danger that requires her to *need* upgraded security. In *Indecent Behavior* (Lawrence Lanoff, 1993), a sex therapist, Rebecca Mathis (again, Shannon Tweed), can experience her growing relationship with a police detective only while he is investigating the murder of one of her patients. And in *Dead Sexy* (Robert Angelo, 2001), Detective Kate McBain (Tweed, again) starts to fall for Blue, a murder suspect, and the film reveals that Kate had to leave her last job for similar reasons. For the heroine of the erotic thriller, love and romance are fundamental goals, but these goals cannot be separated from an ever-present threat of danger.

Unlike hard-core porn, the erotic thriller requires a sustained, feature-length narrative to maintain coherence; yet, soft core is also episodic, for it is structured by a series of sexual spectacles that break the flow of the narrative. Critics of soft core have stated, "The story is negligible. The characterizations are sketchy at best," or "It's long on atmosphere and heavy breathing, short on story and logic. You're supposed to be too swept up in the anything-goes, sensual atmosphere to notice that things don't make much sense."[65] The common characteristics of "quality" narrative films—well-written scripts, brilliant acting, realistic drama—are absent from the erotic thriller. Instead, the film's murder/suspense plot works alongside a series of romanticized sexual spectacles; the sex numbers within the erotic thriller provide the fundamental structure for the narrative. Criticism regarding the fluctuation of spectacle and narrative in the soft-core genre film echoes derision leveled at other "popular" genres. As Linda Williams describes it,

> Now it is commonplace for critics and viewers to ridicule narrative genres that seem to be only flimsy excuses for something else—musicals and pornography in particular are often singled out as being *really* about song and dance or sex. But as much recent work on the movie musical has demonstrated, the episodic narratives typical of the genre are not simply frivolous pretexts for the display of song and dance; rather, narrative often permits the staging of song and dance spectacles afforded by the story line. Narrative informs number, and number, in turn, informs narrative. Part of the pleasure of the movie musical resides in the tension between these different discursive registers, each seeking to establish its own equilibrium.[66]

As in the musical, the two components of the erotic thriller, spectacle and narrative, are deeply intertwined, creating through their collision the requisite pleasure/danger genre syntax. These spectacular images of sexual encounters are not only significant in their obvious divergence from "reality." Structurally, spectacle creates certain gaps within the narrative flow that cause erotic scenes to become momentarily frozen within the course of the soft core's narrative. While Laura Mulvey relies upon a paradigm of male spectatorship and female objectification for the understanding of spectacle, she meaningfully points out that a woman's "visual presence tends to work against the story line, to freeze the flow of action in moments of erotic contemplation."[67] Sexual spectacles, such as the prolonged sex scenes in films such as *Secret Games 1–3* or *Animal Instincts 1–3,* momentarily halt the narrative flow. These spectacles would seem to disengage the spectator from the sutured identification of the narrative *as well as* instill a certain amount of erotic contemplation. As Gina Marchetti states in her analyses of spectacle and ethnicity, "spectacle opens up the text to a contradictory play of possible viewer positionings and multiple interpretations."[68] Spectacle, like the masquerade, through its very excessive constructedness, sets a distance that prohibits the spectator from overinvesting in the image.[69] Likewise, the mutability and multiple interpretations that soft-core spectacle offers hinges on its play of surfaces, rather than depths; again, this mutability allows more possibilities of erotic contemplation for the female spectator.

Narratives and narration in soft core, visible in the erotic thriller and the erotic anthology series, focus on the sexual lives and emotional involvements of women. While this focus occurs occasionally in hard core, the subjectivity and point-of-view identification for the spectator is still mostly gendered male. In contemporary soft core, the heroine's subjectivity provides the narrative trajectory, and the heroine often narrates her sexual adventures through voice-over or diary entry. These women are thus portrayed as active subjects, even though they also exist as desirable objects. The premise of a dichotomy between male subject and female object that was common to 1970s psychoanalytic film theory is undermined by the repeated use of female point-of-view shots in contemporary soft-core films. Women are constantly watching and deriving pleasure from looking at male and female bodies. These heroines are voyeurs, who experience the distance from the image necessary for the objectification of the other. Soft-core film's viewing practices and narratives encourage identification and allow the spectator, explicitly addressed as heterosexual and female, to possess the active power of "the gaze."[70] Still, the erotic thriller's narrative works to constrain the gaze of the female lead (and the female spectator), for active sexual desires always run in conflict with the economic and emotional independence of the heroine. The tensions that erupt as the boundaries between public and private spheres shift and blur are represented through the film's visual strategies; the heroine's subjectivity proves questionable and unreliable, her gaze simultaneously pleasurable and dangerous.

ZALMAN KING'S WORK AS A DISTILLATION OF SOFT-CORE STRATEGIES

While the larger part of my analysis focuses on the soft-core erotic thriller, residing in a place between the hard-core episodic film and the R-rated Hollywood narrative, I wish to focus now on the erotic anthology series/episodes as a distillation of the various strategies and practices utilized in soft core. The erotic anthology episodes that populated late-night cable television in the 1990s, and also had a brief run in 2002–3 with *Chromiumblue .com,* are now available on VHS and DVD. Shows such as *Love Street, Erotic Confessions, Red Shoe Diaries,* or *Women: Stories of Passion* all maintain narrative and visual devices shared by the erotic thriller, providing distinctive alternatives to the aesthetic practices of hard-core porn.

Zalman King, who produces and often writes and directs the erotic anthology series *Red Shoe Diaries* and *Chromiumblue.com,* is considered "the soft-core potentate," "the sultan of erotic moviemaking," or the "reigning auteur of erotic fantasy," and he has been the stylistic leader of the erotic soft-core genre for over twenty years.[71] What started in 1985 with the theatrical release of *Nine ½ Weeks* (Adrian Lyne, 1986), a tale of one woman's brush with sexual obsession, quickly became a pattern for Zalman King and Patricia Louisianna Knop, a husband-and-wife team. After writing that screenplay, they went on to write, produce, or direct a slew of soft-core stories about women and their passions: *Two Moon Junction* (1988), *Wild Orchid* (1990), *Wild Orchid 2* (1992), *Red Shoe Diaries* (1990), *Lake Consequence* (Rafael Eisenman, 1993), *Delta of Venus* (1995), *Shame, Shame, Shame* (1998), *Business for Pleasure* (Rafael Eisenman, 1997), and *Women of the Night* (2000). The first three films and *Delta of Venus* were released in theaters but quickly moved to home video, where they seemed to find a devoted following, as do many such films after a less than successful box office theatrical release. A series of half-hour vignettes, representing female diary entries, was brought to the screen in 1992 on Showtime cable network as *Zalman King's Red Shoe Diaries;* they elicited such a strong demand that Republic Pictures continued to release and distribute collections of the episodes on video and DVD after 2000, and King was still producing episodes as late as 2001.[72] Attesting to the show's popularity, Republic Pictures also sponsored a *Red Shoe Diaries* contest in 1994; women could send in accounts of their sexual fantasies and possibly have them produced for Showtime. In 2000, Showtime teamed up with Cybergrrl and FanciFull in launching MyRedShoeDiaries.com, an online community devoted to the series.[73] Shortly thereafter, King joined with Showtime once again to produce *Chromiumblue.com* (2002–3), a new erotic anthology series with a connected Web site that would sell some of the luxury products shown in the show's episodes. Unfortunately, Showtime canceled the series after half the episodes had aired. In 2005, King produced and directed *Forty Deuce,* a four-part reality series for the Bravo television network that focused on Ivan Kane's glorious burlesque club and its dancers; the cameras followed Kane and his group as they attempted to open another burlesque nightclub in Las Vegas.

Zalman King openly admits in interviews that he deliberately shows sexual experiences through women's eyes, claiming that both "men and women are much more interested in the erotic journey of women rather than men. I just think that's where the heart of eroticism is. Following a guy fucking a lot of women is interesting but it can get old."[74] King does not dispute those who term his work "a little romance novel-esque," and he points out that his showcasing of burlesque dancing on a series such as *Forty Deuce* is essentially about female empowerment—women freely experiencing the world sensually, rather than representing victims of exploitation.[75] In describing *Delta of Venus* (1995), King asserts the sexual politics behind the majority of his erotic work.

> *Delta* is probably the most significant piece because the way we chose to do the story was about a woman who gives up the idea of romance for her own sexual liberation. She even gets a chance to get it back. It really is a feminist movie in a way, because [Elena] becomes disillusioned in a way with her own weakness thinking that a man will supply this romantic idea that she has. As the film progresses, she becomes more and more in touch with her sexuality and sensuality. She takes control of it, and by the end of the film, she is on her own and forsakes her lover because she's having too much fun being liberated.[76]

King's depiction of *Delta of Venus* explicitly connects sexual exploration and power with feminist values, and this point of view colors not only his work but the majority of DTV erotic thrillers currently available.[77] Still, King's unique stylistic vision sets his work apart from that of the many soft-core filmmakers who have followed. He consistently creates a recognizable visual elegance and upscale beauty that is always associated with the Zalman King brand, exemplified by films that highlight exotic locations, stunning actors, and sensuous mood music.

Although the erotic anthology series consists of short films, what prove interesting for an analysis of the erotic thriller are the pronounced aesthetic, structural, and narrative similarities between the erotic anthology episode and the erotic thriller. Zalman King's film *Red Shoe Diaries* (1990), the precursor to the cable series, focuses on a female protagonist, but the murderous tension of the erotic thriller is supplanted by explicit flashback and fantasy sequences. In this sense, much of Zalman King's television work—the erotic anthology episodes in particular—lacks the suspense elements and plot twists to sustain a ninety-minute narrative.[78] Still, the conflicts the heroines experience within their respective abbreviated narratives, as well as the narrational strategies used to convey these conflicts, are analogous to those in the erotic thriller. In the film of *Red Shoe Diaries,* the "real time" of the narrative occurs after the heroine's death, told in flashback by the intermingling of the subjective, narrational voice of the heroine (Alex) with the voice of her fiancé (Jake, played by David Duchovny) as he reads her diary entries. Through Alex's diary, Jake learns the reason for her suicide: she was fulfilling her desires outside of their relationship as well as within it. Faced with her own guilt, she decides not to choose between two men but to kill herself. Thus, she is punished within the narrative for her active sexual desires.

At the highest point of Alex's confusion, she expresses a desire to reach out to strangers, and she places an ad for women to send their diaries to her so that she can learn from their experiences. After her death, Jake, in *his* anguish and confusion, fulfills that desire for himself. His ad states, "Women. Do you keep a diary? Have you been betrayed? Have you betrayed another? Man, 35, wounded and alone, recovering from the loss of once-in-a-lifetime love. Looking for reasons why. Willing to pay top dollar for your experiences. Please send diaries to Red Shoes . . . all submissions are strictly confidential." This ad is the jumping-off point for the cable series *Red Shoe Diaries.* Each thirty-minute installment consists of one woman's diary entry as she responds to Jake's ad. While the series highlights "sexual fantasies" from female diary entries, Jake's particular interest lies in the structures of heterosexual love, creating conflict in the subjective control of the narrative. Ambivalence is maintained throughout the series, as any freedom of sexual expression exhibited in the diary entries is impinged upon by Jake's own subjective desires and imperatives as his voice brackets each episode. Unlike Alex, who through her ad wanted "clues to [her] own dark pain and passion," Jake wants to know why he has lost a "once in a lifetime love," thereby shifting the focus from sexual passion to love, female desire to male loss.[79]

The *Red Shoe Diaries* series contains many characteristics of "women's" genres, constructed from aesthetic and narrative qualities of romance novels and inscribed with the narrative logic and heterosexual imperative located in the woman's film. Although the heroines of *Red Shoe Diaries* dress lavishly in designer suits and long, slinky evening dresses and live exciting lives encountering mysterious, attractive men, their lives remain full of conflict; the nature of these conflicts is the force the narrative exerts on the heterosexual couple versus the autonomy of female personality, agency, and desire—a consistent conflict for heterosexual women in these erotic narratives. Inevitably, in each *Red Shoe Diaries* episode, the female character is neatly absorbed into communion with the opposite sex, despite any game playing or erotic intrigue that previously ensued. *Red Shoe Diaries* combines the conflicts of choice and sacrifice (themes common to the woman's film) in its respective episodes, although usually these choices are seen as desirable to the heroine. For instance, in the episode titled "Safe Sex," Joan Severance and Stephen Bauer play a game of anonymity; they know nothing of each other—no names, no past history. But Joan's character ultimately wants more than casual sex, even though *initially* she contributed to making the game's rules. Similarly, in "Double Dare," the female ad executive plays visual "bare-all" games with a man in an office in the opposite building, but ultimately this ersatz sexual expression only helps to solidify her relationship with her husband. The sex scene (and there is always one explicit scene in every episode) is not with "the man next door" but her husband, thereby legitimating the heterosexual couple.

A quest for an autonomous self combined with the fulfillment of sexual desire is the most common theme of *Red Shoe Diaries,* and this journey is very important in the construction of a heterosexual female identity. Yet, these narrative goals are rarely reached, for the narrative's momentum is based on the conflict between the two desires. For example, in "Double or Nothing," the female character is a pool shark whose "entire identity was defined by the man I was with at the time. There was no me . . . I was just a prop." These inner thoughts are taken directly from the character's diary and are read in her voice. As the narrative progresses, she gets into trouble during a pool game and is saved by a handsome, male pool shark. He offers her a place to stay, but she is hesitant. She is currently living on the streets, having left her last lover to *find* herself. Eventually the two team up to con people together, but the woman is torn between her growing love for the man and her dislike of his control of her autonomy through his occasional paternalistic, teacher-like attitude toward her. She leaves him but then finds him again to challenge him to a pool game. The stakes are that if she wins, he cuts the attitude, but if *he* wins, "he has her soul." The point of the narrative is that she cannot have both. If she sexually desires this man and wants him, she must "sacrifice" her independence. She loses the pool game, and the episode ends.

Because women write these diary entries, one can assume that subjectivity is assigned to the heroine. However, as in most cinema, the object of the gaze fluctuates within the narrative; more often than not, women are the objects, even though they are narrative subjects. As John Berger has stated, "A woman must consciously watch herself. She is almost continually accompanied by her own image of herself."[80] *Red Shoe Diaries, Cosmopolitan* magazine, and the Victoria's Secret catalog are filled with sexual female objects, but these are objects consumed by as many women as men, if not more.[81] The reversal of female object to male object is not an easy one, for the role of woman as object has become ingrained in contemporary culture.[82] *Red Shoe Diaries* positions the female spectator (addressed as heterosexual) to gaze at the female characters, but the series focuses upon men as objects as well. In fact, the majority of Zalman King's work features extremely striking, chiseled, bare-chested men (such as Costas Mandylor, Gary Stretch, Billy Zane, and Richard Tyson), who often disrobe in front of women, or take steaming hot showers, where glistening streams of water cascade down their naked bodies. Although there may not be much uncovered, women are shown as looking and deriving pleasure from looking.

In the series *Red Shoe Diaries,* female bodies are largely left uncovered. Breasts, buttocks, and thighs are common sights, but these visions of flesh are intimately connected to experiences of sexual pleasure for the heroines. Some episodes not only offer women a controlling gaze, but also overturn common psychoanalytic film theories of voyeurism. Cinematic voyeurism is thought to be impossible for women due to the "overpresence" of their own image; because of this implicit closeness, women are unable to maintain the gap or distance from the image—"the essential precondition for voyeurism."[83] This argument assumes that *only women* can be objects within the film text (due to the fetishism and disavowal strategies of the male viewer in relation to castration).[84]

If one puts aside the Freudian scenario of the castration complex as not completely useful for the female subject, women's pleasure in looking can be explicitly examined in *Red Shoe Diaries,* especially in the "Double Dare" episode. Both voyeurism and exhibitionism are seen as highly pleasurable fantasies for the heroine (and may signify that there are opportunities, as such, for the female spectator as well). The main character remains anonymous as she describes her narrative in vivid detail. When she first spots her sexual object in a lighted office across the street, she describes him as "striking, mysterious looking, brooding, almost cruel. I couldn't take my eyes off him" (a description similar to that of typical male heroes in the erotic romance novel). When the man catches her looking at him, the game begins—a game of "Double Dare." Although he initiates the game by sending a fax asking her name, she changes the rules and makes them sexual by faxing to him "No Name. Take Your Shirt Off. Double Dare." Visually, the spectator is *always* with the heroine. While the viewer sees the man consistently veiled by the window and the venetian blinds of his office (through the eyes of the heroine), the spectator never sees a view of the woman from a distance. His agency, through faxing, is only a catalyst that triggers her fantasies of voyeurism and exhibitionism. At one point in the game, he is stripped down to his underwear, while she merely unclasps the front of her bra, never fully unclothing herself. In voice-over, she lovingly describes her adolescence, when she lived across the street from a boys' boarding school and would undress in front of the window: "It excited me then, and it excited me now."

Most important, this episode highlights not only the female gaze, but also the process of construction of fantasies based on real desires. When, at one point, the heroine sees him having sex with a woman on his desk, she pointedly closes the curtains and refuses to open them again, stating that this is "not a part of *my* fantasy." He later tries to meet her in person and corners her near her car. Her fantasy has crossed over into reality; it is only the fantasy and the *distance* involved in her voyeuristic game-playing that are pleasurable. Again, delayed gratification and a distance from the sex act through anticipation are the true forms of titillation. She is not interested in the "reality" of sleeping with this man *or* cheating on her husband. This episode exemplifies the pleasurable possibilities of fantasy construction for heterosexual women, while affording the spectator a certain amount of vicarious pleasure in identifying with the heroine's active desires and gaze.

Although the heterosexual couple is foregrounded in many of these episodes, the turn-on is often outside this realm and seen as forbidden or taboo. The taboo is also an extremely common element of the erotic thriller, in which heroines often cheat on their husbands, lead secret lives as exotic dancers, or masquerade as prostitutes (none of which are wholeheartedly acceptable to contemporary American social mores). Many of the heroines in the *Red Shoe Diaries* episodes remain nameless to their sexual game partners (as in "Double Dare" or "Bounty Hunter") and most sex occurs outside of marriage. The heroines enjoy the escape into forbidden desires outside the monotony of their jobs or monogamous relationships. Fantasy allows for the vicarious experience of taboo practices, for "fantasies are illicit in a way that dreams are not—they span a space between self-indulgence and public restraint."[85] The turn-on for the woman in "Double Dare" is not only in watching a man undress, and in turn being watched; it is that she is forbidden to express and experience these desires while sustaining her marriage. Breaking a taboo can cause guilt, and yet it can create arousal through the existence of that guilt. As Paula Webster explains, "Women's relationship to erotic taboo is complex. For some, playing with the distance from or proximity to the forbidden is a tension-filled turn-on. Without taboo, sex might not feel so delicious. Naughty feels nice, and just 'bad' enough to be intensely pleasurable. Taboo thoughts about taboo people, acts, situations and words are often nurtured, honed and elaborated to heighten our fantasies, again and again."[86] This tension-filled turn-on is essential to the erotic thriller, and it is frequently exhibited in the erotic anthology series. Taboo is important through its utilization in the formation of fantasy, in which *everything* should be allowed; as in the case of fantasies of scenarios such as rape, submission, and bondage, fantasy is uniquely structured outside of reality and not necessarily *directly* connected to reality-tested wish fulfillment.

The *Red Shoe Diaries* series, and many erotic thrillers, deals with certain transgressive ideas of sexual behavior, but those ideas are always neatly positioned within a heterosexual discourse, diffusing their transgressive and political qualities in favor of more utopian heterosexual fantasies. The episode "Another Woman's Lipstick" is just such a case. This fantasy scenario deals with the diverse conflicts of adultery and lesbianism within the parameters of a heterosexual relationship between Zoë and Robert. What Zoë believes to be the "perfect" relationship—she has loved Robert since she was eleven—becomes tarnished in the wake of Robert's infidelity, an infidelity she discovers by finding traces of another woman's lipstick on his collar. Zoë fulfills explicitly voyeuristic desires by following Robert to a smoky bar where he meets "the other woman." Robert and his lover are oblivious to Zoë's gaze, or the gaze of the spectator. The subjective camerawork is highlighted by the passing shadows and dancing bodies that intermittently obstruct Zoë's voyeuristic view (again creating the play of surfaces common to the soft-core genre).

What becomes the chief element of this particular scenario is not the pain of infidelity, but the possibilities of female same-sex desires. Zoë encounters the other woman in the bathroom of the bar, and a highly eroticized moment occurs; the woman tells her that she has "beautiful lips" but recommends a darker shade of lipstick. She proceeds to take Zoë's face in her hands and puts the lipstick on her lips for her. When Zoë initially pulls away, the woman tells her not to be such a "scaredy cat," issuing a challenge in experiencing this same-sex erotic contact. The notion of lipstick and makeup as mere accoutrements for male attraction is problematized within the homoerotic moments between the two women. As the mystery woman states, "It's as simple as that. Change your lipstick and you change your life." Zoë turns to face her reflection in the bathroom mirror in an attempt to reconfigure her sexual identity in relation to this experience. A change of lipstick has indeed changed her life.

When Zoë follows Robert and the woman to a motel, where she spies on them through the blinds, she actively describes her fascination with the woman. Jealousy *of* the other woman is not as intrinsic to the fantasy as identification *with* Robert through the sharing of an object of desire; in fact, the jealousy involved may be directed at Robert. The heroine's look through the blinds captures the exotic other woman performing an erotic dance for Robert; the woman is dressed in black stockings and lingerie and holds a light next to the taut curves of her body. Zoë states in her diary entry, "I watched her, and so did he. She hypnotized us both. I couldn't move, and neither could he." She parallels her voyeuristic experience of the woman with that of Robert, momentarily transgressing gender boundaries. The closeups of the woman's body are presented for an ambiguously defined gaze; although the narrative of the episode is constructed from a heterosexual woman's point of view, the specific objects of desire (the woman *or* the sex between the woman and Robert) play into certain "perverse" fantasies.

Although Zoë's mental flashbacks/fantasies initially focus on her romantic moments with Robert, her fantasies shift to the "other woman." She states, "Every day, night and day, all I could think about was her," thereby excluding her husband (and infidelity) as the object of her fantasies. The erotically lit images of a woman's body are positioned for the female lead/spectator, and the pleasure received by the male character becomes superfluous.

Zoë builds upon her fantasies by dressing as a man and arranging a meeting with this mysterious woman, for she "wanted to touch her." Her transformation of gender through masquerade only highlights the feminine qualities Zoë is trying to cover. Step-by-step closeups of dressing and undressing focus lovingly on the designer lingerie she sheds while stepping into the male role—this is undeniably a woman *pretending* to be a man. She takes off women's stockings and lace underwear and puts on silk boxers and men's socks; she removes her lace bra and binds her breasts before putting on a man's white shirt and tie. The "masculinization" of woman and the revolutionary and political qualities of cross-dressing create the opposite representation; lesbianism becomes as easy as dressing up or wearing another woman's lipstick.

Zoë goes to the same bar as before and "picks up" the woman, stating in her diary, "Now I knew what it was like to be him. There was no resisting her." This entry further signifies her apparent jealousy of Robert, possibly of his role as the unfaithful man who takes his pleasure where he pleases; this pleasure is not so readily available to women in contemporary society without negative consequences. The two women move to a secluded office near the bar, and Zoë orders the woman to take off her clothes. She seems to enjoy the voyeuristic control that appears to come with male privilege. Still, the desire lies within a same-sex relationship, and Zoë's identity is revealed. The woman removes Zoë's hat, and Zoë's wavy blond hair falls around her face. She knows Zoë is "his wife," knows Zoë was watching them outside the motel, but points to the question of desire when she asks, "Who were you watching? Him . . . or me?" This unmasking triggers the sex scene between the two women, which, in line with standard soft-core filmmaking, never reveals anything beyond a kiss, or a hand on another's breast. The titillation of the fantasy, where no real risks are taken, overwhelms any possible political resonances that may occur.

Ultimately, the heterosexual relationship is strengthened by Zoë's foray into lesbianism. Robert and Zoë forgive each other, as they have both "learned a lesson," and Zoë believes that she "got an education."[87] The same-sex interlude becomes just another spicy alternative in the realm of heterosexual experience, not a political or emotional question for the female protagonist. Although the ambiguity of the narrative and the gaze leaves open the possibilities for same-sex desires through fantasy for the spectator, the restrictions of the heterosexual relationship bracket the liberating moments of this episode. Further possibilities for exploration are denied by an explicitly heterosexual resolution. Lesbianism becomes a safe, momentary fantasy.

Red Shoe Diaries appears unique in presenting women as subjects in sexual discourse.[88] However, this discursive power is misleading, for the narrative control is not solely the heroine's in each episode. As in the original film, the narrations of these fantasies are bracketed by the "reading" of the diary entries by Jake, the anguished and confused man who "lost a once in a lifetime love." Jake's character is not heroic in any sense. Having lost his love, he has given up his prestigious job as an architect, avoided all his friends, and retained the sole companionship of his dog, Stella; he now devotes his entire life to "understanding the reasons why," to the point of obsession.[89] His position within the narrative is minimal, yet pivotal. Even though he does not have much to say, and is mostly reading the very beginning and end of each diary entry in the diegetic narrative, his is the final voice of moral judgment in each episode. This narration is not merely a simple structuring tool; because of this bracketing of the female narrative, Jake subverts the power structures of subjective female experience and exhibits ultimate narrational control. This structure is strongly articulated in Michel Foucault's theories on the confession and its importance in sexual discourse, for "it is in the confession that truth and sex are joined, through the obligatory and exhaustive expression of an individual secret."[90] Through the structure of confession, the heroines lose the power of their voices, for they are ultimately telling their stories to an interpreter—and the interpreter is the one who dominates the discourse. "The confession is a ritual of discourse in which the speaking subject is also the subject of the statement; it is also a ritual that unfolds within a power relationship, for one does not confess without the presence (or virtual presence) of a partner who is not simply the interlocutor but the authority who requires the confession, prescribes and appreciates it, and intervenes in order to judge, punish, forgive, console, and reconcile."[91]

Jake has this power to "judge"; in fact, his only role in each episode is to embody a superego that judges and problematizes the fantasies each woman has constructed. This position completely clouds the liberating potential of the narrative. As Molly Haskell describes it, "sex is difficult to generalize about, or to politicize into male/female polarities. The minute you describe a sexual experience to another person, it is transformed by the listener or reader into something else, in accordance with her or his fantasy life."[92]

Jake's moralistic control over female fantasy is exemplified within the episode "Bounty Hunter." The fact that the heroine, Evan, is a "bounty hunter" and that the action takes place in a truck stop or diner, reminiscent of the situation in *The Postman Always Rings Twice* (Tay Garrett, 1946), is meant to subvert some typically male stereotypes and genres. The hunted man is a gigolo of sorts; he sleeps with women, cons them into believing he loves them, and then steals their money. This episode constructs its sexual objects in a unique way. As Evan's voice-over is presented, the camera introduces the spectator to the object of the hunt, Oliver Dunbar. The camera pans lovingly over his "pretty boy" face and holds on him as he spots the truck arriving with our heroine masquerading as a "stranded" passenger; it seems her car has broken down. Evan's job is to track down this criminal, and she uses the best bait available: herself. But this is no mission of mercy, for she has been following him for several months, and she has let him go for the sheer joy of being able to watch him, follow him, hunt him, thus delaying her gratification. Oliver knows nothing of Evan's game, seeing her as just a beautiful victim ripe for a con. The heroine situates herself as the sexual object, but she controls her objectification and his gaze through her every move, purposely playing to his "uncontrollable" desires. In a scene where she tells him she is going to the "ladies room," she lifts her leg up high while cleaning off the road dust; he can glimpse her thighs, positioning him in a place of weakness in terms of narrative knowledge in the film.[93] Her objectification is not passive; in fact, she appears to use him.

Oliver seems the hapless victim when at one point Evan sits across from where he stands and spreads her legs, inviting him to touch her. This move leads to a weakening in his resolve and gives her the opportunity to pull a gun on him while "reaching for a condom in her boot." Still, sex is not her only weapon, just the one Evan finds especially useful in fulfilling *her* sexual desire for *him*. The two battle it out for control, and once Oliver frees himself from his handcuffs, he turns the tables on her. But in true noir/adventure form, she is able to uncuff herself, and she recaptures him. She drags him back into the diner after chasing him down in the pouring rain, only to have to listen to a song and dance about how he is "falling in love" with her—to which she replies "bullshit." He points out that she could have captured him a while ago, but did not since "she saw something in him." She states, "You mean a beautiful whore. Yeah, I did," and firmly situates him as the *object* of her desire. She then initiates sex and appears to enjoy him thoroughly.

During sex with Oliver, a car pulls up, and Evan's male accomplices, accompanied by Evan's client Francine, bang on the door to the diner and force their way in. When they finally break in, Evan and Oliver are both dressed. Evan hands Oliver over to Francine, the last woman he conned, in exchange for fifty thousand dollars. Evan's final words are, "Love and money. Money and love. When push comes to shove, I think I'd rather have a new Porsche, wouldn't you?" Not only does she deny the importance of heterosexual bond formation (Oliver offers her his love and domestic bliss), but she gets to have her cake and it eat too—sexual desire and autonomy.

Of course, this moment dissolves when Jake as interpreter comes into play and problematizes the sexual expression and autonomy existing within her narrative. Exchanging point-of-view, shot–reverse shots with his dog, he says, "Tough stuff, Stella. Maybe too tough. I wonder if she ever felt anything at all for him. I wonder what it is that made her turn him in. If you ask me, I think it was because he used the same line on her as he used on all the other women. She just couldn't stand it. Maybe it was the money. It's a dog-eat-dog world, Stella."

Here the spectator experiences Jake's narrative control, for it acts as a censure of the sexual expression the women exhibit in describing their fantasies. If the female heterosexual spectator is "finding her place" in this narrative and not solely identifying with the female character, Jake's words of wisdom reflect the contradictory characteristics of heterosexual female desire: there are many outside influences that impinge on a woman's freedom to construct *any* fantasy. *Red Shoe Diaries* thus seems to exemplify the double standard for women in terms of sexual representation. At times the heroines possess the gaze, but ultimately their sexual bodies are far more exposed than the male bodies. They seem to relay their fantasies to the spectator, but at the same time these women confess their sexual desires to a man, who will then pass judgment on whether their actions are right or wrong. In fact, it can never be completely determined that the visual fantasies shown in the series are not constructed in Jake's mind as he reads these female fantasies, although the specific appeal to typically female genres belies this idea.

The ways in which the series focuses on fantasy and escapism elide the racial or political concerns that could occur in specific sexual representations. Even in an episode with a black heterosexual couple ("Emily's Dance"), the questions and problems of their race are constructed as secondary to those of their sexuality and desire. The series makes no attempt to confront the interconnected oppressions of race and gender that exist in contemporary U.S. culture. White upper-class heterosexual heroines are predominantly the possessors of the gaze. This racial imbalance could be attributed to the considerable veering away from political and social resonances within hard-core and soft-core genres. Both genres are largely utopian narratives, where the focus on spectacle and sex number overrides the discussion of race and ethnicity in these films. Most commonly, when soft core exhibits nonwhite ethnicities, in films such as *Wild Orchid* or *Lake Consequence,* they exist as backdrops, to overtly sexualize the scenario with glimpses of exotic others. The erotic thriller does not utilize race to the same extent, often forgoing multicultural representation altogether in its persistent interrogation of white womanhood. The "other" is usually somehow sexually deviant or more experienced than the heroine, providing the film's exoticism and "spice."

Zalman King's later Showtime anthology series, *Chromiumblue.com,* still visualizes female sexual fantasies as told to a curious male character, but it distinguishes itself from *Red Shoe Diaries* by including cutting-edge digital aesthetics and maintaining a more light-hearted and self-reflexive tone. Still, the series' jumping-off point is laden with romantic tragedy. A jet-setting fashion stylist, Vivian Vadim (Erica Prior), is hired to style some fashion models for a shoot held on self-made billionaire Henry Brooke's (Shane Brolly) luxury yacht, the *Chromium Blue* (figure 2). In the course of this adventure, Vivian meets and brings along the polymorphously perverse recurring characters who are part of the series' weekly episodes: Henry's tough and beautiful chauffeur, Maria (Summer Altice); his gay mentor, Sir George (Ian Abercrombie); Vivian's equally gay fellow-stylist, Popo (Domi Arcangeli); a gigolo (Jens Nagel); a mischievous bisexual ghost named Owen (Dominic Keating); and later Cybervixen (Annette Culp), the bodacious digital beauty who is part of the chromiumblue.com Web site. Once Henry Brooke spies Vivian, he informs Sir George, "I'm going to marry that girl," spurring the more traditional heterosexual narrative common to *Red Shoes.* Yet, Vivian is a very different type of heroine; she is attracted to Henry, and interested in sex, but she foils Brooke's plans for marital bliss, mocking him with the mantra "Henry Brooke. Came. Saw. And took," and writing messages such as "Too heavy for me, hombre," with lipstick on his bathroom mirror. Vivian finds him seductive, but she is not ready to settle down.[94] Henry, who appears lovestruck, insists on pursuing her to Bali, and he consequently has a debilitating motorcycle accident.

Figure 2. Vivian and Henry in *Chromiumblue.com* (2002).

From the seclusion of his palatial manse, he sends a letter to Vivian (which is heard in voice-over):

My Dearest Vivian,

   The dark clouds of self-pity have finally lifted. Hope rules, and I'm healing . . . We are the same person. What you see, I see. What you feel, I feel. I'm proposing an adventure—a wild plan. I'm sending you *Chromium Blue*—it will be a matter of faith between us. Be my eyes, my ears, my tongue. Feel for me, live for me . . . I need you to be strong. I believe in your strength. Take the *Chromium Blue* and her crew, and round up people. Put them in see-through dresses and march them down the crowded streets. Put them in wigs and dark glasses. Get them high, get them hard, get them wet. Film it, photograph it, burn it into the back of their retinas so when they croak, it's the last thing they see. Do it. And tell me all about it in excruciating detail.

Thus, the setup for *Chromiumblue.com* is for Vivian to guide women (through an Internet site) onto the *Chromium Blue* in order for them to achieve their wildest sexual fantasies *so that Henry can experience them vicariously.* Vivian is the conduit for these experiences—his eyes, ears, and tongue.

Aesthetically, the series is clearly a Zalman King enterprise. The show takes place in exotic locales throughout Europe and promotes a glamorous lifestyle without financial limits. The clothing comes straight from the world of high fashion, and as King himself has said, "It's really . . . like Dolce and Gabbana ads that just come to life."[95] King uses rapid-fire montage sequences to display the show's fantasy world, and he deeply connects the show's music to its visuals by displaying the group name and song in the lower left-hand corner of the screen (very similar to a technique used in music videos). The careful viewer will also recognize images that have appeared in previous Zalman King productions. In "The Eternal," parts 1 and 2, when Maria goes out into the night, she drives through an underground area where street toughs play with long fluorescent light tubes. This scene is recycled from the King-written-and-produced *Business for Pleasure* (1998), when Alex (Jeroen Krabbé) and Anna (Joanna Pacula) first find the handsome Rolf (Gary Stretch) while driving among the same street toughs. Similarly, in the same *Chromiumblue .com* episodes, when Maria goes out to a dark, throbbing nightclub, scenes of a giant, pulsing, colorfully lighted warehouse space are shown. These same scenes are first shown in *Business for Pleasure* when Isabel and a colleague go out dancing at a nightclub, accompanied by the same music ("Instigator"—Keri Rose, with Hypnogaja).[96] This recycling of sounds and images is astute, both financially and aesthetically. Once King has the rights to use certain songs for his films, he saves money by reusing them. More important, King ups the recognition factor for the spectator in the know, creating a consistent and recognizable brand of erotic entertainment that fulfills spectator expectations.

The close connection between sound and image in Zalman King's work creates a synaesthetic effect, where the eye hears and the ear sees. This experience is tied to the way his actors move onscreen, often in a seductive and intimate dance for the camera/spectator. Sex scenes are lovingly choreographed, and poses shift in slow motion or are freeze-framed to capture the characters' graceful movements; these movements are common to both female and male characters, who are artfully composed to create sinuous patterns across the film frame. Each sex scene in one of King's erotic films has a seductive rhythm, as the warmly lit bodies are cut in time to the music, thus providing flashes of experience, glimpses of fantasy.

Chromiumblue.com differs most significantly from the *Red Shoe Diaries* series in its shift in both sexual politics and tone. While *Red Shoes* invests in romance and romantic fantasy, *Chromiumblue.com*'s interests are hedonistic; as King describes the show, "It's not about soul, it's about partying. Good time sex."[97] This fun-loving attitude is reflected in the zany humor present in almost all the episodes, an attempt by King to "put romantic comedy with sex."[98] In the episode "Barcelona Bologna," three wild, soon-to-be-wed women all fantasize about "doing it" with the Spanish movie idol Alfredo Garcia, projecting themselves into the shoes of his leading lady, Carmella Rios. The three dress in identical Carmella Rios outfits (yellow dresses with big blue polka dots) and matching platinum wigs, and they zip around on scooters on a hunt for Alfredo. They are stopped by a man, a fellow Carmella lover, who surprises them by cross-dressing (in identical Carmella wear) and by bringing out a bong. They all proceed to get very stoned. Soon, everyone is dressed in the Carmella outfit—female, male, and transsexual alike. Even Vivian and Maria get into the spirit by donning costumes, although they pepper their conversation with witty, ironic remarks, keeping the fantasy participants at a distance. The episode climaxes with an all-out same-sex orgy on the beach, and the show's Cybervixen narrates in voice-over as these three women engage in a lesbian encounter—girls who have been hopelessly in love with each other since a fifth-grade slumber party. The next morning, the three women have suffered a drug-induced mass blackout, and none of them remembers the orgy of the night before; same-sex desire is reduced to a drunken revelry without consequences, indicative of the show's hedonistic, utopian leanings.

When characters experience negative consequences for their sexual forays, the concern is over financial exploitation, not gendered victimization. In the King-directed "I Like to Watch," a beautiful woman named Rachel toys with mild bondage fantasies and sadomasochistic desires, when a couple at a cafe, Blithe and Charles, pay her to watch them have sex (and secretively film her for future blackmail opportunities). Rachel enjoys the experience so much that she approaches two women at the same cafe, strangers, and offers to pay them so she can film them making love to a man. Soon the four are doing shots of alcohol and rolling around on a bed, a writhing tangle of lips, hands, and unclothed bodies. When Blithe and Charles request Rachel's presence a second time, she readily agrees, telling them she would like to give up control. Maria, undercover as a bored, rich housewife, also connects with the scheming couple, telling them of her need to dominate. The couple hastily set up a rendezvous where they can film the two women and thus blackmail them.

The rendezvous between Maria and Rachel exemplifies the aesthetic of the *Chromiumblue.com* episodes, while also recalling some of King's previous work. Rachel is shown in a diaphanous white dress, clutching the bars of a makeshift cage, while four women in varying forms of fetish-wear writhe nearby. When Maria appears, she is dressed like a man, masked and wearing a wig and a hat to disguise her identity. She sports a white shirt and tie, but the shirt is half-open, revealing a black lace bra and a very feminine body. This visually dynamic scenario highlights the pleasures of role-playing and suggests that passive and active roles are not naturally ascribed to gender roles, but are socially constructed, and therefore, malleable. While Maria is actually there to break up the blackmail ring (which she does by head-butting the videographer and dragging Rachel away), she first takes the time to fulfill Rachel's fantasy of submission, thereby condemning the blackmail scheme but not Rachel's fantasy.

In the same episode, the scene of Rachel's foursome cuts to Vivian seductively addressing the camera as she slowly moves along a wall, pouting and giving come-hither glances; the Cybervixen mimics her movements and her lines as they both say, in intercut scenes, "You are bending me to your will. You are the master and I am the slave." Narratively, Vivian might be addressing Henry through digital communication, or she could be speaking directly to the spectator; either way, her words and actions suggest calculated seduction through role-playing surrender. Vivian continues to writhe against the wall, until Maria's voice is heard offscreen asking, "What the fuck are you doing?" This abrupt switch in tone exemplifies the self-reflexive qualities of *Chromiumblue.com;* recurring characters such as Vivian and Maria frequently break the fourth wall and acknowledge the camera, shifting from coy seduction to ironic, self-conscious wit. The tone of the series switches dramatically from the more serious exploration of sexual fantasy and desire of the *Red Shoes* series. Here, experience is emphasized over emotional connection, adventure over love and commitment.

Still, in other episodes, this tension created by the clash of humor, explicit sex, and romance renders the fantasy awkward and disjointed. In "Cover Me Girls," a female cowboy wants "a Eurostud to fire her gun" and shows Maria and Vivian how to target shoot on board the yacht by imagining the target is "someone who pissed you off." Maria, in typical bad-ass mode, gleefully replies, "I just don't know where to begin, there's so many people I fuckin' hate!" When Vivian momentarily hesitates, Maria taunts her with, "So what if you're all alone, the prime of your life. Sunday pimpin' for some Phantom of the Opera." At this reference to her relationship with Henry, Vivian proceeds to shoot the target right in the genitals. All three women are dressed in bikinis with western-wear gun holsters; it's the Wild West, King-style. Shortly thereafter, an over-the-top Italian spaghetti-western director spies the three women and insists on casting them for his latest film, where Syd (the cowgirl) gets a chance to meet an Italian "stallion" who will "fire her gun." This zany, "anything goes" attitude is countered by Vivian's interaction with a man named Quincy, who tells her that she's his dream girl, and who triggers some of her latent fantasies ("Did I show up naked at your door?"; "Did you do me on the subway?"). Unfortunately, at Quincy's initial tentative caresses, Vivian immediately flashes back to lovemaking with Henry, and she tells Quincy that she cannot encourage him. Later, when she files her digital report to Henry, she speaks of her temptation but says that she could only think of him, explaining, "Maybe that's what love is. Not wanting to be with anybody else."

This conflict between unbridled, carefree sex and the pull of love and romance might have been the series' undoing. Perhaps King's core female audience became confused and uncomfortable by the series' schizophrenic tone and jumbled visual noise as the pace of images steadily increased. The repeated cutting to the show's Cybervixen and her topless dancers—often crass, big-breasted female stereotypes more at home on a porn set—is jarring for viewers accustomed to the svelte, small-chested, exotic women more common to King's oeuvre. Further, the self-reflexive humor and the more outrageous fantasies undermine the powerful love relationship and more subtle sexual desires that Vivian and Henry represent, a relationship that is the backbone for the entire series. As King himself explains, "I loved it but Showtime didn't. It's putting romantic comedy with sex and it worked very well. It's almost broad romantic comedy and extremely sexy. I guess there is no genre to classify it as. It seemed to confuse Showtime; I think they were expecting *Red Shoe Diaries* again. I didn't want to do that, I wanted to do something different. I hope someday TV will catch up with it. It's an acquired taste."[99] *Chromiumblue .com* illustrates the ways in which a known brand and aesthetic, such as Zalman King's erotic films and cable episodes, can both construct niche markets (by repeating distinctive generic elements and storylines) and undermine new aesthetics through the same entrenched genre conventions. While *Red Shoe Diaries* produced sixty-six episodes, *Chromiumblue.com* ran only to thirteen.

Both *Red Shoe Diaries* and *Chromiumblue.com* offer brief narratives about the importance and construction of fantasy in the private lives of women, and both series represent women as subjects with a sexual desiring gaze. The soft-core erotic thriller exhibits the same visual and aesthetic characteristics of the erotic anthology series, but it channels its sex numbers into more elaborate narrative forms. Stories of female sexual awakening are stretched to ninety-minute formats, and the high production values of soft core are accompanied by denser characterization, the suspense-building of a "thriller" structure, and a string of B-level actors well known for their continued involvement in these films.

The soft-core genre, and the erotic thriller in particular, uses aesthetic and narrative strategies familiar to consumers of "women's genres" to create pleasure through the reintegration of generic techniques. The combination of the genre's specific semantic elements and its corresponding syntax situates the erotic thriller within contemporary film forms, especially those attempting to produce sexual entertainment directed toward heterosexual women. Contemporary cultural shifts in sexual responsibility highlight the sexually adventurous and knowledgeable woman who appears in the genre. Erotic anthology series, as well as mainstream narratives such as the erotic thriller, reinforce the questions surrounding heterosexual female identity. As mainstream media struggle to define women's roles within the culture, sexual entertainment reproduces the very fear of female empowerment it simultaneously works to construct. Furthermore, the DTV erotic thriller text helps to maintain normative definitions of the feminine by using stereotypically feminized conventions and by manipulating female subjectivity and identification processes within its structure. Thus, the political resonances of the genre raise questions about female heterosexual identity while simultaneously attempting to constrain femininity within formulaic romanticized narratives.

HOW TO BE A GOOD FEMALE HETEROSEXUAL: THE EROTIC THRILLER'S INSTRUCTIONAL DISCOURSES

*I*n Gary Delfiner's film *Teach Me* (1998), a young couple is in the throes of sexual problems. Janine, the film's heroine, is uptight and inhibited in bed. Her husband, Keith, under-stands, but even therapy is not helping this "problem." Janine dresses up in sexy lingerie one night, bathes their room in candlelight, and tries to seduce him, but she grows distracted and unresponsive as they start to make love. When she expresses her fear in disappointing Keith, he exclaims, "This isn't about me, Janine. It's about us. Don't do it for me unless you can do it for yourself!" Janine needs to move beyond codependency and toward fulfilling her own sexual desires.

Enlisting the help of Marta, her sexually experienced girlfriend, Janine travels to an abandoned warehouse loft to begin her "sexual education" and lose her inhibitions. At the loft, a disembodied voice informs her not to be afraid, that he (the voice is digitized, but apparently male) will be a teacher and guide. Informing her that her experience will be "a different kind of therapy," the voice insists that in order to fix her "problem," she must follow certain rules and instructions. In the course of three nights, she will "let her-self go" and "begin to unlock the door to [her] sensuality." Through a series of titillating sex numbers, Janine gains more and more sexual knowledge, culminating in a final party scenario, where she meets her "disembodied voice" and seduces him. He turns out to be her husband, Keith.

The film structures the heroine's sexual education and knowledge ac-cording to a series of titillating, romanticized sexual scenarios. In some in-stances, Janine only voyeuristically watches the action unfolding around her, and at other times, she participates. While Janine experiences these sexual scenarios—light bondage, dressing up in lingerie, experimenting with other women—these moments are always couched discursively as "lessons." The rhetoric throughout the film suggests that Janine, for her own empowerment, must get in touch with her sexual needs and desires. In order to gain sexual agency, she must embrace these lessons with a "do-it-for-yourself," self-help zeal, following the instructions of the disembodied voice in order to experience what's "good for her." In the end, she not only experiences sexual pleasure, but also resolves the sexual problems that were undermining her marriage.

The instructional discourses apparent in this film, which are more explicit than in other erotic thrillers, indicate a certain "education of desire" and suggest regulatory practices of sexual behavior.[1] While couched as erotic entertainment, films such as *Teach Me* (Gary Delfiner, 1998), *Virtual Encounters* (Cybil Richards, 1996), *Forbidden Passions* (Jackie Garth, 1996), *Shame, Shame, Shame* (Zalman King, 1998), *Voyeur Confessions* (Tom Lazarus, 2001), and *Personals 2: Casualsex.com* (Kelley Cauthen, 2001) all explicitly construct each heroine's narrative trajectory or journey as a series of lessons that have to be mastered in order to obtain the heroine's goal: sexual fulfillment. While each film focuses on the heroine's search for sexual knowledge, the narrative's discourse takes great pains to emphasize the importance of sexual fulfillment *for the heroine's* empowerment and self-growth. Each lesson the heroine learns makes her more of a "sexual agent."

The discursive emphasis on sexual agency, empowerment, and better sex in the erotic thriller stems from very specific contextual influences that contribute to the construction of normative female heterosexuality in contemporary U.S. culture. The instructive course of the erotic thriller arises at a very specific moment within feminism and feminism's representation within popular culture. Beginning in the 1990s, women's magazines and pop feminism maintained an explicit focus on sex and sexual practices, most specifically on how heterosexual women can achieve sexual pleasure and knowledge in the name of their own empowerment. The pursuit of sexual pleasure, or "better orgasms," appears to be the current requisite goal of enlightened heterosexual women. Since that time, younger feminist writers, often aligned with third-wave feminism, have come to embrace this focus on sexual expressiveness, and champion a version of empowerment closely aligned with female sexual pleasure.

Since Tad Friend coined the term "'do-me' feminism" in 1994, the term and its connotations for both female heterosexuality and feminist rhetoric have continued to resonate within popular mass culture and the discourses constructing the erotic thriller. Friend wrote:

> Those "sexual agency" or "sexual empowerment" agitators have no collective platform, they often strongly disagree, and they hate being indiscriminately lumped together. But from lesbian eroticist Pat Califia to Clark University professor Christina Hoff Sommers there's a commonality of interest strong enough for us [*Esquire*] to do some discriminate lumping and declare it a movement, a movement proclaiming sexual liberation, sexual equality, and the reclamation of men from the scrap heap of theory. Call it "do-me" feminism.[2]

Friend's eager emphasis on "sexual liberation" and men reclaimed from "the scrap heap of theory" situates his idea of this "new" feminism in opposition to popular stereotypes of feminism that circulated (and continue to circulate) within mainstream media. Primarily, Friend's concept stems from media and press coverage of the 1980s "sex wars," which were highly publicized contentions between feminists over the role of pornography within popular culture.[3] While many writings indicate the highly varied positions feminists held on pornography, reports from the mass media contended that antipornography feminists maintained the dominant feminist position on the issue.[4] As Friend declares, "For years radical feminists such as Catharine MacKinnon and Andrea Dworkin have held sway, declaring sex bad and men worse, but now comes a generation of young women who have read the theory, thought about it—and rejected it. That purposeful hammering spreading across the land, bedroom by bedroom, is the sound of those young women beating their swords into bustiers."[5]

Friend's article suffers from the same type of overgeneralization that the pornography debates experienced in the 1980s, and it lumps a series of quite disparate women together under the rubric of "pro-sex" discourse. The difference between Pat Califia, a lesbian S/M activist from the second wave of feminism, and Katie Roiphe, a young woman barely coming of age during the "sex wars," is highly significant.[6] Similarly, bell hooks and Rebecca Walker, although both black feminists, come from very different generational histories. The feminist media scholar Elayne Rapping criticizes Friend's use of bell hooks's work on this front: "The quotation from bell hooks was the most outrageous, 'We need versatile dick who . . . can negotiate rough sex on Monday, eat pussy on Tuesday, and cuddling on Wednesday,' she says in an excerpt from her work. No doubt it fueled the fantasies of a lot of men—men who would not understand a word hooks said if they actually met her."[7] Katha Pollitt pinpoints Friend's claim of a pro-sex attitude change as "The New Blather," Ruth Shalit describes "do-me" feminists as "plucky, confident, upwardly mobile, and extremely horny," and Lois Leveen states that "we must be skeptical when feminism becomes reduced to a chatty, phallocentric article in a popular men's magazine."[8]

Yet, Friend has not only spurred hot responses from the feminist community, he also crucially points out an oppositional movement in which the mass media and feminist discourse intersect. This opposition responds to the prevailing media stereotype of feminists as antipornography. Or as Lois Leveen states, "in the popular press, young feminists are described as pro-sex (and therefore against date rape and sexual harassment awareness campaigns) *against* a construction of older, established feminists as sex-negative (dare I say man hating?)."[9] While Friend quickly embraces the "pro-sex" supporters as a new wave of feminists, he attributes these changes in cultural attitudes toward sex as a shift "from the failures of men to the failures of feminism," thereby contributing to "post-feminist" rhetoric.[10] What Friend alludes to, but never teases out in his eagerness over all the feminist "locker-room talk," is the conflict in contemporary feminism that hinges on a feminist generation gap, in which the label "feminist" is seen as a contested term, and one that is loaded with negative cultural connotations. Some members of this new generation of feminists, often labeled third-wave (for the generation after the supposed second wave of feminism in the seventies), conceive themselves as opposing a feminism of the past—a less sexually expressive feminism. As Astrid Henry explains, "Rather than seeing themselves as part of an ongoing debate within feminism—one that can be traced back to the first wave—about the meaning of sexuality for women's liberation, some third-wavers describe as a generational perspective what is more accurately a particular feminist philosophy of sex. These 'women of the New Girl Order' celebrate sexuality as the third wave's particular contribution to feminism, that which makes third-wavers unlike the feminists who came before them."[11]

Third-wave feminists grew up during a period of intense cultural contradiction and media backlash, in which they simultaneously experienced "the conservative backlash and the AIDS epidemic, the queer movement and genderfuck. We got divorced parents and 'family values,' homophobia and lesbian chic, 'Just Say No' and Ten Ways to Drive Him Wild."[12] These contradictions, exemplified by the presence of the porn star Jenna Jameson's memoir *How to Make Love Like a Porn Star: A Cautionary Tale* on the *New York Times* bestseller list during the same year as the uproar over Janet Jackson's notorious exposed breast (2004), are ever-present in contemporary U.S. culture.

Many writers, both popular and academic, have utilized the term "postfeminism" to explain a cultural attitude toward the women's movement as well as to mark feminist discourses since the 1990s. While the term's definition is unfixed and mutable, "post"-feminism suggests a time period after the necessity of feminism, in which the goals of gender equality that propelled the feminist movement have been systematically reached. As Ginia Bellafante suggests in a controversial *Time* article, "Some would argue that if the women's movement were still useful, it would have something to say; it's dead because it has won. Some wags have coined a phrase for this: Duh feminism."[13] The need to express an "end" to feminism or to discuss its "failure" suggests that the movement is alive and well and continues to threaten gender hegemonies; but the generational differences between second-wave, or 1970s, feminists and those now seen as the third wave prove significant to the way feminism is represented, especially within mass cultural forms.

Wendy Kaminer comments on feminism's "identity crisis": "As Karlyn Keene, a resident fellow at the American Enterprise Institute has observed, more than three-quarters of American women support efforts to 'strengthen and change women's status in society,' yet only a minority, a third at most, identify themselves as feminists. . . . If widespread support for some measure of equality reflects the way women see, or wish to see, society, their unwillingness to identify with feminism reflects the way they see themselves, or wish to be seen by others."[14]

To take a stand against powerful cultural ideologies and align oneself with a politically active movement such as feminism is rarely an easy decision, especially when there exists a strong degree of stigmatization. If normative femininity defines itself through a construction of rigid gender roles and boundaries, then to move outside that norm becomes a struggle. As Kaminer suggests, "When women talk about why they don't identify with feminists, they often talk about not wanting to lose their femininity."[15] Yet, a move back to the "feminine" and an embracing of women's "sexual power" suggests that the focus of "do-me" feminism is to "return sex from the political realm to the personal," which opposes "the personal is political" position of the second wave.[16]

"Do-me" feminism has its advantages as an ideology within contemporary mass culture. Since the term comes from a men's magazine, it implicitly promotes good relations with men. Media celebrities such as Naomi Wolf, Camille Paglia, and Katie Roiphe all fit under the term's broad umbrella. Most significantly, the term posits a pro-sex attitude, and other contemporary cultural barometers—women's magazines, talk shows, and mainstream film and television—can attest to the importance of sex as power and knowledge. Still, the focus upon sex by this group of women elides other issues equally important to feminism, a point Friend does not omit from his article: "Adds Rebecca Walker, the twenty-four-year-old founder of the New York–based feminist activist group Third Wave and the daughter of novelist Alice Walker: 'You can't have sexual agency if you have little exposure to ideas, you're being beaten, and you don't have enough money to eat.' Do-me feminism, then, is chiefly the preserve of a white female elite."[17]

Rebecca Walker points out that a focus on "sexual freedom" entails an elision of issues dealing with race, class, age, education, and *sexual preference.* Third-wave feminism is known for its vested interest in racial politics and inclusiveness, and some young feminists are unfairly aligned with an implicitly "girlie" feminism: "Girlie encompasses the tabooed symbols of feminine enculturaltion—Barbie dolls, makeup, fashion magazines, high heels—and says using them isn't shorthand for 'we've been duped.'"[18] Still, as Jennifer Baumgardner and Amy Richards wisely admit, "Girlie is pretty much an all-white phenomenon, and black women have never made such a big deal about the implications of wearing nail polish or makeup."[19] In this sense, "do-me" feminism's chief concern, in its embracing of the "feminine," is the construction and regulation of white female heterosexuality.

In focusing upon the media representations of feminism and female sexuality, articles such as Tad Friend's are important producers of contemporary popular discourse. Most of the women Friend discusses in his piece are high-profile media celebrities who have written best-selling, popular books and appear on talk shows and political debates to support their well-publicized opinions. As Naomi Wolf points out in *Fire with Fire: The New Female Power and How to Use It,* "At the end of the twentieth century, mastering the media is inevitably a form of seduction, no matter who you are or how important the message is."[20] Popular feminist discourse directly connects to the amount of media exposure involved in its circulation.

For simplicity's sake, I use the term "pop feminism" to contextualize the varied feminist discourses that affect the production of the erotic thriller within popular culture. Pop feminism is just one strand of feminist discourse, the popular media representation of feminism that intersects, yet also can diverge from, academic feminism and activist feminism. What differentiates pop feminism from other feminisms is its accessibility to the mainstream. Pop feminists such as Naomi Wolf and Camille Paglia write for *Mademoiselle* and have appeared on Bill Maher's now cancelled *Politically Incorrect* or his HBO series. They are as reachable as the daily newspaper or *Oprah*. This idea of accessibility also impinges upon other circles of feminist thought, including academe. As Catherine Orr explains in her investigation of third-wave feminism,

> Accessibility seems to be the watchword of the third wave. And when issues of accessibility to feminism are foregrounded, chances are that academic feminism's exclusivity and excesses lurk in the background. Many of these young women may devote themselves to feminism, but only insofar as they are able to "relate" to it on their own terms. . . . For a significant number of them, those terms include eschewing anything that alludes to academic feminism. . . . What feminism in the academy comes to mean in the larger society, then, is determined by those who can speak in the language talk show audiences can understand and *Cosmo* readers can appreciate.[21]

Pop feminism is intrinsically tied up with consumption and with the production of femininity through the purchase of various products, media, and other commodities. Talk shows and women's magazines both belong to a cycle of women's culture and consumption, and the parameters of pop feminism are drawn from these cultural artifacts and the consumer products they try to push (products from the beauty, self-help, and entertainment industries). Katha Pollitt points out that for "do-me" feminists, "it's feminism as book tour, a market-segmentation strategy (how to position the product to appeal to upscale under-30s, to conservatives, to bondage fanciers, whatever)."[22] She further specifies, "What the media call feminism is mostly sex chat and book promotion by a handful of writers (Camille Paglia, Katie Roiphe, Naomi Wolf, Elizabeth Wurtzel), some of whom are really antifeminists and none of whom have much to do with serious intellectual inquiry."[23]

Still, what the media deems "feminism" helps to construct the media products that utilize feminist rhetoric and terminology within their discursive structures. These "media maids" are the contemporary spokesmodels for a specific product—contemporary female heterosexuality.[24]

SEX BY NUMBERS: HOW TO HAVE BETTER ORGASMS

Contemporary women's magazines play an important role in both constructing and providing information on female heterosexuality and sexual practices, adding to pop feminist discourses on sexual exploration and empowerment. Indeed, fashion magazine editors often consider their publications to be "feminist." Gay Bryant, then *Mirabella*'s editor-in-chief, stated, "We assume our readers are feminists with a small 'f.'"[25] When Ruth Whitney was *Glamour* magazine's editor-in-chief, she said that "I would call *Glamour* a mainstream feminist magazine, in its editorials, features, fashions, and consumerism."[26] These ubiquitous messages permeate women's everyday lives. As Connie Schultz has noted, "Sometimes it seems as if sex is everywhere but in our bedrooms. Take the grocery store, for example. There's a lot of sex in the checkout line, where women's magazines that used to tout the perfect potpie now cook up recipes for everything from fiery foreplay (think chocolate) to clever costumes (think plastic wrap) to hour-long peak experiences (think unlikely)."[27]

Any analysis of popular media (including the erotic thriller) requires serious and sustained examination of the crucial role women's culture serves in constructing female identity; women's magazines are just one part of the mass cultural web. As Naomi Wolf exclaims, "Many feminists advocate rejecting women's magazines and daytime talk shows. These media are now the heart of feminism that is shaking the country."[28] The kind of feminism Wolf refers to is generally a gender-based bourgeois feminism, or what Ann Kaplan defines as "women's concern to obtain equal rights and freedom within a capitalist system."[29] As previously suggested, the definition of feminism is not monolithic or fixed, but feminists interested in class are especially suspicious of products that serve and promote commodity capitalism in the guise of feminist rhetoric. What women's magazines seem to promote is a feminine status quo, based on the consumption of products specifically marketed to women. Even purportedly feminist products are not immune to these criticisms, as there is "a danger that Spice Girls Pencil Set syndrome will settle in: girls buy products created by male-owned companies that capture the slogan of feminism without the power."[30]

Still, this particular "brand" of feminism (to use an appropriate capitalist term), selling sex in the name of female empowerment and self-growth, is rooted in women's advice columns in periodicals of over a century ago. In her historical contextualization of television talk shows, another highly popular form of women's culture, Jane Shattuc comments that in the 1880s United States, "articles that dictated correct behavior were the overall favorite of women readers," and that "these columnists functioned to promote women's rights as well as to control women."[31] What Shattuc discusses in reference to early tabloid culture is still useful when analyzing contemporary women's magazines and their effect on women's culture, for the popular press maintains a consistent instructional and regulatory tone, especially in how the media deals with sexuality. Articles touting "The Six Best Sex Positions," "Toys in Babeland," "Take Your Climax to the Max," "46 Things to Do to a Naked Man," "3 Steps to Your Best Orgasm Ever," and "Blab Your Way to Better Sex" all express a "how-to" discourse, implying that women readers need and desire more sexual experience, and that women's magazines can provide the "experts" to teach them the rules.[32] These "how-to" guides each provide specific physical techniques for better orgasms, with pop psychology surrounding gender behavior; they especially focus on female-gendered attitudes about sexuality and highlight the importance of romantic settings and romanticized fantasy scenarios. When comparing the contents of women's and men's magazines, one finds that women's magazines are much more invested in "how-to" sex articles and issues regarding "relationships" than men's, even though, if media stereotypes hold, men are supposedly more interested in sex.[33] In this respect, women's magazines intersect with "pro-sex," "do-me" feminism, suggesting that the responsibility for female (and male) pleasure lies in women's capable hands. Women's magazines' monthly bombardment of "sex instructions" at the checkout aisle signifies the weighty importance placed on female sexual knowledge in constructing female heterosexual identity. In a quest for sexual knowledge and empowerment, they suggest, women are in charge of what happens in the bedroom.

The popularity of sex advice and self-help in women's magazines extends to the video realm, as "how-to" sex videos in series such as "Better Sex" and Playboy's "Couples Only" also saturate the video/DVD market, sold in places from the Sharper Image to Borders. The two types of sex instruction videos vary, as the "Better Sex" line is much more explicit in its "instructional" qualities, often using the voice-over or appearance of psychologists, doctors, and medical experts to validate the information being presented (which is very similar to the way material is presented in women's magazines). Playboy's "Couples Only" series, while still coded as a "how-to" series, is much more connected to the realm of titillation and erotic entertainment for which *Playboy* magazine is well known. Like the "Ordinary Couples, Extraordinary Sex" series, "Better Sex" attempts to use "ordinary" people as their subjects, pulling the focus away from the glamour and romance of sex, and emphasizing technique and skill over mood and setting. Still, this type of technical hard sell has its drawbacks. As Peggy Kleinplatz writes in the *Canadian Journal of Human Sexuality*, "By focusing so heavily upon technique, many videos suggest that sex equals performance. They offer mechanical instructions rather than sexuality education. They describe and demonstrate correct technique and form for engaging in intercourse, manual, oral and anal stimulation, and occasionally, self-pleasuring. This tends to perpetuate the belief that there is a right way to do 'it,' as opposed to fostering sexual exploration, communications and pluralism."[34]

In contrast, Playboy videos such as *101 Ways to Excite Your Lover* and *How to Make Love to the Same Person Forever 1* and *2* emphasize a mise-en-scène of desire, focusing more upon setting and mood than specified techniques. According to Playboy's public relations director, Jim Nagle, "Our programs are produced with R-rated guidelines. . . . These are not so much sex manuals as advice on how to use sex to keep the spark in your relationship, by using sex games, body oils, dressing up for your partner."[35] Available at the Sharper Image stores and catalogs, the Playboy videos are easily accessible and focus more on cultivating fantasy scenarios. According to Nagle, 50 percent of the tapes' sales are to women.[36] Stimulation of the five senses—smell, taste, touch, sight, and sound—is explored in *101 Ways to Excite Your Lover*. One scene shows a woman blindfolding her partner and then having him smell and taste different foods.[37] Other scenarios show couples bathing each other, stroking each other with feathers, or staging impromptu photo shoots where both partners model a variety of different underwear. Each of these three scenarios relies on mood, romance, and communication to express sexual and sensual pleasure, leaning heavily on the importance of foreplay in reviving the passion of a relationship. The films rely on a fantasy realm to get their point across, and while they may be instructional in tone, this educational quality is covered over by the gloss of sexual entertainment.

In the Playboy series, "normal couples with real-life problems are replaced by drop-dead-beautiful actors skinny-dipping in a million-dollar swimming pool and making love in a penthouse hot tub. No children, dirty dishes, or piles of unpaid bills are in evidence."[38] Like romance novels and erotic thrillers, Playboy's home videos tend to disguise any overt instructional quality that may inhibit the spectator from being stimulated. The films provide ways to practice voyeuristic pleasure without retribution. As Robert Eberwein explains in his analysis of sex instruction videos, "Sex therapy videos occupy a unique cultural space. At least in conception, they offer viewers an opportunity to watch explicit sexual activities as students seeking information rather than voyeurs."[39] While a female spectator studies each scenario for ideas on how to "spice up" her relationship or seduce her next date, the video also serves double duty as soft-core pornography, stimulating arousal through its high-quality production values and eroticized aesthetics.

Playboy's "Couples Only" series shares many semantic elements with the erotic thriller genre—both in the way the video's "suggestions" are hidden under the guise of entertainment, and because the romanticized fantasy scenarios are tools for constructing female heterosexual identity. As in *101 Ways to Excite Your Lover,* couples showering together, blindfolding one another, caressing each other with feathers, and participating in erotic photo shoots are common tropes in the erotic thriller. *Teach Me* (1998) uses blindfolded caresses with feathers and the erotic photo shoot as ways to get Janine in touch with her desires.[40] The shopping for and trying on of erotic lingerie, another trope in the erotic thriller, also contributes to the genre's instructional quality, as "dressing up for your partner" constitutes one of Playboy's suggestions.

Still, Playboy's *101 Ways to Excite Your Lover* is a documentary, even though the lovemaking scenarios are staged and fictionalized. The film may be erotically stimulating, but its explicit goal is to inform and, by extension, to solidify and regulate normative sexual relations. The erotic thriller more frequently combines fictional suspense narratives with a heroine's path toward the gaining of sexual knowledge. Each sex scene, then, becomes a lesson on how this sexual knowledge can be obtained and of what it should consist. Combined with the therapeutic treatment of a problem—usually issues of sexual dysfunction, low self-esteem, or inhibition—the instructional erotic thriller utilizes instructional discourses to both titillate and educate the spectator, as the heroine in the film achieves both erotic and emotional fulfillment.

Films such as *Nine ½ Weeks,* a mainstream soft-core film that has provided the essential structure for numerous erotic thrillers, have become famous for their "food" scenes, "striptease" scenes, or "blindfold" and "ice cube" scenes. These films are all suggestive, creating through their fantasy scenarios a "try this at home" discourse, which contributes to the regulation of female heterosexuality. If a certain "technique" is repeated in a range of films over and over, these erotic suggestions become coded into mainstream culture as signs of "good sex," and they then produce a homogenization of sex and eroticism based on media representations. Furthermore, if certain scenarios are repeated in women's culture—a scenario from a romance novel is translated into a magazine article, which shows up in a "how-to" video and is then visualized in an erotic thriller—the question of what women want becomes indistinguishable from what they are told to want through media and product consumption. For instance, in an article focusing on Shannon Tweed, the "Queen of Erotic Thrillers," Donald Liebensen describes the erotic thriller *Cold Sweat* (Gail Harvey, 1993): "There are enough 'good parts' to satisfy her fans, including an outrageous sex scene involving dayglo paint. 'I loved that,' [Tweed] exclaimed. 'The idea for that scene came from the director, who is a woman. And you just wait. There's going to be a big budget picture that copies it.'"[41]

In a repeating, circuitous process, mainstream media produce and are constructed from a variety of competing discourses and popular trends. Films like *Flashdance* (Adrian Lyne, 1983) produce a vogue in torn, off-the-shoulder sweatshirts; and in the same vein, the seductive use of candle wax in *Body of Evidence* (Ulrich Edel, 1993) might encourage spectators to try this technique during at-home seduction. While both of these films are examples of medium-budget Hollywood films, the erotic thriller—their low-budget, B-grade sister—manages to exist within this same circuitous cycle of production and consumption. The instructional erotic thriller provides suggestions, non-explicitly, on how to gain sexual self-knowledge, thus producing an active spectator who uses entertainment for educational purposes. While this quest for sexual knowledge does connect with discourses on female empowerment and self-growth, this same knowledge must be recognized as participating in the regulation of female heterosexuality and, through consumption, constructing heterosexual female desires.

IN ORDER TO BE GOOD, YOU HAVE TO LEARN TO BE BAD

Pop feminists, beginning in the 1990s, tended to identify triumphantly with the bad girl. Elizabeth Wurtzel, in her appropriately titled book *Bitch*, gripes, "All this I'm really a lady, I'm really a nice girl crap—who needs it? It really is nothing more than surrender."[42] Camille Paglia champions the bad girl as well, stating, "I want a revamped feminism. Putting the vamp back means the lady must be a tramp."[43] Even Naomi Wolf, formerly skeptical of the beauty industry's overt sexualization of women, points out that "the bad girl is sexual. . . . The sex icons of this awakening are in charge of their own sexuality and enjoy it shamelessly."[44]

An ironic contradiction is built into the logic behind "do-me" feminism's rhetoric about "reclaiming the bad girl." As suggested earlier, this "revamped" feminism is an oppositional strategy, a media response to the contemporary representation of feminism's stereotyped alignment with a sex-negative attitude, especially regarding heterosexual sex and the gender inequalities (and differences) it entails. In order to be "good" heterosexual women, in touch with their own sexual empowerment, according to "do-me" feminism, women have to be "bad" or celebrate their "shadow slut."[45] Ironically, the attempted response to the so-called dogmatic prescriptiveness of feminist rhetoric, anti-sex in this case, is replaced by a discourse equally dogmatic and regimented. If pop feminism suggests that focusing on women's sexual power is "bad," or involves being a "bad girl," then the madonna/whore dichotomy that these women attempt to undermine is substantiated. Merri Lisa Johnson, a third-wave feminist, is wise to these contradictions inherent in "do-me" feminism, and she is also aware of the ways in which pop culture and pop feminists exacerbate supposed feminist battles for media attention. Commenting about her book *Jane Sexes It Up,* she says, "When I first imagined this project I thought that in writing it I would force feminism's legs apart like a rude lover, liberating her from the beige suit of political correctness. I wanted feminism to be *bad like me.* A young feminism, a sexy feminism. I found myself saying things like, 'I'm not *that kind* of feminist,' all sly innuendo and bedroom eyes. Early in my research, however, I discovered that *that kind of feminist* is mostly a media construct—oversimplification spiced with staged cat fights."[46]

Wolf stumbles into one of these contradictions in *Promiscuities.* She states that "in the wake of the sexual revolution, with the line between 'good' and 'bad' girls always shifting, keeping us unsteady, as it is meant to do, it will not be safe for us to live comfortably in our skins until we say: You can no longer separate us out one from another. *We are all bad girls*" (emphasis mine).[47] While Wolf initially recognizes the shifting nuances and malleability of female sexuality as something unstable and unfixed, she concludes that this shifting is "unsafe" and aligns herself clearly with bad girls. Along with Wurtzel's praising of "bitches" and Paglia's celebration of "vamps and tramps," the prescription for contemporary enlightened women is a reversal of societal puritanism. Yet, this reversal entails an indelicate slippage from the social to the biological, as sexuality moves from an unfixed, unstable social construct to a biological imperative. The sexual power that Camille Paglia refers to is essential, where prostitutes and seductresses "wield woman's ancient vampiric power over men."[48] Acting as purveyors of active sexual power, pop feminists contribute to a normative understanding of femininity; instead of destabilizing gender by suggesting a multiplicity of sexual practices and attitudes, they focus on "the natural interest in female badness" and suggest that biology (and sexual difference) is destiny.[49]

Pop feminist discourse concurrently embraces the *active* sexual woman, a figure repeatedly represented in soft-core erotic thrillers. As Nancy Friday remarks in her collection of women's sexual fantasies, *Women on Top*, women no longer see themselves as the passive recipients of sexual pleasure, but as active participants or initiators. Pop feminism has depicted this turn toward the active in popular "erotic" literature and other forms of women's culture as an example of female sexual empowerment or "liberation." Sexual empowerment becomes "essential" to women's identity, and the sexual woman turns into an unproblematic and "positive" representation. In turn, the contemporary sexual woman channels this "goddess"-like power, maintaining an ability to control men through sexual wiles.

Camille Paglia and Elizabeth Wurtzel embrace Madonna, Drew Barrymore, Sharon Stone, and other performers who utilize their sexuality in their roles and personas. In an analysis of Madonna, Camille Paglia states, "The old guard establishment feminists who still loathe Madonna have a sexual ideology problem. I am radically pro-pornography and pro-prostitution. Hence I perceive Madonna's strutting sexual exhibitionism as not cheapness or triviality but as the full florid expression of the whore's ancient rule over men."[50] For Paglia, Madonna's sexual persona is her power; women are encouraged to exploit their sexuality for their own purposes. As Naomi Wolf expressed in the quotation given earlier, sexual icons "are in charge of their own sexuality and enjoy it shamelessly." Thus, being in charge, using one's sexuality, is a valuable skill, one that can be cultivated. Women's magazines also stress the importance of learning to be a good lover, of being responsible for one's orgasms (and his, too). Under the rubric of feminist code words such as "empowerment" and "liberation," pop culture provides guidelines for female heterosexuality—and a rhetoric that finally allows women to "shamelessly" enjoy being "bad."

The soft-core erotic thriller emerges in this cultural environment as yet another outlet for sexual instruction, replicating the trajectory of sexual in-experience to sexual fulfillment common to self-help videos, while using the formulaic narrative and representational strategies common to the erotic thriller's structure. The soft-core film differs distinctively from both the educational sex video and hard-core porn, maintaining a blurry line be-tween the integrated sex numbers and their supposed instructional purpose. It never crosses into the explicit penetration of X-rated films, and it clings firmly to melodramatic narrative. The role of fantasy serves as the chief dif-ferential between overt and covertly instructional sex films (with Playboy's "how-to" videos riding the line between both types). As previously stipu-lated, in soft-core film, and the erotic thriller in particular, fantasy is exactly the point. Because of the erotic thriller's highly formulaic structure, repro-duced in multiple sequels (for example, *Secret Games 1–3*), these films are not rented to provide some kind of reality check. Instructional soft-core allows vicarious experience of commonly demeaned but titillating sexual practices (stripping, exotic dancing, and prostitution), presented within a narrative framework of female sexual fulfillment and empowerment. Entering the world of a strip club or topless bar as one of its participants promotes a fantasy of exhibitionism and sexual expression without societal punishment or retribution. Furthermore, the films allow a glimpse—albeit fantastical, glamorized, and unrealistic—at traditionally heterosexual male enclaves, places where women are often rendered uncomfortable or unwelcome.

One of the most striking aspects of *Lap Dancing* (Mike Sedan, 1995), which will be explored in some detail, and other erotic thrillers such as the *Secret Games* series, *Carnal Crimes* (A. Gregory Hippolyte, 1990), *The Dark Dancer* (Robert Burge, 1995), *Visions of Passion* (Randall St. George, 2003), and *For-bidden Sins* (Robert Angelo, 1998) is that they deal with women who escape from dull, un-erotic professional or domestic lives by moonlighting as high-priced call girls, nude models, or exotic dancers, all in the process of getting in touch with their more sexual side or fulfilling their fantasies. The encroach-ment of sexual self-help rhetoric contextualized within the current surge toward women's sexual knowledge creates a genre that provides instruction on how heterosexual women should achieve sexual fulfillment. Ideologically, these films suggest that to be "good" or "healthy" sexually and emotionally, you've got to learn to be a "bad, bad girl," chiefly because "bad girls," or sex workers in this case, know sex best (figure 3).[51]

Lap Dancing (Mike Sedan, 1995) provides an ideal case study, since it ex-emplifies some of the formulaic tropes of the erotic thriller while explicitly

Figure 3. Kate watches a stripper perform in *Dead Sexy* (2001).

dealing with "bad girl" sexual terrain—the world of the exotic dancer or lap dancer. Typically, a sexual or professional empowerment plotline combines with the necessary narrative trajectory toward the heroine's sexual experience. In this case, the film opens with Angie (Lorissa McComass), a struggling actress, failing miserably at an audition where a certain amount of (implied sexual) "experience" is necessary to play the role. Success, here in terms of acting, can only occur when one has fully developed sexual knowledge. Angie's naïveté and lack of street smarts are revealed through her sweet personality, in direct contrast to Claudia, her sarcastic lap-dancing roommate (Shannon Tweed look-alike Tane' McClure), who represents the sexually experienced other woman necessary to lead Angie to sexual knowledge. Claudia suggests that Angie come to the club she works at, in order to prepare her for more sophisticated acting roles, and so begins the heroine's sexual instruction within the "other world."

Lap Dancing replicates the structure of some better-sex documentaries, which must provide the credentials and expertise of their requisite sex therapists in order to be utilized as instructional tools.[52] In the soft-core film, sexual instruction and "lessons" are frequently taught by the women, who represent so-called experts in their field. (A similar motif appears in erotic thrillers that deal explicitly with therapeutic situations, where the heroines are sex therapists or sexologists.) Also, as in many instructional videos, *Lap Dancing* tends to displace voyeurism (here female) within an "educational" or "instructional" context. Within the erotic thriller, the tensions between voyeurism and instructional looking become even more apparent, just as sexual performances within narrative film are predicated on a level of voyeurism. These tensions are played out in the character of Angie, who is always caught between titillation—or getting in touch with her sexual side—and her education as a necessary step toward her professional success and self-development.

Claudia, the woman of experience, repeatedly refers to the sex numbers in the film as "education." During an eroticized moment in their apartment, Claudia tells Angie to close her eyes while she softly touches the surfaces of Angie's body. Claudia seductively asks, "When was the last time your heart was beating so fast, you thought you would explode," instructing Angie to focus on her body's sensations, her breathing, and her heartbeat. While Claudia's hands do touch Angie as she teaches her, the touch is not as much intimate as instructional. The film never indicates that Claudia's motivation for helping Angie is anything more than "sisterly" or friendly.

During Angie's first official lap dance, as in her acting audition, she appears awkward, stiff, and uncomfortable. When Claudia takes over the lap dance for her, she orders Angie to watch. The camera focuses on Claudia's body moving over the sprawling customer, but through Angie's gaze. Angie never appears titillated by watching, as if she is studiously taking mental notes; yet, later she does have fitful, sex-filled dreams and explains how she's so "worked up." As Claudia performs the lap dance, she talks to Angie, further breaking the voyeuristic fantasy, like breaking a fourth-wall boundary. The customer upon whom she gyrates is only a pawn in Angie's quest for self-knowledge, useful for purposes of illustration but without any gaze or subjectivity of his own. Furthering this uneven power differential are the rules of lap dancing. Claudia informs the man, "Don't touch. I can touch. You can't. Got it?" Within lap dancing, men are passive, unable to be active or aggressive.

Another dancer, Sandy, teaches Angie about sex by blindfolding her and having her listen to the sounds of her and her boyfriend having sex. Even though Angie admits, "I just don't know how much more educated I could possibly get tonight," the scene illustrates the dual functioning in the erotic thriller of titillating erotic entertainment combined with instructional discourses. In this scene particularly, Angie becomes obviously stimulated and turned on, even though she cannot see what's happening—she's educated aurally. Again, Sandy addresses her voyeur by communicating her desire to Angie throughout the sex act, indicating the underlying exhibitionism inherent in sexual instruction. While characters such as Sandy and Claudia perform as instructors, the narrative makes clear that these women are enjoying their roles as sexually experienced mentors throughout their performances.

Later that evening, after Angie comes back to the club from Sandy's apartment, Claudia drags her out into the back alley, stating, "O.K. Angie. Time for a little more education." Angie becomes "educated" as they watch Irene turn a trick with a john; they both voyeuristically absorb this sight (since Irene is "caught unawares"), all in the name of instruction. The two characters are never punished for their voyeuristic looking, for the looking is couched in educational terms, serving a higher goal.

Lap Dancing provides an elaborate spin on stripping and prostitution as safe pursuits, and therefore as havens for the playing out of fantasy. Still, through the film's positioning of female empowerment as its narrative drive, certain moral boundaries (and feminist values) are maintained. For instance, Sandy's abusive boyfriend is stridently despised, as is Angie's domineering ex-boyfriend, who is dumped very early in the narrative. Codependency is continually critiqued in these films. In *Teach Me* (1998), for instance, Janine is frequently told that it is not enough to please her husband; she must learn to lose her inhibitions for herself.

In *Forbidden Passions* (1996), the film's entire narrative motivation is built around teaching its heroine, Mara, how her life is negatively influenced by her codependency problems. The film even implies that she dies because of this ignorance. After her boyfriend unceremoniously deserts her, Mara despairingly turns to her virtual reality (VR) program for comfort (she's a VR designer). While in this virtual world, her apartment catches fire, and she dies. Mara is trapped in the virtual world, and the rest of the film consists of her attempts to leave it by helping people (often sexually). After she learns her lesson—that she must experience pleasure and make decisions based upon her own needs—she can finally leave VR purgatory. This critique of codependency serves a dual purpose. For one thing, it supports the self-help, self-esteem rhetoric reiterated in women's magazines. In addition, the film's discursive strategies promote the idea of "sexual empowerment" and experiencing sex actively, "for yourself," which substantiates "do-me" feminism.

In *Lap Dancing*, stripping is always contextualized within certain instructional contexts, and exotic dancing and prostitution are never completely condoned as fully legitimate lifestyles; the job is just a means to an end. While Claudia and Angie both value their experience as exotic dancers, the narrative makes clear that these women are interested in higher-profile careers (Angie as an actress, Claudia, a singer). In fact, to promote the profession's legitimacy, Angie serves as the investigator within the story (and a stand-in for the spectator), asking Claudia and Sandy why they dance, and why Irene "has sex with men for money." Still, Irene insists that she "likes it," that she's doing it for herself, which follows the erotic thriller's formulaic credo toward sexual fulfillment: exploring this part of your fantasy life or sexuality is "good" for you, no matter how you go about doing it.

In recent years, lap dancing has maintained this glossy do-it-for-yourself mythology not only within the erotic thriller, but also within the popular press and the culture at large. James Langton interviewed strippers and dancers who worked at Scores, the high-class club on Manhattan's Upper West Side where Demi Moore took "lessons" in preparation for her role in *Striptease*. When he asked a dancer what advice she gave Moore, she replied, "I approached her, took her hand, and said: The most important thing I can tell you is always dance for yourself. I always dance for me. And what man can get off on a woman who doesn't get off on herself."[53] (See figure 4.) The article further explains that in lap dancing "it is a naked woman who controls the dance, not the man before her."[54] Claudia demonstrates this concept in the film when she shows Angie how to lap dance. Both of these discourses on stripping serve as support for the narrative and fantasy role-playing present in *Lap Dancing*'s rhetoric of female empowerment. In order to gain sexual satisfaction, "sisters are doing it for themselves," as the song says, and not in order to please men, even though it is men who demonstrate their economic power by purchasing lap dances and prostitution services as commodities.

The film posits that exotic dancing and stripping are just useful tools or performances that trigger self-exploration. Still, the female stars of the instructional erotic thriller only dip into this sexual netherworld—researching for an acting role, in *Lap Dancing;* moonlighting while finishing an MBA, in *Lap Dancer;* or providing an outlet for an unfulfilled college professor, in *The Dark Dancer.* These women never remain within that world; instead, it provides a necessary escape valve from their unfulfilled sex lives and is only a spicy diversion to them, not a career move. *Lap Dancing* constantly reminds us that Angie's stint as an exotic dancer is temporary, even though her encounters with her sexuality will last forever.

Figure 4. Claudine dances "for herself" in *Kiss of Fire* (1998).

The sex scenes in *Lap Dancing,* and all the sex numbers in these films, signify the conflicting discourses surrounding the construction of hetero-sexuality within the instructional soft-core film, and within "do-me" femi-nism as well. In a scene where Irene is dancing onstage, Claudia instructs Angie to "look at her . . . she has no inhibitions." While Claudia suggests that Irene feels sexual, and that her sexiness is "real," "something that you can't fake," she simultaneously shows Angie, through demonstration and various tips and advice, that sexual experience is "learned" and a "skill." She tells Angie, "It's real. It's honest. She feels it." Yet, what Claudia reveals to Angie in lesson after lesson is that sex is a performance, an "attitude" or mask that one can put on and take off—that heterosexuality is not natural or "real." This conflict also lies within Angie's quest for self-development, for the only outcome of her lap-dancing experience is the further instability of her fixed heterosexual identity, even though she is now able to free her formerly inhibited, "innate" sexuality. In the end, Angie auditions again for the part she was too "inexperienced" for before. She lands the role, but not without reiterating that her more nuanced "performance" is what helps her achieve her goal.

Lap Dancing and other films that deal with "bad girl" fantasies are easily dismissed as exploitation and sexist trash, but the focus on female sexual subjectivity and fulfillment in these films collides with the discourses on female heterosexuality that circulate throughout popular culture. For instance, Christie Hefner writes in *Cosmopolitan,* "That which is sexual—including sexual imagery and words—is positive and healthy. For an emotionally healthy woman, sexually arousing material—whether it's a magazine, book, or film—may add profoundly to a good relationship. So rather than expending energy attempting to label and suppress the sexual fantasies of others, women and men alike would do better to explore and celebrate their own sexual fantasies and desires."[55]

Christie Hefner's celebration of sexual imagery reveals her political and economic stake, perhaps hidden within her veneration of rampant sexual freedom. The coincidence of her position as head of Playboy Enterprises, Inc., and her presence in a magazine such as *Cosmopolitan* exemplifies how the market produces materials that stimulate a need and desire for sexual instruction, the defining of boundaries, and the construction of a fixed sexual identity. What is promising is that these materials, through their constant production and proliferation, focus on the skills of "sexual performance" and thereby call into question fixed sexual identities.

Still, the recurring focus on the acquisition of sexual experience and knowledge within these films, sustained as a move toward the goal of "sexual empowerment," deserves skeptical investigation. Nor should the fact that the term "do-me" feminism arises from a popular *men's* magazine, *Esquire,* be ignored. In all the discourse surrounding women's sexual agency and aggressiveness, those who stand to gain the most from women's being "bad girls" might be heterosexual *men* (as Tad Friend's eager embrace of the new feminism attests).

Pop feminism's focus on sexual agency is an important consideration for sexually active women. Yet, "do-me" feminism serves as another "instructional discourse" that dictates a set of rules for appropriate behavior. The erotic thriller's structure and narrative reflect this same system of regulation that governs the construction of contemporary female heterosexuality. In interrogating these different pop cultural forms, their intermingling similarities suggest certain ideological definitions of gender. The representation of sexuality is constantly changing, as women's lives inform the media and vice versa, but the two are no longer separable or distinguishable from each other. As Meryl Altman explains, "The way a woman experiences her sexuality, the ways we represent our sexuality to ourselves and enact that representation, are almost impossible to separate from the representations our culture makes available to us."[56]

While "instructional discourses" within sexual materials can encourage more experimentation and communication in the bedroom, the underlying message behind the instruction, an attempt to contain inappropriate or deviant behavior, must also be interpreted. Although the mass media help to produce the contemporary "sexual woman," they can never be certain that women are "doing it" for themselves.

THE SUBJECT OF PASSION, THE OBJECT OF MURDER: REFASHIONING THE GOTHIC AND FILM NOIR GENRES

A woman flees a dark house and the murderous clutches of her husband. A police detective attempts to uncover a murderer but risks being seduced by the killer. An enchanting femme fatale manipulates a man with her sexual wiles, laughing inwardly as she emasculates him. These narrative examples contain certain themes—murder, sex, and a threatened subject—as well as some generic archetypes of the female gothic (or paranoid woman's film) and film noir: the curiosity-driven young wife, the sexually vulnerable police detective, and the duplicitous, seductive woman. All of these generic narrative tropes contain a sexual threat, as the main character's subjectivity becomes clouded by the pursuit of the object of desire. These generic tropes are common to film genres established primarily in 1940s Hollywood. Since then, spinoffs of these genres have emerged, serving as contemporary retellings of familiar stories. Most recently, the contemporary soft-core erotic thriller borrows and manipulates some of the same dark, corrupted elements that brought the thrill to these established genres.

REUSABLE GENRES

Genres do not merely reflect the current ideology of a historical moment; they also produce that ideology.[1] Two 1940s Hollywood film genres have re-emerged into a specifically *contemporary* sexually oriented genre, indicating a refashioning of generic elements within a new but related sociocultural context. Gothic and noir versions of the erotic thriller convey anxieties regarding the definition of women's role within both the public and private spheres. This "socio-symbolic message," as Fredric Jameson describes such a specific generic narrative component, stems from strong generic predecessors.[2] Genres related to 1940s Hollywood developed from film industry practices within a specific sociocultural moment, and there was a simultaneous transformation and persistent reestablishment of gender roles. In the 1940s, women became a necessary part of the workforce and subsequently changed the film audience of that era, indicating a period of gender role instability.[3] The threatened wife of the gothic film and the dangerous femme fatale of film noir became archetypes symptomatic of a threatened sexual division of labor; separations of the public and the private were under siege.

The "woman's film" sparked another 1940s Hollywood phenomenon: narratives directed toward audiences that were increasingly female. Still, the "paranoid women's film," or "gothic," described by the theorist Mary Ann Doane did not typify the melodramatic associations of the "woman's film."[4] The themes of love and harmony coexist with violence and fear in the gothic. Doane admits that the female-driven thriller is "infiltrated by the conventions of the *film noir* and the horror film."[5] While these films focused on female subjectivity, this focalization was always threatened or questioned by dark forces (patriarchal ones, such as the murderous husband). While issues of marriage and family share generic connections to melodrama, the fear and anxiety that shadow the gothic film reveal acute anxieties surrounding the heroine's sexual and emotional subjectivity. Her role as wife remains uncertain or questionable, reflecting her unstable relationship to her own femininity.

The more recent DTV gothic erotic thriller, or "neo-gothic," continues to represent the heroine's subjectivity as the dominant mode of focalization; as in the paranoid woman's film, the neo-gothic heroine experiences curiosity in tandem with palpable fear (and often guilt). Spectator identification occurs through the restricted narration of the film's female protagonist, however uncertain or questionable this narration becomes. While neo-gothic films occasionally exhibit omniscient narrative strategies, and point-of-view structures are sometimes playfully manipulated, the heroine's plight as simultaneous hero and victim, subject and object, remains the trajectory of the narrative. Structural differences in the erotic thriller rely on the repeated positioning of sex scenarios within the story. Thus, the anxiety entrenched within the neo-gothic has as much to do with the heroine's being the subject of passion as with her being the object of murder.

Erotic thrillers with gothic-infused narratives specifically allude to women's genres; yet, the refashioning of a male-oriented genre such as film noir also contributes to an expanding interest in female-driven narratives. Substantive narrative and structural changes to established genres thus indicate the continued appeal of these genres, as well as their necessary contextual transformation. This transformation also produces new formal possibilities: the noir detective becomes female, and her voice-over and point of view reveal the narrative's trajectory. She now grows vulnerable to the sexual advances of the duplicitous man (and sometimes woman) who threatens her authority. Similarly, erotic thrillers with male detectives/investigators reveal the femme fatale's narrative control. The male protagonist often exists as a pawn in the woman's sexual adventures.

The postmodern situation complicates the matter and creates a certain logic regarding originality and "original" forms; contemporary film is embedded with a history of generic forms, producing consistently hybrid genres. The DTV erotic thriller thus represents a merging of the past and present, utilizing traditional Hollywood narrative strategies while producing new forms of sexual and social discourse. Jameson argues that "the relationship of the 'third term' or historical situation to the text is not construed as causal . . . but rather as one of a limiting situation; the historical moment is here understood to block off or shut down a certain number of formal possibilities available before, and to open up determinate new ones."[6] Formally, the DTV erotic thriller overtly embraces a more sexually explicit aesthetic, while hints of other contemporary women's genres—the erotic romance novel, the soap opera, and the talk show—lurk within its structure. Still, the 1940s female gothic and film noir remain the most persistent undercurrents within these films, translating gender instability and female audience interests into a more contemporary, yet strikingly familiar, format.

The tensions between pleasure and danger that exist within the erotic thriller remain crucial to the syntactic structure of the genre, since they convey the formal and textual limitations of the historical situation. Whereas the sexual themes of the 1940s gothic and film noir genres were essentially submerged, albeit erupting throughout the text, the heroine's sexuality becomes the focal point of the soft-core genre. While the heroine's sexual desire drives the narrative forward, the institutions and regulations that mark her role as "woman" threaten the story's resolution. She can no longer be contained within the roles of wife or mistress, yet her troubled relationship to economic and emotional independence does not disappear. Whether the heroine is a sexually frustrated wife, a horny police detective, or a treacherous femme fatale, her desire for sexual gratification must always be linked to danger and dread.

SOFT-CORE GASLIGHTING, OR THE NEO-GOTHIC

The image of a young, attractive woman fleeing a forbidding castle or mansion, her nightgown blown by the gusting wind, is a common trope of the modern gothic romance. The woman runs from the house that entraps her, symbolically escaping the marriage that threatens her.[7] Her husband displays suspicious motivations, hints of possible murderous intentions; yet he remains an enigma, a mystery the heroine determinedly explores. This narrative paradigm creates an important subjective space for the gothic's heroine: she is simultaneously the curious, investigating subject and the threatened victim. Her flight from her home also suggests a troubled relationship to domesticity. A woman's traditional realm of security becomes threatening and unstable, and consequently her role as wife disintegrates. Her diaphanous clothing suggests her problematic relations to her sexuality as well.

My interest in the female gothic genre lies predominately in mid- to late twentieth- and early twenty-first-century versions of this romantic narrative. But the form's historic precedents during the mid- to late eighteenth century provide a ground for understanding the genre's reemergence within contemporary formulations, specifically in the context of changing economic and leisure circumstances of women during these different periods. The literary historian Kate Ferguson Ellis suggests that increased industrialization, the population's movement to urban areas, and the increase of a servant class in eighteenth-century England produced a group of new readers; work moved out of the home and into industrial areas, creating separate spheres of existence for men and women.[8] Ellis points out that "'domestic happiness' emerged toward the end of the eighteenth century, as the middle-class home, distanced in ideology and increasingly in fact from the place where money was made, became a 'separate sphere' from the 'fallen' world of work."[9] Leisure increased for middle-class women as they were released from previous physical work duties, and they now became the primary keepers of the hearth or home and the moralities that were contained there.[10] Changing gender roles encouraged this push, as "a well-regulated home . . . was an outward sign of male competence and trustworthiness, a valuable economic asset in a situation where traditional markers of reliability were inappropriate, inadequate, or breaking down."[11] If a woman was middle class, her labor role was transformed into mothering and moral integrity. A division in gender roles, and in class distinctions, became more pronounced.

The construction of separate spheres during the second half of the eighteenth century proved symptomatic of the unstable gender boundaries of this period. Likewise, the movement from countryside to urban centers accompanied by changes in technology created social violence and unrest. The home, as a place of safety for women, was to be secure from danger outside its borders. As Ellis argues, "It is when the home becomes a 'separate sphere,' a refuge from violence, that a popular genre comes into being that assumes some violation of this cultural ideal."[12] Thus, in the gothic genre, the home develops into a threatening and unstable environment, becoming a castle or prison, with danger lurking within its very walls. Similarly, the conflict revolving around the heroine's social role permeates her subjectivity. As a moral guardian, she must suppress her desire; her temptations are suffused with fear. Domesticity thus becomes fundamentally feminine and potentially dangerous.

The themes of the eighteenth-century gothic and its problematic relationship to women's domestic role translate directly into the (literary and filmic) modern gothic romance; the reemergence of the gothic in the contemporary DTV erotic thriller explicitly reveals these connections. The 1940s female gothic film grapples with similar tensions, as women were forced to exist within both public and private spheres while men were at war. A persistent relationship must be drawn between the two genres of the woman's film, for not only do the female gothic or "gaslight film" and the neo-gothic erotic thriller appeal directly to women through similar narrative techniques, but they both also continue lines of inquiry about the changing social role of women in relation to economic alterations.

Soft-core cinema's contemporary co-opting of the gaslight film conveys familiar problematic relationships between the heroine and her husband, and her uneasy containment within her marriage. Like the heroines of *Rebecca* (Alfred Hitchcock, 1940) or *Secret beyond the Door* (Fritz Lang, 1948), the heroines of the gothic erotic thrillers—*Sexual Response* (1992), *Sexual Malice* (1994), *Illicit Dreams* (1994), *Nightfire* (1994), *Carnal Crimes* (1990), *Night Eyes 2* (1992), *Intimate Obsession* (1992), and *Two Shades of Blue* (James Deck, 2000)—all have a troubled relationship to the past. Within the gothic's 1940s and contemporary permutations, the husband is often more sexually experienced, emotionally dominating, and frequently paternalistic toward the younger bride—traits subtly revealed, but relentlessly ignored, during the early period of their relationship. These women are nostalgic for their courtship days with their husbands, when the love between them was consistently available. Similarly, the husband has a dark past, although in the erotic thriller the heroine inevitably discovers this skeleton too late.

While the 1940s gothic film and the contemporary erotic thriller share similar strategies, they strongly differentiate themselves by their respective enigmas. The heroine's enigma in the 1940s gothic is her husband and his mysterious motivations. Her pursuit revolves "around whether or not the Gothic male really loves her."[13] Often a woman from the past—Rebecca, Alice Alquist, a controlling mother-in-law—stands in the heroine's path toward achieving this goal. In contrast, for the soft-core heroine, the narrative enigma shifts to the woman's sexual fulfillment, consistently experienced outside her marriage (again, the institution serves as a symbol of containment). The heroine's enigma is no longer her husband's inner life, but *her* sexual life. The husband's indifference no longer drives the heroine to discover the origins of his behavior, for they have been married for a while; instead, her lack of gratification and sexual communication with her husband drives her into the arms of another. Self-knowledge through sexual pleasure is the heroine's explicit goal, and her husband's (still malicious) motivations are an accidental discovery.

The notion of separate spheres prevails today, especially within contemporary neoconservative ideological discourse, but the continuing strides of the women's movement have caused these gendered divisions to blur and dissolve. As Diane Waldman explains, gaslight films reveal a tension between the sphere of production, outside the home, and the sphere of reproduction, within the home.[14] The conflicting role definitions surrounding the working woman of the 1940s are even more pronounced regarding the contemporary working woman. The erotic thriller's protagonist is torn between her productive, and lucrative, public persona—lawyer, writer, sex therapist—and her private persona: sexually frustrated wife. This public/private, exterior/interior tension appears within the soft-core text, represented through the figure of the house and the body of the woman.

In the eighteenth and nineteenth centuries, the house developed into the sphere of womanhood; a woman was judged by the successful management of her husband's house and material possessions. These themes carry over into the 1940s gothic film, where the young newlywed encounters the forbidding ancestral mansion and must learn to manage its staff and herself with the proper decorum. Ed Gallafent argues in his analysis of *Gaslight*

(George Cukor, 1944) and *Rebecca,* "What is being underlined is the function of the bourgeois wife as a point of connection between sexual desire and the household's systems of exchange. Her role as a protector or preserver of the objects of the house reflects on her guardianship of that other 'treasure,' her sexual virtue. . . . coupled with this is the fear of the woman who possesses the treasures for herself rather than on behalf of her husband, and exercises her sexuality outside the terms imposed by a dominating male."[15]

The fear and threat of the woman in possession of her own treasures, inside and outside the home, becomes a powerful source of conflict within the gothic erotic thriller. The neo-gothic heroine now works within the public realm; the house signifies the heroine's own material successes in the outside world. Her high-powered job or business acumen has made her the primary breadwinner of the couple, which thereby emasculates the husband. Her success in the business realm is not only acutely resented by her husband, but also provides a source for her dysfunctional management of her home and marriage. The success of the woman outside the home is proportional to her lack of success in the bedroom. The female protagonist's sexual frustration then produces the dynamic anxiety surrounding domesticity that always structures the gothic; her adulterous needs catalyze the murderous feelings the husband carries toward his successful wife. Because the heroine's goals have shifted from love (traditionally evoked through the heterosexual couple) to sexual gratification, the marriage bond proves an impediment to the heroine's narrative trajectory. Murder becomes the only way of resolving these apparent social conflicts.

Sexual Malice (Jag Mundhra, 1994) replicates the themes of domestic upheaval and sexual distress common to the DTV gothic erotic thriller; indeed, the fundamental building blocks of the gothic genre are laid out within the first five minutes of the film. The shadowed, soft-focus figures of a couple making love foreground the intended subject matter of the film: sex.[16] The narrative opens with the film's heroine, Christine, telling her story to several male police detectives in an interrogation room. She decides to start at the beginning—"I guess it started at a party"—and immediately the spectator enters into her restricted narration as she describes the events that led to her arrest. Female uncertainty, a crucial component of the gothic's structure, emerges through the heroine's troubled retelling. Did the story occur this way, or is she imagining things? The use of restricted narration introduces the crises of subjectivity layered throughout the neo-gothic and the woman's film in general—a subjectivity where "the woman's exercise of an active investigating gaze can only be simultaneous with her own victimization."[17]

In *Sexual Malice,* the story world then evolves into the introductory party scene. Christine's party, set in a sprawling mansion and attended by lavishly outfitted guests, sustains the conflict between her public and private personas. Her tactless boss jibes at Richard, her husband, about his inferior existence as a college professor (who earns a third of what his successful lawyer wife does). Through this unsettling comparison, the house no longer indicates masculine financial success (of which the "trophy wife" plays a crucial role). Instead, Christine's success emasculates Richard, stripping him of necessary phallic power. He proves unable to function within his social role of breadwinner, and he subsequently fails in his sexual role as well. Christine has achieved a level of status that moves her beyond domestic duties connected to the house; servants and caterers are in charge of running the house, distancing her from the traditional feminine role. Furthermore, children are not even mentioned, so motherhood does not serve as a feminizing tool.

While the source of Richard's dissatisfaction apparently lies in his wife's economic success, his motives and thoughts are never explicitly voiced or revealed. He remains enigmatic and unreachable. When Christine enters the upper reaches of her house, looking for him, she encounters her first voyeuristic sex scenario, which sets the film's true enigma into motion. The heroine stumbles upon her boss's sexually frustrated wife having sex with the caterer, frolicking among the billiard balls on the pool table. The scene's shots are through Christine's point of view as she gazes at this sexual display. This sex scenario serves several purposes. It acts as titillation to Christine (and to the spectator), reminding her of her own needs. In fact, the woman's adulterous behavior foreshadows Christine's own foray into infidelity, and the scene serves as an instructive moment, leading the heroine to increased sexual knowledge.

Christine's initial act of sexual voyeurism also suggests the incompatibility of sex and love—an essential theme of the soft-core narrative. This troubled distinction commonly manifests itself through relations between the female protagonist and the "experienced" woman. The presence, whether real or implied, of the other woman connects the heroine with a sinister and mysterious past. Never is this connection more apparent than in Hitchcock's *Rebecca,* for the deceased Rebecca's sexual experience and sophistication defines the heroine through the negative: everything the other woman is, the heroine *is not.*

This enigmatic female character translates into the heroine's promiscuous friend in the erotic thriller. The female protagonist appears always naïve and sexually repressed, only developing sexual wants through repeated interactions with a series of phallic women. Christine's first encounter with this type of woman begins with her voyeuristic view of her boss's wife. Still, most of her sexual knowledge is imparted by her best friend, Nicole. The film repeatedly establishes a marked contrast between the two characters. As the two size up men at Christine's party, Christine accuses Nicole of being a "nymphomaniac" for openly expressing her desires. Later, on the terrace, Nicole gives Christine some worldly advice:

Nicole: Leave him.
Christine: I can't. I still love him.
Nicole: Honey, if this is love, I'll stick to sex.

While Christine remains the focalized source for the narrative, Nicole emerges as Christine's idol and sexual role model, the woman she aspires to be. Unfortunately, the heroine cannot become satisfied within the confines of her marriage, a condition with which Nicole, like all other gothic bad women, is familiar. Later Christine expresses her disgust at her boss's wife's actions (fooling around with the help) and remarks on the woman's married state. Nicole can only laugh at Christine's naïve idealism toward the institution. The heroine longs for a time when her husband's love was available and apparent, a time when she did not question his motives or desires.[18] The difference between the renditions of the 1940s and the contemporary gothic rests on the decision the heroine makes regarding her fears and anxieties. While the 1940s heroine must find love at all costs, the contemporary heroine gives up on love and focuses on the more instantaneous gratification of sex. Indeed, within the erotic thriller, love and sex are mutually exclusive.

Since the film is filtered through Christine's restricted narration, the spectator exclusively experiences her subjective development. Therefore, the heroine's introduction to the male sex object, Quinn, marks the explicit objectification of the male body. Quinn is a male stripper, an erotic spectacle, and thereby feminized. The camera focuses for long periods on the removal of his pants and shirt as his body writhes to some music; he has no other purpose than to be Christine's object of desire. Every sex scene in Christine's narration places her as the subject of passion (figure 5). Unfortunately, because of the film's limited point-of-view structure, Christine (and the spectator) does not realize that she has been betrayed. Richard has paid Quinn to seduce her, to prejudice the divorce settlement, and then subsequently frames Christine for her lover's murder, which places her in jail when the story begins. The film

Figure 5. Christine and Quinn have wild sex in *Sexual Malice* (1994).

slips into omniscient narration at two pivotal points in Christine's narrative. Once, when she's on the phone with Quinn, the narrative reveals Richard listening on another phone, unbeknownst to Christine. At another point, Quinn blindfolds Christine while they are having sex, and he takes pictures of her for purposes of blackmail. Both instances reveal Christine's victimization in tandem with the restriction of her active, sexually investigating gaze.

This combination of pleasure and danger within the erotic thriller works to substantiate Christine's faltering subjectivity. She may provide primary access to the film's visual world (although her narration is twice disrupted), but she loses this control as she languishes in jail. This is where the male rescuer/love interest figure common to the gothic becomes necessary. The heroine cannot rely on her own investigations, for as Mary Ann Doane explains, "Quite often the female protagonist is endowed with the necessary curiosity and a desire to know but is revealed as impotent in terms of the actual ability to uncover the secret or attain the knowledge which she desires."[19] Christine may actively pursue her sexual desires, but she remains oblivious to the danger lurking within her home, from her own marriage. The film requires two male rescuers: Christine's old lover, Jack, a police detective who jilted her at the altar, and her younger brother, David.[20] The two men set out to discover who framed Christine, and then they must trap the criminal. The film's climax reveals Richard fooling around with Nicole, Christine's promiscuous friend, having planned to divorce the heroine and destroy her financially. Here the submerged noir elements of the gothic rise to the surface—the femme fatale gets the man, and the desire for wealth, not love, stands as Richard's motivation. Richard states, "I never loved [Christine], but I grew to love her money," thereby proclaiming that love and marriage threaten the contemporary heroine's life, autonomy, and economic independence. The male rescuers kill the gothic villain, but only after his murderous intentions are finally uncovered.

The narrative of *Sexual Malice* suggests that the heroine experiences punishment for her sexual explorations outside of marriage, as infidelity leads to murder; yet, the *marriage* proves to be the really fatal element for Christine. After she tells her husband of her infidelity, her husband miraculously forgives her. He creates sexual scenarios in the outdoor Jacuzzi and within their lavish bedroom, and Christine is lulled into imagining that love prevails. As she sleeps contentedly in the bed they share, Richard kills her lover and frames her for the murder. Christine's trust in her husband and their monogamous love relationship has led to murder. The heroine's marriage instigates the crisis her subjectivity undergoes; in order to achieve personal autonomy and sexual fulfillment, she must leave her "love" relationship behind.

While Christine's husband remains enigmatic and unknowable until the climax of *Sexual Malice,* another strain of both the gaslight film and the DTV gothic erotic thriller displays a less ambiguous, more clearly vindictive husband. In films such as *Dragonwyk* (Joseph L. Mankiewicz, 1946) or *Gaslight,* or in more contemporary versions such as *Illicit Dreams* or *Sexual Response,* the audience experiences near omniscient narration by witnessing the husband's murderous intentions. This narrative structure, which I will call the "abuser" narrative, is also common to the made-for-TV "female-in-jeopardy" (fem-jep) movie (with its explicit address to a female viewing audience) and to a lesser extent, the slasher film.[21] All of these narratives create a masochistic engagement with the heroine's plight as she experiences her terror. In the abuser gothic, the spectator knows that the husband is evil, often from the outset, yet enjoys watching the heroine suffer, hoping that she will be rescued or prevail in the end.

Within the abuser narrative, the heroine retains a more clearly drawn relationship to the house, the symbol of entrapment in the gothic romance.

As discussed earlier, the role of the heroine as protector of the house and its objects remains as a symbol of the husband's masculine control over both the public and private spheres; he must keep these realms separate in order to sustain his masculine identity. The treasures of the house (the wife being one of them) are rigorously regulated by the abusive husband, as he delegates domestic responsibilities to his wife with great importance and vehemence. In both *Illicit Dreams* and *Sexual Response,* for instance, the heroine is required to serve her husband domestically and sexually, although in each film the protagonist is frustrated by her husband's cavalier treatment of her desires (in *Illicit Dreams,* the husband carries on with his secretary in the heroine's home). The economically independent heroine only compounds the abuser's anger and resentment, thereby creating further demands that she fulfill her traditional role as wife, domestic laborer, and sexual slave.

The tension between the productive realms and reproductive realms, expressed in the management of the gothic house, becomes directly proportional to the heroine's sexuality inside and outside the marriage. Sex and love, as well as financial success and marriage, cannot coexist for the heroine. The instability of these dichotomous terms becomes insurmountable, and the narrative often resolves itself through murder. For instance, in the neo-gothic *Sexual Response,* Dr. Eve Robertson (Shannon Tweed) works as a radio talk show sex therapist while simultaneously attempting to fulfill her role as wife to her husband, Philip. She must report to him her actions outside the home and provide his meals and comfort whenever necessary. She soon enters into an adulterous yet sexually fulfilling relationship with Edge, a drifter she encounters at a bar with her promiscuous friend from work, thus further separating her work life from her home life, and sexual pleasure from confinement within marriage. Eve begins to neglect her marital life, and as Philip discovers her infidelity, his homicidal tendencies are triggered; he had killed his previous wife under similar circumstances. In the film's climax, Eve's husband and several other characters are murdered, and the narrative resolves through destroying the marital institution and leaving the heroine sexually knowledgeable and able to fulfill future sexual desires. Tensions can be dissolved only after the heroine's domestic role has been eradicated, for she cannot exist successfully within both public and private spheres.

Similarly, Moira (Shannon Tweed, again) in *Illicit Dreams* (Andrew Stevens, 1994) must also fulfill her abusive husband's desires, even though *his* infidelities and obsessions are allowable within their marriage. She explains to her promiscuous friend Mindy that divorce would not be possible, because if she tried to leave, Daniel would kill her. At one point, the heroine overhears her husband having sex with his secretary in her home, and shortly thereafter her husband demands she serve both of them coffee. Moira does not work within the public sphere, which means she must succeed in her role as wife and caretaker of the house; as Daniel points out, "You have nothing to do all day except take care of the house." As in all DTV erotic thriller narratives, the tension between public and private spheres revolves around shifting definitions of gender roles. As Daniel's business falters, he obsessively attempts to regain control by abusing his wife within the private sphere—forcing her to clean at 3 A.M. and becoming enraged when his eggs are cold. Moira's psyche, like that of an abuse victim, compensates for domestic terrorism through dream work, which creates the guiding subjectivity of the narrative.

"The uncanny" has always been a major component of the gothic genre, usually manifesting itself within the heroine's own unstable subjective space.[22] While the heroines of *Dragonwyk* and *Gaslight* are hounded by imagined ghosts and evil curses within their gothic homes, the abusive husbands proceed to carry out their schemes to rob their wives of their innocence, their sanity, and their money. The contemporary erotic thriller toys with the uncanny most frequently through dream sequences and fantasies, outlining the heroine's subjective processes. *Illicit Dreams* reveals the heroine's troubled subjectivity by combining both pleasure and danger within its opening moments. Moira glides in slow motion through a blue-tinted room, a breeze flowing through her hair and her lingerie. Candles flicker and the room is draped in swathes of drifting gauze. She approaches a man whose back is to her, and she reaches out to embrace him. They kiss in shadow, with the man's face hidden. Suddenly the breeze increases to a strong wind, blowing out the candles and causing the woman to stir in fear and terror. Someone, something threatening is approaching. She turns from her lover and flees down an endless, shadowy hallway to the courtyard . . . and then she wakes. It was all a hideously beautiful nightmare.

The film's narrative and aesthetics lean heavily on the "woman in peril" tropes of the modern gothic romance (woman in nightgown fleeing castle) and highlight the heroine's repressed sexual desires by making these images a recurring dream, in a sort of return of the repressed.[23] Throughout the film, Moira continues to dream the same images from the film's opening, and they gradually increase in sexual explicitness and danger. The repetitiveness of the dream and its psychic connection to Nick (Andrew Stevens), her extramarital love interest, reveals the heroine's subjectivity and visually reproduces her wish. Slow motion, distorted sound, and shadowy images clearly indicate the scenario as a dream, and reality intrudes only when Moira wakes to her husband sleeping beside her. Beyond linking the film to the uncanny, this dream produces several key threads of the narrative. Initially, the man in Moira's dream is a mystery, a man without a face; yet he is clearly not her husband, suggesting both the heroine's sexual frustration and marital unrest. Again sexual fulfillment and threat are linked. In addition, because the gothic house signifies domesticity and domestic space, Moira's flight from its confines foreshadows her eventual disassociation from her "proper" female role as wife and mistress of the house—a role created by the marriage contract. Furthermore, Moira's active exploration (through point-of-view shots) within the dream leads her to Nick, an investigation that is at odds with the threats of the narrative, represented by her husband, which are experienced through omniscient narrative devices.

The themes of destiny, psychic telepathy, premonitions, and mysterious doppelgangers also link *Illicit Dreams* to the realm of the uncanny. Moira's love interest/rescuer initially emerges within her dream and passes her the key to the dream house, similar to a gothic mansion, in her sleep. She investigates this odd occurrence with a psychic, who informs her that this man "loves her" but is separated from her by a "dark, evil force." As "destiny" would have it, Moira subsequently encounters the dream house and Nick, a handyman who happens to be fixing it up; her key, of course, happens to fit the lock. Nick has been dreaming nightly of Moira as well, although we never experience those dreams through his point of view. Because of Nick and Moira's psychic connection, they are doubled characters; Nick is a male version of the sexually frustrated housewife: he watches the home shopping network, calls his promiscuous male friend a "pig," and dreams about finding true love with his fantasy woman (Moira). When Daniel forces Moira to clean in the middle of the night, the film cuts to Nick donning rubber gloves in the middle of the night to scrub his sink. Nick provides a sharp contrast to the abusive husband, while he also leads Moira toward marital infidelity, which is the necessary prerequisite for sexual fulfillment.

Still, the "true love" represented by Nick and Moira is always counterbalanced by their foray into adultery, a theme that also emerges through their interactions with their promiscuous friends. Moira's friend Mindy has been through several marriages, and Nick constantly interrupts his friend Reed's sexual interludes by calling him in the middle of the night. Thus, masculinity and femininity maintain unstable boundaries, for the promiscuous friends remain phallic foils to Moira and Nick's feminized romanticism. Yet, in order for Moira to experience sexual fulfillment, she must simultaneously step outside her marriage and sleep with another man. Her dream explicitly outlines the consequences of her active pursuits, for she always experiences temporary satisfaction, only to be threatened by the shadowy force that comes between them, in the shape of her marriage and her husband.

The tensions between Moira's subjective fantasies and desires and the danger within the thriller narrative manifest themselves through the force of narration. While the spectator is positioned to experience identification primarily through Moira's subjectivity, the revelation of Daniel's intentions through omniscient narration undermines her narrative authority and increases suspense. The spectator knows that Daniel is having Moira followed during the romantic moments she and Nick share. The viewer also witnesses his discovery of her whereabouts immediately before the film's climax at the dream house. At one point, the film expresses its self-reflexive awareness of tension-creating techniques by using a stalking, subjective camera (similar to that in slasher films) to hunt down Moira within her home as she packs to leave Daniel. Mindy turns out to be the mysterious pursuer, signifying her role as phallic woman and also contributing to the masochistic thrill of the narrative.

The film's climax and resolution further problematize the themes of "true love" and the restrictions of marital fidelity raised in *Illicit Dreams.* Moira's nightmare comes true as she awakens in the dream house; hearing a noise, she finds Daniel's secretary dead and her own husband stalking her. As she flees the gothic mansion, reenacting her fantasy, Nick feverishly races against time to save her; he manages to staple-gun Daniel to death just as the latter is about to shoot Moira. Again, the narrative is resolved by murder. Still, love and sex are incommensurable elements within the erotic thriller, and the ending of *Illicit Dreams* maintains this same implication. As Nick and Moira embrace in triumph, Moira awakens suddenly . . . from a dream. Next to her, Daniel groggily inquires, "Whatsa matter, honey? Having a bad dream? How about some coffee?" She remains married, true love does not conquer all, and the narrative proves unresolved in its resolution; for the sexually frustrated wife, there is no easy escape.

THE FEMALE INVESTIGATOR AND THE LAW OF DESIRE

For the classic film noir detective, the seductive femme fatale is the enigma of the story, making film noir and the gothic two sides of the same generic coin (both exhibit active investigators who pursue enigmas, usually of a romantic nature). In fact, Murray Smith suggests the symbiotic relationship of these two genres in his analysis of *Deception* (Irving Rapper, 1946): "In most films from one or the other genre there is a ghost narrative of the other form. . . . In *Rebecca*, for example, the story of Maxim's relationship with Rebecca constitutes the skeleton of the noir's actantial structure—the man who is destroyed by the duplicitous woman."[24] Similarly, in the DTV gothic erotic thriller, the different generic tendencies underline each other: the cheating wife produces the murderous husband; the husband attempts to kill the wife, or frame her, in order to get her money; the female protagonist, through her husband's indifference, becomes involved in corruption while appeasing her sexual appetite. For those erotic thriller films that approach narrative through noir tropes, the female detective pursues the *homme* fatale, but her active investigation is undermined by male authority figures, and she is ultimately deceived or betrayed through the pursuit of her sexual desires.

The distinctions between productive and reproductive realms, and the tensions that ensue when masculine and feminine roles become unclear, permeate the film noir texts of the 1940s *and* their current incarnations. In the 1940s and 1950s, the femme fatale and the vulnerable male detective archetypes were symptomatic of the influx of women into the wartime work force, where women's economic power persistently threatened gender roles. More recently, increasing pressure on the glass ceiling by economically independent women has allowed the femme fatale icon to reemerge. The strong female protagonist within film noir—combined with the frequent spectacular display of the *male* sex object, especially within the erotic thriller—has moved beyond the role of seductress and into that of the police detective. Still, with the erotic thriller's explicit focus on sex acts and sexual fulfillment for the heroine, the tension between "worker" and "woman" serves to undermine the female protagonist's narrative authority.

Female subjectivity remains the crucial structuring tool in the noir erotic thriller, whether the heroine is the genre's police detective or investigator— *Criminal Passion* (1994), *Bodily Harm* (1995), *Desire* (1995), *Dead Sexy* (2001), *Forbidden Sins* (1998), and *Pendulum* (James Deck, 2001)—or the femme fatale who manipulates the emasculated man, as in *Body Chemistry 1–4* (1990–95), *Scorned* (1993), and to some extent, *Sexual Predator* (2001). Still, what Mary Ann Doane has outlined as the crisis of subjectivity for female protagonists in the woman's film continues within the DTV female detective erotic thriller.[25] The female detective's sexual desires constantly interrupt her investigative process, subverting her authority as a representative of the law. She proves increasingly susceptible to the seductive charms of her suspect, who often has the money and power to get away with murder. The heroine's emotional and sexual involvement with a possible killer, as in the gothic genre, replicates the pleasure-and-danger scenario of the erotic thriller, the two terms existing interdependently.

The opening sequence of *Criminal Passion* (Donna Deitch, 1994) outlines the crucial struggle between subjectivity and objecthood so prevalent within the genre. A point-of-view gaze reveals a police officer, Melanie Hudson (Joan Severance), driving aimlessly through the city streets, her voice-over recounting the pleasure she takes in the night, "curious to know what goes on in the dark." She refers not only to the crimes of the city, but the passion that exists "in the dark." Unfortunately, that same darkness serves to obscure her vision, as well as the spectator's, as the scene cuts between her driving and a vicious murder. Suddenly, a subjective camera view opens the gates to a courtyard and moves toward one of the apartments. This camera movement initially suggests that this may be the heroine investigating "the dark," but soon the camera's view floats through a window and circles above in an "eye of God" maneuver (a camera movement reminiscent of the opening scene of Hitchcock's *Psycho* [1960]). The switch from voice-over narration to omniscience reveals the problems within the "female detective" erotic thriller: the heroine can never maintain control of the narrative. The view moves past a couple making love, then out the window to an apartment across the courtyard, where neighbors look out the window, disturbed by the sensual moans of Isabella, the woman across the way. In the darkness, the lovers' faces are shrouded in mystery; as the woman's pleasure turns to terror, the camera flies to the neighbors reacting to and then investigating the screams. The scene fades to black as a body is discovered, obscuring the sight from the spectator. The shifting from Melanie's active subjectivity and voice-over to omniscient narration signals the dissolution of the heroine's narrative control and points to her future victimization.

As in other female-driven action narratives, *Criminal Passion* explores the uneasy gendering of the female protagonist, with the narrative compensating for any masculine qualities by providing requisite feminine ones. This balancing reveals itself through the tensions between the detective's authority and duty and her role of woman as a sexually desiring subject.[26] Melanie immediately introduces herself as a tough character, a woman who will not allow herself to get close to a man. When some small-time hoods give her trouble, stating they want to "give her some," she pulls a gun on them, verbally taunting them. Later, when another detective calls her "honey," she grabs him by the testicles and squeezes, violently putting him in his place. Still, because the erotic thriller must maintain a focus on sexual explorations, the heroine must be a sexual woman as well; this feminization wreaks havoc on her masculine authority within the law.

Inevitably, in every DTV female detective erotic thriller, the heroine's authority is undermined by her sexual history; either she used to be involved with her work partner, creating suspicion regarding her working with him again, or she had some kind of sexual involvement with the chief suspect, undermining her authority in handling a case against him. In *Bodily Harm* (James Lemmo, 1995), Rita (Linda Fiorentino) was married to one cop while having an affair with another. When her infidelity is discovered, her husband kills himself, and she must suffer the guilt as well as the censure of her fellow officers on the force. Within the real time of the story world, she and her partner investigate several brutal murders, possibly perpetrated by her former ex-cop lover; the investigation is further compromised as she becomes involved with him again. The heroine of *Dead Sexy,* Detective Kate McBain (Shannon Tweed), is transferred to the police precinct in the film's story world because of her previous personal involvement with a suspect. Before long, she falls under the sway of the mysterious Blue, the chief suspect in another rash of murders. While investigating him, she becomes his lover.

In *Criminal Passion,* Melanie was previously involved with her partner, Nathan, and he still tries to pursue her. When officers are assigned to investigate the brutal murder of Isabella (the woman in the opening scene), the captain threatens to take the heroine, rather than her male partner, off the case. The female detective is repeatedly accused of being too personally involved, and she must prove beyond a doubt that she is capable of handling her role as enforcer of the law. Yet, in order to fulfill the goals of the erotic narrative, she must follow her sexual desires and become vulnerable to these claims. Melanie can never rest comfortably in her roles as cop or woman, revealing the ever-present tensions between the public and private spheres for the erotic thriller's protagonist.

Melanie's inability to maintain a successful romantic relationship with a man leaves her hopelessly flawed, and every man within the film (her partner, her best friend, the killer) insists she must overcome her "trust issues" and deal with this handicap. These instructions from "helpful" men indicate the heroine's naïveté regarding sexual issues and point to the path toward sexual knowledge that Melanie must traverse. She becomes drawn to the chief murder suspect, the architect Conner Ashcroft, who actively engages her in innuendo-filled conversations and penetrating gazes. Throughout the first half of the film, Melanie's voyeuristic gaze positions Conner as the male object of desire, as she simultaneously investigates him as a suspect and explores her own desires. As Nathan and Melanie show up at Conner's house to ask him some questions, the architect happens to stroll by naked in front of her inquisitive gaze.[27] Later, during one of her aimless drives, she arrives at Conner's house and greedily watches him making love to his lawyer by the pool—he appears to be irresistible to all women. In these moments, the heroine experiences both identification with the female object and the desire of a female subject. On all counts, Melanie possesses an active voyeuristic gaze.

Conner does his best to lure Melanie into bed with him, often through the technique of the "twice-told" tale; he describes in a sensual voice differ- ent sexual scenarios and games, implying that he will seduce her through these techniques in the future. This discussion provides verbal foreplay to the sexual acts that occur later in the film for both the spectator and the heroine. The narrative again discriminates between sex and love for the heroine, leaning heavily on the necessity of "great sex." When the detectives interview several of Conner's old girlfriends, these themes are reiterated. As one woman explains, "Dating a man like that is an affair, period. Take it for what it is—great sex." Other women concur that they have experienced "great sex" with Conner, leading Melanie to explain in voice-over, "He knew exactly what a woman wanted; that's what all his girlfriends said. Where did Ashcroft learn so much about what women want? He must have learned it from women. I had to find out." When Melanie does decide to "find out," she places her desire over her duty, and both her narrative and visual author- ity become undermined.

When Melanie finally has sex with Conner, she appears as the aggressor within the scenario. He is swimming outside in his pool, naked and vulner- able; she strolls nearby in an evening gown, taunting him, asking to be in- vited in. She ultimately climbs into the pool, fully dressed, and takes control. While they seem to be mutually satisfied, it is Conner who appears to lose control, moaning as Melanie grabs him. This struggle for control emerges through the shift in subjective visual strategies within the narrative; suddenly, Melanie becomes a victim and an object, caught unawares or watched from a distance. After Melanie misses the captain's party while having "great sex" with Conner, Nathan grows suspicious of his partner's behavior. When the two are interrogating another possible suspect, one of Conner's ex-lovers, the woman confronts the heroine with "He's good, isn't he? She understands." Nathan and Melanie proceed to have a violent verbal exchange, seen through the one-way mirror outside the interrogation room. A younger detective, Michael, eavesdrops both visually and aurally on the conversation, objectifying Melanie in turn. Later, Melanie arrives home to a ringing phone. When she answers, headlights from a passing car illuminate her from outside her window, rendering her as an object. Subsequently, the view suggests Conner's gaze, as he asks whether she wants to come out and "play."

The battle over the visual field most explicitly plays out when Melanie enters Conner's construction worksite, a well-known masculine enclave. There, Melanie's point-of-view shots dominate the scene, yet her eyes are repeatedly met by the curious and often hostile stares of the workmen around her. Suddenly, Conner appears and helps her into an elevator, instigating another sex scene. They fool around in a rising elevator, while all the workmen watch as they pass. Melanie faces them, her eyes meeting theirs. The spectator sees through her point of view behind the elevator screen, but she becomes the exhibitionistic object for the gaze of the other men; they are ultimately the voyeurs within this sexual scenario even though the viewer sees only through Melanie's eyes. This shifting of the visual field sets up Melanie's transformation from the subject of passion to the object of murder.

At this point in the narrative, the heroine's voice-over narration disappears, to be replaced with more omniscient narrative strategies or scenes from Nathan's point of view. While this loss of narrational control happens intermittently throughout the film, that technique becomes predominant after Melanie sleeps with the suspect. Now Nathan takes up the essential role of active investigator/male rescuer within the film, substantiating Melanie's position as victim. Shortly after Nathan and another detective, Jordan, discuss the heroine's dangerous situation, someone breaks into her apartment. Suddenly, the viewer identifies with Nathan as he hears about the break-in from Melanie; the spectator does not actually witness the discovery through her eyes. Later, when the scorned ex-lover, Tracy, shows up and threatens Melanie, the heroine quickly takes control of the situation and shoots Tracy in the leg. Nathan insists that she was set up by Conner, but she refuses to consider this idea, naïvely trusting a suspected murderer. Shortly thereafter, Melanie and Conner play sexual power games with a straight razor (which he described doing to her earlier), and Nathan and Jordan uncover a woman's fingerprints on the murder weapon—a straight razor. While the spectator remains "in the dark" as to the killer's identity, Melanie no longer plays an active role in his pursuit (she places herself "on vacation" after her initial spat with Nathan). Only in the film's final confrontation does Melanie once again take an active stance.

The resolution of the "female detective" erotic thriller rarely confirms "happily ever after" ideals. In *Criminal Passion,* the heroine's exploration of desire ends in betrayal and murder, as her love object turns into a violent, psychotic killer. The narrative never explains Conner's motives for murdering five different women, beyond vague hints regarding something to do with his mother; ultimately, his motivation proves unimportant to the film. For Melanie, Conner's murderous passion confirms the invalidation of her own intellectual certainties—her instincts are proven false, misleading, and ultimately destructive. She is left to drive aimlessly through the dark city streets, returning to her beginnings.

Similarly, in *Bodily Harm,* Rita dismisses her lover from her life, forgoing his "love" and her own sexual pleasure for safety and solitude, even though he is no longer considered a suspect. Even here, the erotic thriller ends ambiguously; like the infamous ice pick under the bed, at the end of *Basic Instinct* (Paul Voerhoven, 1992), the murder weapon is left lying in the glove compartment as Rita's lover drives off. Thus, the heroine unwittingly allows a killer to go free. Likewise, at the conclusion of *Dead Sexy,* Kate believes that the murders were committed by her colleague, Detective Rackles, who was supposedly framing Blue. But as Kate leaves with Blue at the film's end, a moment of omniscient narration clues in the audience to Blue's guilt: a bagful of the "Burgeon Rouge" lipstick, a shade worn by all the victims, hangs from the back of Blue's door. While these endings leave the film open to a sequel, they also reveal the inability of the heroine to experience romantic narrative closure. In choosing between the public and private, her career (masculine) and love life (feminine), she can never experience a balance of both worlds. These tensions dissipate only in the face of betrayal and destruction.

THE DTV NOIR EROTIC THRILLER AND THE NEW FEMME FATALE

The essential ingredient for the successful noir thriller remains an acute instability within assigned gender roles and women's uncertain access to power. The police detective, a role commonly represented as one of authority, becomes exposed as corruptible through gendered inconsistencies.

Whether the detective is male or female, sexual desire proves dangerous to the protagonist, stripping the detective of narrative knowledge, authority, and conferred privilege. The neo-noir, especially in its DTV erotic thriller formula, represents a response to the shifts in gendered power throughout the last twenty years. As I suggested previously, even feminism (academic and popular) struggles with the difficulty of establishing a locus of female power. For women, success remains tainted with "either/or" restrictions, based on the troubled integration of separate spheres. The erotic thriller repeatedly articulates these tensions, especially through the evolving role of the femme fatale within the erotic noir.

The femme fatale of 1940s film noir remains well-traversed theoretical territory for feminist film theorists, primarily because this symbol of seduction maintained a unique magnetism, exuding a power rarely found in women on the Hollywood screen.[28] Still, the femme fatale of 1940s noir does not actively wield her power—she is merely its symbol. Or, as Mary Ann Doane has indicated in her analysis of this erotic icon, "Her power is a peculiar sort insofar as it is usually not subject to her conscious will, hence appearing to blur the opposition between passivity and activity. She is an ambivalent figure because she is not the subject of power but its carrier."[29] In contrast to her previous function within the narrative, the contemporary duplicitous woman who lures the male detective to his demise has undergone significant transformation, proving more successful and more manipulative than her historical antecedents. These changes are manifested in two distinct narrative strategies: (1) the male protagonist's increasingly restricted narration as male voice-overs vanish from the erotic thriller, and (2) the film's open-ended narrative resolution, in which the femme fatale is ultimately not destroyed.

As in most film noir, the spectator of the noir erotic thriller experiences the restricted point of view of the male protagonist, for on one level he remains the narrative's active investigator; yet, the focus on the sexual gratification and conquests of the femme fatale creates another level of narration for the audience. The dangerous woman overwhelms the male character through the pressure of her own subjectivity; she holds the plot points of the film together through her active manipulating and plotting. Thus, the film's pleasure shifts from the man pursuing the femme fatale to the woman, revealing the male character's weakness through repeated acts of shame and humiliation. The male "hero" believes in his own intellectual and moral omnipotence, which only makes his fall from grace, marked by his infidelities, that much sweeter. The male detective, usually a formerly faithful husband, becomes a sex object for the femme fatale and a "victim" of desire, hers and his. She is the object of his point of view, but she simultaneously exists as the subject of the narrative's authority. Because of the male protagonist's victimization, the femme fatale provides an active identificatory source for the spectator. In an inversion of the female gothic's structure, this time the *male* protagonist's perceptions and investigations become repeatedly invalidated; this invalidation commonly occurs when his subjective narration and point of view slip away from him—a trait that emerges in the "female detective" erotic thriller as well. The most likely reason for these narrative shifts remains the instability of the boundaries that surround the traditional subject/object dichotomy of narrative cinema, which was formerly bound by rigid gender roles.

The femme fatale of the contemporary erotic thriller also wields greater economic and intellectual power than her predecessor. No longer does this woman struggle for security by attaching herself to a wealthy man; her material success is generally her own. Whereas the 1940s "spider woman," in films such as *Out of the Past* (Jacques Tourneur, 1947) and *Double Indemnity* (Billy Wilder, 1944), used her sexual wiles to gain economic independence and security, the contemporary erotic femme fatale uses her economic and political power to gratify her sexual urges. She uses her intelligence to get what *she* wants, while allowing the male protagonist to initially believe he has control of the situation. Claire Archer, the heroine of *Body Chemistry 1–4*, epitomizes this new breed of femme fatale. A renowned and successful sex researcher, she begins the series as the head of a research department and finishes as a successful author with a TV movie based on her life, with sequels still possible. Along the way, she leaves a trail of men, victims of her aggressive desire; for the series' successful continuation, she can never achieve the unity of the "happy couple," since she remains the overt symbol of its opposition.

The crisis for the seductress of the DTV erotic thriller remains the tension between love and sex, a repeated theme within the genre. While the female character single-mindedly pursues her sexual conquests, the desire for possession of the man, couched as a monogamous love relationship, drives her to murderous extremes. Again, love and sex cannot coexist within the narrative, and murder becomes the outcome of societal tensions. Because the focus of erotic noir is on its elaborated sex scenes, the murders involved become secondary to the narrative drive of the film, the femme fatale's pursuit of pleasure. Thus, the strength of the male protagonist's narration is diffused and ultimately destroyed, overpowered by the force the female character exerts on the narrative. This shift in narrative power occurs most dramatically at the end of the film. The distinctiveness of the contemporary noir erotic thriller lies in the narrative's resolution: the emasculated husband/detective/lover generally dies, and the femme fatale lives to kill again—and again.

While this narrative structure could be explained as a vehicle by which to create sequels to the film, the subjective pleasure of watching a woman get away with murder still remains for the female spectator. Likewise, in order to identify with the male protagonist who ends up dead, the spectator must assume a passive, masochistic engagement with the character, which does not follow the forward progression of the narrative. The femme fatale's need for sex may not be satisfied, but she goes unpunished for her active sexual desires; instead, the *male* character's infidelities are punishable by death. This subversion of gender and generic roles speaks of a genre specifically constructed to appeal to heterosexual female viewers, an audience that may find pleasure observing repeated male humiliations.

The original *Body Chemistry* (Kristine Peterson, 1990) raises important themes that proliferate throughout the other *Body Chemistry* films. Men are never shown in a positive light; instead, they are a combination of a lust-crazed animal and a "lying, cheating bastard." The opening of the first film illustrates these stereotypes through a sex experiment, with men as subjects. Their hands methodically clench and unclench, their pupils dilate, and they practically drool while watching a porn movie in the film's primary location—the research lab. When Claire Archer (Lisa Pescia) decides to use the lab to collect data for her sex experiments, which attempt to dispute the causal relationship between viewing sex and acting out violence, she encounters her first male victim, Tom Redding (Marc Singer).[30] Tom is a happy, hard-working family man, with a pretty wife and cute little boy; nonetheless, his picket-fence lifestyle proves unsatisfying and he quickly and thoughtlessly begins an affair with Claire, ignoring any possible consequences.[31] Because the male protagonist in this erotic series believes he is always in control, he acts with impunity, lying and cheating on his wife while having guilt-free sex with another woman. The *sex* is not punishable, for the femme fatale always makes the sexual advances, choosing where and when to fulfill *her* desires; from the very first film, the male character always appears to be a pawn, a sex object. Instead, the male character is punished for his ignorance, his inability to recognize that things have changed. His roles as family man, breadwinner, and sexual dominator no longer apply; thus he incurs punishment by the femme fatale—the key figure of societal transformation and gender imbalance. Like the DTV gothic erotic thriller, the noir version of the genre reveals the same proliferating tensions: the boundaries that maintain gendered, separate spheres blur, and the traditional identification with the active male protagonist of conventional narrative cinema proves inadequate to the genre's "visual pleasure."

Claire Archer continues to wreak havoc in each of the *Body Chemistry* films, ridding the world of "lying, cheating bastards" over and over again. In *Body Chemistry,* the main character is a family man; in *Body Chemistry 2* he is trying to get together with his high-school sweetheart, and in *3* and *4* he is married. Each man either exists within the "happily ever after" scenario or aspires to it; still, he never has the slightest qualm about infidelity, appearing to have no self-control or will. Claire exposes the flaws of all these men, and, as the sequels progress, her explicit goals combine sexual pleasure with increased male humiliation. As *Body Chemistry 3* and *4* reveal, Claire Archer no longer maintains a semblance of respect for these male characters, openly taunting them and smirking in reaction to their fears and anxieties. She brings new meaning to the label "sex toy," as she uses these men for her own pleasure and discards them when she is finished. Similarly, the narrative always hints at the male protagonist's lack of intelligence. In *Body Chemistry 4* (Jim Wynorski, 1995), Simon Marshall, Claire's lawyer and latest pawn, remains completely oblivious to her machinations, to the point of hilarity. Female characters within the film, quick to understand Claire's abilities, repeatedly point out his lack of intelligence; only when Simon finally realizes how he has been manipulated does he state in an appropriate analogy, "She maneuvered me like a rat through a maze." The male protagonist's emasculation is essential to the strength of the femme fatale in the noir thriller. Because these male characters are so weak and ineffectual, narrative interest remains strongest when the femme fatale is on screen.

Body Chemistry 3 (Jim Wynorski, 1994) displays all of these key themes, but does so with an ironic nod toward the genre, recognizing the formula of these films and highlighting DTV erotic thriller conventions. Alan Clay (Andrew Stevens), the "happily married" television producer, begins his descent into infidelity by pursuing the rights to a possible "made-for-television" fem-jep movie about a woman who has lost two lovers under tragic circumstances—one she had to kill in self-defense (*Body Chemistry*), and the other was killed when police fired on him while he was trying to strangle her (*Body Chemistry 2*). This "true story" is about Claire Archer, the possible future subject for a "woman-in-peril" erotic thriller. Alan meets with Freddy

Sommers, who formerly worked in the lab with Tom Redding (the male love interest in *Body Chemistry*) and now wants to break into screenwriting, beginning with Claire's story. The connection to the previous films serves a dual purpose: it provides exposition for those viewers unfamiliar with the genre and the series, but it also gives a nod to the genre's ironic viewer, the spectator "in the know." Bringing these characters back from the past indicates there will be more of the same, substantiating the film's formula.[32] Initially, Claire says no to their project, but later that night during a fierce lightning storm, she and Alan have sex, constituting the first sex number in the film. She makes the first move; even though Alan has just spoken to his wife, Beth (Morgan Fairchild), on the phone, he shows no hesitation toward infidelity. So begins the revelation of the "lying, cheating bastard."

By *Body Chemistry 3*, Claire Archer has developed a following, especially since she always gets away with murder. The pleasures of the narrative thus become less about what will happen to the femme fatale, and more about *how* the male protagonist will be duped, set up, and humiliated; Alan Clay's lack of narrative control and unwitting victimization are expected. The setting out of the scenario creates the "forepleasure" Elizabeth Cowie discusses in "Fantasia," where the goal of the narrative (already known) becomes secondary to its process.[33] The contemporary femme fatale is always one step ahead of the male protagonists and the other characters, omnisciently predicting their every moves.[34] Claire excels at appearing unexpectedly and catching Alan off guard. At one point, he enters the house to get her phone call and finds her calling him from *his* bedroom. She proceeds to seduce him, in front of open windows looking out onto the tennis court where his wife and his boss play a match (figure 6). The tension within the noir erotic thriller, especially in the later *Body Chemistry* sequels, revolves primarily around whether the male protagonist will be caught with his pants down. While Alan and Claire have sex in his bedroom, his wife and company walk up the path toward the house, the bedroom in clear view. Will they look? Will they hear Claire's moans? The scene cuts rapidly between the two, dividing the safe world of marriage from the exciting life of sex.

In another scene, Claire and Alan visit Beth, who is an actress, on the set of the TV drama *Empire* (again parodying another women's genre—the soap opera). As soon as the cast takes a break, Claire seduces Alan on the empty set. Suddenly, Beth realizes she left her script on the set, and the scene cuts again between Alan and Claire passionately embracing and Beth walking down the hall perhaps to catch them. While Alan quickly emerges with Beth's script,

Figure 6. Alan and Claire are almost caught in *Body Chemistry 3* (1994).

stopping her in the hall, the camera reveals Claire around the corner, smoking a cigarette and smiling to herself. She derives pleasure not only from her sexual encounters with Alan, but also through his repeated fear and possible humiliation; her reaction to his panic indicates her desires.

The appeal of the successful, seductive career woman, unencumbered by marital ties or motherhood, manifests itself within this film through the relationship between Beth and Claire. While Beth has a successful career on a nighttime soap, she feels dissatisfied because her roles are always limited to the "good girl" or victimized wife; she wants to play a bitch, and she believes that the role of Claire in Alan's TV movie would allow her to break out of her type. The film again nods toward the "in-the-know" spectator, for Morgan Fairchild, who plays Beth, is a popular nighttime soap actress, well known for playing the bad girl. The film explicitly examines the attraction of the femme fatale through Beth's fervent desire to become one. When Alan arrives home after having sex with Claire, Beth, after reading the script, stops him in the hall. Dressed in black lace (very spider-like) and backlighted, she claims, "I'm Claire." When the two make love (Alan is the fantasy man who can "do it" forever), Alan's desires are uncertain—is he making love to Beth or Claire?

Beth becomes increasingly persistent about winning this role as the story progresses, practically pimping Alan out to Claire, using him as an object of desire to get Claire to sign over her rights to the story. The male protagonist is now the pawn being bartered and manipulated; in a sense, he must sleep his way to the top (Claire) in order to achieve success in his career. The femme fatale remains the film's narrative interest, giving the narrative meaning and momentum. Beth's desire to "become" Claire illustrates how identification functions for the spectator; the femme fatale is the narrative subject, the male protagonist, her object. In the end, after Alan's death (by Claire's hand, although it cannot be proven), Beth's wish is fulfilled and she gets to play Claire in the TV movie of her life. The final scene of the film visually mirrors the framing and images of the final confrontation between Alan and Claire, except this time, the story has subtly changed and actors play their parts (in a film-within-a-film structure). Claire produces the television movie and murder becomes lucrative, providing the requisite ending to the ultimate "woman-in-peril" erotic thriller.

The tensions between the domestic space, where the wife of the cheating husband resides, and the public sphere, where the femme fatale competes with and overpowers her male counterpart, arise in the erotic thriller through the repeated invasion of the male protagonist's home. In *Body Chemistry,* Claire parks a van outside Tom Redding's house, then chains him to the inside wall and has sex with him, offering to invite his wife to watch. Later, she drops in on a party at his home and then sets fire to his outdoor deck. In *Body Chemistry 2* (Adam Simon, 1992), Claire ties Dan Pearson to the stairs, pours hot wax on his body, and then later handcuffs him to a lift in his garage, leaving him half-naked for his "good girl" girlfriend to discover. Claire invades Alan's home repeatedly in *Body Chemistry 3* and manages to have sex with him in his bedroom. In the last installment of the series, *Body Chemistry 4,* Claire mysteriously materializes in Simon Marshall's home again and again, first leaving threatening messages for his wife, trashing their office, turning the gas in the kitchen on, and finally shooting Simon in cold blood in his bedroom. Each time, and within each sequel, the home becomes more and more dangerous, less of a stable, reliable environment for the man. Claire Archer is literally a "home wrecker," but the boundaries of the home are already weakened through the narrative's disinterest in representing a successful, monogamous love relationship, and through the narrative control the femme fatale exhibits throughout the film.

In addition, the *Body Chemistry* series emphasizes the greater intellectual depth and strength of the femme fatale character, always representing Claire Archer as smart, successful, and able to get her man (at least for sex). Claire's repeated attempts at involvements with married men indicate her distrust of marriage and point up the restrictions the role of "wife" provides. The noir erotic thriller carries the same message as the gothic—sex is best experienced outside of a love relationship, and marriage leads to murder. The goal of the femme fatale remains "great sex"; the toppling of traditional heterosexual romance is only an added benefit.

The *Body Chemistry* series, as well as other DTV erotic noir thrillers, maintain a close resemblance to mainstream Hollywood neo-noirs, especially in regard to their representation of the new femme fatale. What distinguishes a film such as *Basic Instinct* (1992) from the erotic thrillers previously described is its budget, casting of stars, number of sex scenes, and marketing. Star power from Michael Douglas (the epitome of the threatened, emasculated man) and Sharon Stone, coupled with high-budget location shooting and extensive mass marketing for theatrical release, provides a different context for the film's reception; still, the femme fatale's power within the narrative proves strikingly similar to that of her lower-budget relative.[35] While Detective Nick Curran (Douglas) stumbles through the film with a false belief in his own narrative knowledge, Catherine Trammell (Stone) maneuvers him into her bed, into her next bestseller, and into believing she is innocent of multiple murders. She has possibly killed off almost everyone he knows, and he still thinks the two of them will live "happily ever after." Again, the detective's ineffectual weakness draws the spectator into the femme fatale's nefarious machinations. When the closing image shows Trammell's ice pick under the bed, the female spectator might hope there will be more of the same—the femme fatale getting away with murder. While *Basic Instinct* is well known for its explicit sex scenes, the female character's subjective pursuit of pleasure does not constitute a focus for the narrative; neither are there the frequent references to the family and home that indicate the tensions common to the DTV erotic thriller (linking the genre to melodrama). The femme fatale may get away with murder, but the spectator does not experience her subjectivity, just the consequences of her actions.

The femme fatale of the DTV erotic thriller arises at a time when representations of women who derive power from their sexual curiosity proliferate within popular culture. The climate after the sex wars created tensions between the economically independent woman and the sexually independent woman, both roles becoming crucial achievements of heterosexual female identity. Similarly, the pop feminists Camille Paglia and Naomi Wolf, both vocal media icons, rapturously espouse theories on the power of the sexual woman, and *Sex and the City*'s Samantha proved a popular example. Feminist discourses (mainstream and academic) lurk beneath the excesses of the femme fatale, allowing the female character to experience a "both/and" fantasy within a primarily "either/or" reality. This connection to feminist discourses would not constitute these films as "feminist" per se, but the films do indicate the influence of contemporary women's movements in popular media forms. Within these quasi-utopian narratives, the institutions of marriage and family are dismantled, promiscuous sex becomes possible for women, and "lying, cheating bastards" (i.e., men) get what they deserve: humiliation, harassment, and death. Through identification with the femme fatale, the heterosexual female spectator can experience the pleasure of the "bad girl," who goes unpunished for her active desires and is ready to prowl again. Still, beneath the utopian vision of a "bad girl" who can have it all lie the conflicts present in wielding sexual power as a tool for autonomy. The femme fatale of the erotic thriller does maintain the stigma of the "psychopath" or "bitch from hell," a representation that cannot be ignored. Pleasure may be found in the narrative humiliation of men, but it comes at a steep price.

4

VIEWING THE PROBLEM:
THERAPEUTIC DISCOURSES AND SOFT CORE'S
"TALKING CURE"

Indecent Behavior 2 (Carlo Gustaff, 1994) opens with a woman discussing her sex life with her therapist. Initially, only the woman's voice-over provides narrative, but as she continues to talk, to describe "last weekend at a party," the scene begins to materialize visually. The spectator is allowed to experience the woman's confession visually and aurally, but through a unique splitting in identification and point of view, precipitated by the doctor-patient relationship involved in the story's telling. On the one hand, identification begins with the female patient, whose voice-over controls the narration and elicits the accompanying visuals. The film shows the patient, Shoshana, approaching a window to spy on a couple making love outside the party. As she voyeuristically watches the couple, a mysterious man approaches her from behind, and they have sex as well. On the other hand, the visualized scenario may be said to be focalized through the patient's doctor and interlocutor, the film's true heroine, Dr. Rebecca Mathis (Shannon Tweed), who actively listens to the woman's confession. Rebecca's voice repeatedly interrupts Shoshana's story, indicating her role as authority figure within their communication.

Abruptly, Rebecca halts the fantastic narration and reverie to accuse Shoshana of fabrication and deception; Shoshana basically lies and makes up the narratives there in the therapist's office. Unable to locate Shoshana's sexual problem, Rebecca attempts to sever their professional relationship. Later, the narrative reveals that Shoshana is a tabloid reporter trying to dig up dirt on Rebecca for a story. Thus, the opening scenario of *Indecent Behavior 2* reveals several major themes that run throughout the discourse of many direct-to-video "therapeutic" erotic thrillers, a frequent and repeated version of the genre. For one, the films reveal a tenuous relationship between doctor and patient, a relationship loaded with eroticism and possible treachery; the possibilities for transference and countertransference are numerous.[1] This tension is exemplified through the shifting of identification between the character who tells the story and the character who listens. Further, the deception involved in this opening scene indicates the instability of any fixed power relationship. If the telling of sexual secrets reveals sexual "truths," then deception indicates more of an emphasis on titillation and exhibitionistic display.[2] The revealed "secret" becomes less about fixing a "problem" and more about stimulating the therapist (and through identification, the viewer).

The therapeutic erotic thriller can be placed into one of three primary categories, distinguished by each type of film's relationship to therapeutic discourses: (1) the sex therapist/sex surrogacy erotic thriller, (2) the countertransference erotic thriller, and (3) the radio talk show erotic thriller. The sex therapy/sex surrogacy erotic thriller, of which *Indecent Behavior 2* is an example, commonly features a female lead who is a sexologist or sex therapist, and sex surrogates who perform some of the sex numbers. (To clarify this role, a surrogate is someone who has sexual encounters with the doctor's clients as part of their "therapy.") In these films, while the heroine is perceived and recognized as an authority or expert on sexuality, she maintains troubled relationships to sex and love in her own personal life, creating a constant tension between her roles as doctor and as woman. In the countertransference erotic thriller, the female (or in some cases, male) therapist's relationship with her patient, usually a person of the opposite sex, becomes tainted and unprofessional. The mixing of pleasure through romantic involvement with "work" puts the heroine in grave danger. This version of the therapeutic erotic thriller focuses on the heroine's vulnerabilities, as she succumbs to her male client's charms. Finally, the genre includes the radio talk show thriller, where the radio waves contribute to the movement of sex secrets from the private to the public sphere. The therapeutic format elicits seduction, usually through the talk show host's relationship to her or his audience, and exhibitionism, in the way listeners and callers interact with the therapist and other audience members. These forms of titillation are especially significant since the talk shows always include sex talk. Also, while male and female talk show hosts are both working to resolve problems through expertise, they are represented very differently in these thrillers and maintain widely varied relationships with their clients.

The use of therapeutic discourses in the erotic thriller, in which a doctor-patient relationship is constructed and exploited, serves several purposes. For one, in fulfilling the genre's erotic component, the films offer titillation through the telling of sexual secrets and the visualization of sexual scenarios, and at times they use the practice of sexual surrogacy as a way of bringing titillating talk to a visual register. Also, the film's therapeutic structure helps set up different sexual scenarios as "problems" that the therapeutic relationship, through narrative work, can eventually resolve. Still, what is most crucial to the therapeutic erotic thriller is the way the films participate in the construction and regulation of female heterosexuality, which is produced specifically through the tensions and dynamics of therapeutic relationships and their connections to power and gender. The erotic thriller becomes especially important in understanding the construction of ideological sex discourses, for as Meryl Altman suggests, sex literature (and by association, the erotic thriller) "thus combine[s] two of the most sophisticated strategies for inscribing ideology our culture has developed: the fiction which elicits identification and self-modeling, and the discourse of the expert."[3] Similar to the erotic thriller's circulation of instructional discourses, and influenced by the popular representation of "do-me" feminism in the mass media, the therapeutic erotic thriller also provides a way, in the guise of sexual entertainment, to regulate female heterosexuality through its focus on sexual problems and their resolutions.

Since the publication and translation of Michel Foucault's *History of Sexuality*, his model of the confessional has frequently been used as a way of explaining how sexual discourses circulate, and how the power relations involved in confession, between priest and confessor, are reiterated in the Freudian concept of the analyst-and-analysand scenario, replicating therapeutic discourses.[4] According to Foucault, within the confessional dynamic, the individual who hears the confession retains power: "the agency of domination does not reside in the one who speaks (for it is he who is constrained), but in the one who listens and says nothing: not in the one who knows and answers, but in the one who questions and is not supposed to know."[5] While therapy is based on "confessions" from a patient that are interpreted by a therapist, and although the patient becomes cured through that confession in a "talking cure," the therapeutic relationship's dispersal of power is more complicated than the Freudian conception of analyst and analysand, especially in the revisionist use of Freud that is prevalent within the United States. As Jane Shattuc explains, "It is the Freudian analyst who serves as the model for Foucault's powerful social interlocutor whose silence provokes the supine patient into a submissive confessional mode. At issue, then, is whether with the rise of self-determination in American therapy the unequal power relations dissolve. Or are they reinvented in a more complex and insidious form wherein the patient polices himself or herself in the name of 'self-actualization'?"[6]

The representation of the therapeutic doctor-patient relationship in the DTV erotic thriller suggests a shifting in power relations based on the diminished authority of the doctor's role that stems from the patient's increased activity. Within a "self-actualizing" therapeutic process, in which the patient actively pursues emotional growth, the therapist's silent figure is replaced with a more interactive, communicative, and less authoritative role. In the erotic thriller, the role of therapist is usually played by a woman, a heroine who, through working and communicating with her patients, reveals more about her own vulnerabilities than those of the patients who come to her for help. This diminishment of the therapist's authoritative power substantiates the self-help rhetoric of contemporary U.S. culture by reducing the importance of the interlocutor and by undermining female authority through the questioning of the *need* for a "professional." Furthermore, Foucault's confessional model does not explicitly take gender into account, even though it may be understood that only male priests are qualified to hear confession. When a female character is placed in the role of interlocutor, in a role of power, her possession of this authority is often repeatedly questioned and undermined. As exemplified in the opening of *Indecent Behavior 2*, Rebecca effectively recognizes that she is being manipulated by her patient, who is bent on performing a therapeutic tease. Still, the scenario sets up the possibility of deception.

In this film, and the other sex therapy thrillers, the heroine is undermined by her belief in the sanctity of the therapeutic relationship and the patient's need for a cure. Later in *Indecent Behavior 2*, Rebecca is deceived again and again by her patients, or by those who work for her, revealing that her expertise is questionable. In addition, her lack of success in her own sexual and love relationships qualifies her judgment as a "sexpert." And, in films that deal with the therapist's seduction, her inability to maintain a mode of professionalism hurts her further. According to the structure of gender relations in the "therapeutic thriller," the doctor's role is not supported as dominant, as in the Foucauldian paradigm, but is instead riddled by vulnerability, despite her position as expert.

The therapeutic erotic thriller is unique, because it presents its sensual subject matter on an aural as well as visual register. Soft core utilizes the female therapist and confessional discourses as sources of information and titillation. The protagonist, usually a sex therapist, is confronted with her clients' problems, and she encourages her patients to talk through their fantasies and anxieties. Her clients then participate in the therapeutic relation by disclosing their sexual secrets, describing their desires in sensual detail. This verbal foreplay serves a dual function within the narrative. On one hand, it provides pleasurable stimulation through graphic detail; on the other, it outlines the "problems" of heterosexuality explored in the film and lays out the female protagonist's relation to these problems in terms of power and pleasure. The heroine's narrative trajectory is to negotiate the problems of others while embarking on her own quest for sexual fulfillment; the difficulty of succeeding in both narrative threads contributes to the anxiety of the thriller.

Lawrence Lanoff's *Indecent Behavior* (1993), the first film in the series, exemplifies some of the major themes and conflicting discourses in the therapeutic erotic thriller. The film's narrative revolves around a female sex therapist, Rebecca Mathis (Shannon Tweed), and highlights various sessions she has with her clients, as well as exploring her own personal relations with men. Rebecca is unhappily married, and the film's romance narrative focuses on her involvement with a male detective, Nick Sharkey (Gary Hudson). Sharkey becomes interested in Rebecca after one of her patients suspiciously ends up dead. While murder is a major subplot of the narrative, the film only vaguely investigates its cause, choosing instead to focus more specifically on Rebecca's negotiations of her clients' sexual dysfunctions, and on her troubled marriage to Tom (Jan-Michael Vincent).

The film opens with a nightmarish dream sequence that establishes Rebecca's subjective point of view and the markings of a "thriller" narrative. Shortly thereafter, a therapeutic session occurs, and the film provides the titillation of its first verbal confession. The scene begins with Rebecca poised over a notebook as she questions Carol about her sexual "philosophy." Carol reveals that she does not confuse sex with love, and that her training (implied as prostitution) allows her to make these distinctions. Through Rebecca's soft-spoken questioning, Carol seductively begins to reveal the story of her "first time." She revels in the story's minute details, her voice slow and husky as she recounts the ways she was caressed, touching herself while recalling her memories. The camera slowly curls around Carol as she exposes her secret to the therapist, only occasionally reverting back to Rebecca's studied observation of her client. The lighting is hazy and soft-focused, but there is no visual explicitness in this scene. Both women are completely, almost conservatively dressed. Carol's verbal revelation is the film's initial sex number, and its understated titillation indicates the structure of the visual elements to come.

What appears initially as therapeutic self-disclosure, marked as a doctor-patient interaction, is exposed as a job interview; Carol is applying for the position of Rebecca's sexual surrogate. What the surrogate role provides for soft-core film is the visual representation of a talking cure, as the clients act out their problems with a sexual partner for the doctor's probing gaze. The verbal register of the confession can provide only so much information within such an explicitly visual medium.

The introductory scene between Rebecca and Carol constructs its sexual scenario as graphically explicit in detail, but also highly romanticized as it focuses on the mythical romance of one's "first time." At the end of Carol's interview, Rebecca comments that most people spend all their life looking for that "one pure moment." Carol replies, "Even you?" Rebecca ignores this question, but her halting and shy response reveals some of the problems within her character and introduces one of the chief dynamics of the therapeutic erotic thriller. In a moment of identification with her client, Rebecca allows her professional demeanor to slip, relegating her to the role of "woman" instead of "doctor." She quickly attempts to cover her affectivity, but not before her role as authoritative figure comes into question.

Throughout *Indecent Behavior*, Rebecca's identity as a doctor and a therapist is challenged and threatened, thereby undermining the power that usually accompanies the therapeutic relationship. The film underscores a tension between the protagonist's subjectivity and objectivity. Rebecca's objectivity remains intrinsic to her role as doctor, the "subject supposed to know," yet her subjective moments reveal uncertainty or a lack of knowledge. Rebecca's role as doctor elicits confessions from her patients, but the narrative systematically hinders any domination this role would entail. This situation is exacerbated by Rebecca's "expertise" as sexual.[7] Unlike the authority of religion or the law, the authority of the public sphere, Rebecca's authority dwells on the private sphere of the bedroom. Her overt relationship to sexuality and sexology highlights her position as a female doctor, and it substantiates the idea that sexual power rests within the feminine sphere.

Her existence as a professional who deals with the private realm intersects with the difficulties Rebecca has negotiating the two parts of her life.

During one of their first exchanges, Detective Nick Sharkey confronts Rebecca on her choice of profession. He asks, "Why this career? Kicks?" When confronted, Rebecca defensively points out the seriousness of her profession and attempts to halt negative associations connected between gender and subject matter. The distinction is immediately made between the public authority of the law and the private authority of the sex therapist. On first entering her clinic office, Sharkey, who will become Rebecca's love interest, is under the false impression that Rebecca is just a "therapist." He disparages "shrinks" openly and acknowledges his discomfort at having his secrets disclosed. As he struts into the office and greets a city councilman by name, he does not understand the palpable discomfort of Rebecca's clients concerning his public presence in this private clinic.

Rebecca's authority as a doctor is under attack throughout *Indecent Behavior*, as the film's narrative uncovers her scandalous professional past. The film's opening nightmare sequence is a reenactment of the death of a young, attractive man due to an overdose of Extremis, an experimental sex drug. As the narrative unfolds, Rebecca's connection to this sex drug, and her illegal use of it in her therapy practice, as well as for her own sexual pleasure, brings her professional credentials into question. The murder subplot hinges on the death of another of Rebecca's male patients by an Extremis overdose. Rebecca is supposedly the authority on this sex drug, but her possible negligence positions her as a suspect in the murder. Again, it is Rebecca's placement in the private sphere, through her pursuit of the sexual in both professional and personal matters, that puts her in conflict with the public realm. The murder is the punishment for her power.

In *Indecent Behavior 3* (Kelley Cauthen, 1995), the dangerous tension between sex therapy and female authority becomes even more explicitly punishable by death. The narrative again features Rebecca Mathis (Shannon Tweed), who is still practicing sex therapy while performing community service for her illegal dealings with Extremis in the first film.[8] Her imposed servitude to the law traps her, and the police use her as bait for a serial killer, who this time is specifically targeting sex therapists. Significantly, the therapists who are killed are all marked by their crossing of the line between their public work and their private lives; they are killed in their offices, and all have apparently slept with the murderer.

The conflict between the public and private embodied in Rebecca's role as a sexual doctor structures the various tensions of the *Indecent Behavior* series. While Rebecca struggles to maintain her professional status in the first film, her personal, sexual involvement with Nick Sharkey detracts from her authoritative role, as her difficulties with her love life overshadow her professional abilities. This conflict is commonly represented in films that portray female psychiatrists. As Janet Walker suggests in her analysis of psychiatry in the cinema, "The working woman role model is thus consistently undercut by the textual proclivity to designate the woman psychiatrist as more woman than psychiatrist."[9] The film's narrative reveals this "textual proclivity" by alternately focusing on Rebecca's professional interactions with her clients and her personal struggles with Nick and her husband, Tom; the professional and private parts of Rebecca's life have difficulty coexisting. The murder subplot may place a distant third in narrative importance, but it provides the narrative embodiment of a woman/doctor conflict. Placing a woman in a position of medical authority in an erotic thriller can only end in murder. The tensions between these different parts of the narrative pose an explicit challenge to therapeutic power dynamics, where the authority of the therapist is largely unquestioned. Instead, *Indecent Behavior* fixates on the resounding threat of women in positions of authority—Rebecca's professionalism must remain suspect.

The visual strategies and relations of looking that are found in *Indecent Behavior* contribute to this tension between doctor and woman. The disclosure of sexual secrets within a therapeutic relationship participates in mechanisms of voyeuristic pleasure, especially on a discursive, verbal level. As suggested earlier, the cinema's explicit relation to the visual encourages the visual representation of a talking cure, often for the gaze of the female doctor and the spectator. Psychoanalytic film theory generally precludes the possibility of women as voyeurs, for they are the site of visual anxiety (castration threat), and therefore the object of a male gaze. Likewise, women narcissistically identify with their own image and, due to this closeness, cannot experience the distance required for voyeurism.[10] The gendered distinctions of subject/object relations in the cinema become especially crucial when the "sex object" is so prevalent within the soft-core genre.

Indecent Behavior problematizes such theories of gendered looking by repeatedly positioning the female protagonist as watching and studying explicit sexual displays. This observation is carried out secretly, for Rebecca studies her clients' sexual confessions from the cover of a two-way mirror; therefore, her clients are objectified and unaware of her questioning gaze.

Likewise, Rebecca's surrogate also becomes an object for her gaze, but Carol is aware of being watched. Carol is an active *object* and thereby assumes a position of authority over the objectified clients in the film. The cloistered world behind the two-way mirror frames the action in the other room, thus structuring the sex acts as performances, with the area where Rebecca watches and takes notes functioning as a fourth wall.

While Rebecca may participate in highly active looking, a clear division must remain between clinical observation and sexual titillation; while the woman is allowed to look, she is not allowed to derive pleasure from doing so. In one of the film's initial sex numbers, a man enters "the Pleasure Center" with a performance difficulty; he can think only of his partner's pleasure and not his own. To combat this dysfunction, Rebecca and the surrogate enforce passivity and submission in this man by using light bondage restraints; the women render him inactive, a passive object. Upon entering her "observatory," with its two-way mirror, Rebecca encounters her niece, Elaine, gazing raptly through the window at the couple performing sexually, clearly aroused by what she sees. (In this film, Elaine studies sexology in college and interns at Rebecca's office. She is carrying on a very obvious affair with Rebecca's husband, Tom.) Rebecca startles Elaine out of her reverie by accusingly asking, "What are you doing?" to which Elaine hastily replies, "Watching." Rebecca promptly lectures Elaine on the importance of objectivity in this profession, for "there is a difference between watching and *watching*."

As the sex number unfolds in front of them, Rebecca sits upright and alert, taking notes. Elaine, the other voyeur in this scene, represents a foil and a challenge to Rebecca's character. She continually derives pleasure from the confessions she hears or watches, undermining their serious clinical content. She eavesdrops on various sessions or watches avidly, without taking detailed notes. Rebecca is a serious doctor, and her confrontation with Elaine outlines the conflict between serious study and voyeuristic pleasure. This renegade, voyeuristic character is taken up again by Ellie, Rebecca's assistant in *Indecent Behavior 3*. Ellie not only becomes turned on by watching therapy sessions, but she also ends up sleeping with the male sex surrogate (in *Indecent Behavior 3,* there are two surrogates, male and female). Soon afterwards, she is murdered, punished for her crime.

For Rebecca, objectivity and authority are synonymous; she must remain clinically detached from the sex she watches. This clinical framing of sex underlies the tension surrounding sexual pleasure in this film. While sexual surrogacy and a two-way mirror provide a convenient means of voyeuristic inspection, Rebecca counters these pleasures by voicing her clinical observations. This enforced detachment provides the female spectator with a conflicted role as well. Mary Ann Doane believes that in films that utilize a clinical setting, "The audience of the film is thus represented within the text, the doctors taking on the role of audience surrogates or narratees. The spectator's eye becomes that of a doctor, and the spectator is given, by proxy, a medical or therapeutic role."[11] Moments of sheer voyeuristic pleasure are recuperated by the film's discursive system, as the clinical realm provides the guidelines for how sex should be perceived. The structure of the film's sex numbers discourages titillation, emphasizing the importance of diagnosis and cure. As the film vacillates between the protagonist's roles as doctor and woman, it also wavers in its relationship to visual pleasure, prescribing a specific form of watching.

While Rebecca's looking is always "framed" within a clinical realm, her acquisition of any type of powerful gaze must be undermined in order to destabilize any connection she has to visual authority. For instance, the breaching of the film's fourth wall, when a character addresses Rebecca through the two-way mirror, clearly signifies danger and threat. When one of Rebecca's patients (in *Indecent Behavior 2*), Tom, experiences erectile dysfunction in his session, he stops and asks her, "What now, doctor?" looking directly into the mirror and at the audience. This outburst indicates Rebecca's lack of control over the therapeutic scenario, as well as her inability to be a true, invisible voyeur. In *Indecent Behavior 3*, the obnoxious police detective and love interest, Frank, walks into Rebecca's research area while a session is underway, eyes the ménage-à-trois tableau in front of her, and snidely cracks, "So this is what you do all day." His voyeuristic perusal of the session again signifies Rebecca's lack of control over her environment, especially regarding the law, and her repeated breaching of her patients' confidentiality. These scenes are particularly self-reflexive as well for the genre. Not only does the breaking of the fourth wall remind the spectator that she is watching a sexual performance by actors, but the proscenium-like mise-en-scène frames the sex as an "act" to be watched. Furthermore, the way so many characters "get off" or try to remain professional while the sex scenes unfold is a running commentary on the titillating aspects of voyeurism.

Nowhere is the performative aspect of sex more apparent than in the scenes that feature Billy (Doug Jeffery), the male sex surrogate in *Indecent Behavior 3*. While the film frames Billy as a sex object, paid to have sex with female clients (never male) and watched by the female sex therapists, his role as object of a gaze is an uneasy one. Billy takes to his profession like a porn actor and always seems to play to the woman who watches behind the two-way mirror. This knowledge becomes especially apparent, and manipulated, after Billy has sex with Ellie, the therapist-in-training, who is also a bad girl for not acting professionally. Ellie grows suspicious of Billy's constant questions about Rebecca, indicating that he may be the sex therapist serial killer. When she discovers incriminating files in his locker, Billy finds out. (Billy, the narrative later reveals, is actually a reporter, working undercover for a story on sex clinics.) In response to Ellie's breach of his privacy, during his next session, while having sex with a client, he pushes the woman's torso against the two-way mirror, forcing Ellie to watch the sex act while he acts out his own aggressions. As a performer, he takes control of a supposedly therapeutic situation and thus taunts Ellie with his actions. In this instance, Ellie struggles to maintain any kind of clinical distance from the sex she witnesses.

This emphasis on the clinical in relation to sex and love reveals itself through the dynamic between Rebecca and Detective Nick Sharkey in the first *Indecent Behavior*. As Mimi White has suggested in her analysis of Dr. Ruth and other practitioners on confessional television shows, therapeutic discourses tend to transform "stories" into case studies.[12] Nick also becomes a case for Rebecca to cure. Not only does he have a problematic relationship with his father, but he is so obsessed with his career that his wife has divorced him. He cannot seem to "have a life." During a dinner date, Rebecca asks some gentle questions. While Nick initially hesitates to reply, he quickly falls into complete self-disclosure and confesses his problems to her. That night he discloses his sexual secrets as well. He becomes her "patient," a role common to mainstream theatrical Hollywood cinema, for "when the psychiatrist is a woman, the man must take the complementary role of patient, due to the consequences for the therapeutic couple of Hollywood's convention of romance."[13] Rebecca serves as both Nick's therapist and his lover, curing him with her body while pursuing her own sexual desires; her roles as doctor and woman systematically collapse. Her relations with Nick are never purely romantic; they cross over into the clinical, sustaining the tension surrounding the female protagonist's role within the narrative.

A similar relationship develops between Rebecca and Frank in *Indecent Behavior 3*, but this time with much more dangerous results. When Frank solicits Rebecca's help, the narrative highlights the incredible animosity he has toward Rebecca and her "profession." Frank finds her "work" highly suspect, believing that sex therapy is either glorified prostitution (for the surrogate) or game playing (for the rich and bored). As time passes and more sex therapists are killed, Frank starts to divulge his own problems. When their first sexual encounter turns violent, Rebecca realizes that Frank needs help. However, by *Indecent Behavior 3* Rebecca has learned her lesson and sends Frank to Ellie for a consultation. Frank reveals that his mother was raped and brutally murdered by her lover, and that this has scarred him. Only in the very last moments of the film does the narrative reveal Frank as the serial killer, driven to violence by his tormented relationship with his mother (a classically Freudian scenario, taken straight from Hitchcock's *Psycho* [1960]). The final confrontation between doctor and patient is taken to the extreme as Rebecca frantically tries to psychoanalyze and therapeutically calm Frank, while he waves a gun in her face. In the end, Frank is killed by a dying Billy, but by then it is too late for Rebecca's reputation to be redeemed; she never suspects or recognizes the homicidal pathology apparent in Frank's case study. Rebecca's search for sexual fulfillment blinds her to the dangers so close to her.

Contradictory sexual ideologies infuse the first *Indecent Behavior,* elaborated through the problems of the patients and characters within the story world. The film represents the marital relation, the most persistent of heterosexual bonds, at its most dysfunctional and problematic. Not only are the marriages of Rebecca's clients sexually unsatisfying, but her own relations with her husband are strained, as Tom continues to have numerous extramarital affairs. Near the beginning of the film, Rebecca claims she is filing for divorce, which not only highlights her dysfunctional marriage, but also sanctions the sexual relations she will have with Detective Sharkey. Rebecca's reaction to Carol's touching "first time" recitation signifies the loss of her own romantic illusions.

Throughout the film's narrative, a conflict between love and sex persists. When Rebecca hires Carol as her sexual surrogate, she admires the woman's ability to separate the two terms (women stereotypically have difficulty separating "sex" from "love"). She later tells Elaine that Carol will go far, for she maintains a "good philosophy." With the film's negative representations of marriage, extramarital pleasure initially appears positive, and even necessary. Nevertheless, sex as pleasure, devoid of relations to love, is ultimately pathological within the narrative. Elaine, the film's relentless pleasure seeker, is continually reprimanded for her stance. Her illicit sex scenes with Rebecca's husband are always short, abbreviated moments that never reach fruition. In contrast, Rebecca's sexual relations with Nick Sharkey are carefully elaborated, full of romantic promise and sensual detail. Much of their interaction is marked by kissing and embracing, and after their first encounter, they fall asleep together; the narrative emphasizes their developing feelings for each other.

The film's moralistic judgment gets passed on to Carol. Ironically, the woman who could distinguish sex from love is earmarked as the film's psychotic killer, implying that her ability to make these distinctions has enforced her pathology. In fact, Carol's brother is the victim of the Extremis overdose in the first moments of the film, and Carol attempts to frame Rebecca for the murder of one of her clients in order to punish her for her brother's accidental death. Carol injects an overdose of the drug into Detective Sharkey, and Rebecca must battle with her surrogate to save her own life and her lover's. In the end, Carol's murderous sexuality is vanquished, and Rebecca and Nick unite as a couple. The narrative restates the conflict over Rebecca's position of authority when she is charged with illegally using Extremis, a controlled substance. She may lose her license to practice, but she does get her man. While the film remains within a system of inner contradiction, pitting the doctor against the woman, its resolution reinforces the importance of romance to the protagonist.

Still, embedded within the structure of the erotic thriller genre is an implicit contradiction regarding women's relationship to marriage and infidelity. In *Indecent Behavior,* Rebecca is driven into the arms of another man because of her cheating, neglectful husband and unsatisfactory marriage. She also repeatedly advises her female patients to explore their sexuality, even if this exploration takes them outside the boundaries of their marriages. Infidelity is further sanctioned by the allowable excess of sexual surrogacy, where female clients often lose their inhibitions through an interaction with the sex surrogate (either male or female). The structure of the series itself, with its numerous sequels, contributes to the heroine's uneasy relationship with monogamy, or "good sex" inside a relationship. While Rebecca may seem to resolve the film by coupling with Detective Nick Sharkey in *Indecent Behavior,* and with Dr. Liam O'Donnell (James Brolin) in *Indecent Behavior 2,* the very nature of a sequel precludes her making lasting bonds with men. The heroine of the therapeutic thriller, and of many other versions of the erotic thriller, must never fulfill her quest for sexual fulfillment and empowerment within a romantic relationship. She must always be pursuing this elusive narrative goal.

Within the therapeutic erotic thriller, a loss of authority appears inherent in the representation of a *female* therapist. This undermining of the heroine's professionalism evolves explicitly in films dealing with women troubled by countertransference, where the female therapist/heroine unwittingly "falls for" her patient, often placing her in a position of extreme danger. The therapist or psychiatrist's "fall from grace" is a frequently used plot in Hollywood cinema, appearing in films such as Hitchcock's *Spellbound* (1945). As Janet Walker explains,

> Marriages or love affairs between analysts and analysands are common to popular culture representations and are described as transference/counter-transference. It is unclear whether these fictional marriages represent the patient's fantasy or the doctor's. Perhaps [the] popular (and illegitimate, according to professional standards) version of countertransference is partially responsible for the professional assertions of the undesirability of countertransference and for the oft-asserted objectivity of the analyst.[14]

In the *Indecent Behavior* series, the heroine painstakingly verbalizes her rules and boundaries, always reiterating the importance of objectivity and the clinical gaze in her work. The threat of countertransference implicitly plays out in Rebecca's involvement with Detective Nick Sharkey (who models himself as a case study), but it becomes explicit when she unwittingly sleeps with Frank, the psychotic killer in *Indecent Behavior 3*. The heroine's "slip" within these films reveals a profound skepticism about maintaining professionalism in a vocation devoted to sex. Problems in countertransference appear more likely when the talking cure is of such an intimate nature. Again, these tensions stem from the power relations involved in the doctor-patient dynamic common to therapeutic discourses, except that the relationship stressed in the erotic thriller always focuses on the heroine's vulnerabilities.

Within the countertransference erotic thriller, the relationship between doctor and patient masks an all-out gender war. The male characters in films such as *Profile for Murder* (David Winning, 1997), *Sexual Intent* (Kurt McCarley, 1994), and *The Dark Dancer* (Robert Burge, 1995) play the role of the *homme* fatale, or the "fatal man," within the narrative. (These films retain a narrative structure similar to that of the film noir–oriented films discussed in chapter 3, in which the heroine investigates and the man is the object of her scrutiny.) In countertransference erotic thrillers, the heroines are assigned to these men because of their problems or pathologies. While the narratives are not as focused on sex talk, as in the sex therapy films, the conversations between doctor and patient evolve into verbal titillation, as the male character carries out the seduction of his doctor. The films usually construct the female lead as a workaholic, badly in need of a vacation, and uninvolved in a successful love relationship. In *Profile for Murder,* Dr. Hannah Karras (Joan Severance), a criminal psychology expert, is coming off the eighth month of her divorce and an unsuccessful fling with a police detective, and she chats about a vacation with Michael, the assistant district attorney. Following the structure of the DTV erotic thriller, Hannah's goal sustains two narrative threads: she must find a serial sex killer and fulfill her own sexual needs. Both goals are entwined in one character: Adrian Cross (Lance Henriksen), the fatal man. The film represents Hannah as smart and strong in her profession and simultaneously vulnerable and needy in her love life, a necessary tension for her to succumb to countertransference. In these narratives, "As lovers themselves, the psychiatrist characters cannot remain omnipotent, objective professionals, but become vulnerable to mental instability."[15] The heroine's apparent devotion to her career cannot be maintained, and she is eventually punished by her fall from grace.

Fairly early in the film, the heroine's professional and personal lives intersect when she "takes her work home with her." She begins to fantasize about her male patient, a situation he instigates, and places herself within the disclosed secrets and narratives he tells her. These stories are invariably seductive and loaded with sexual detail. For instance, in *Profile for Murder,* Hannah falls quickly for Cross's charms, as the narrative implies in the opening scene that Cross is a ladies' man who can pick up any woman whenever he wants. The film opens with his arrival at a nightclub, where he pulls an attractive blond out of the crowd, dances with her, and then brings her home for sex. This sex scene becomes not "twice told" but "thrice told" within the film. Initially, the viewer watches the action unfold in the film's opening scenes, voyeuristically indulging in the sex scene. Shortly thereafter, Cross narrates the intimate details of the scene when Hannah questions him in his prison cell.

While Hannah asks him about what happened, his story digresses into sensual details—the taste of the woman's skin, the feel of her lips, the caresses of his hands on her body, the type of music pounding in the background. As Cross confesses his secret, the film revisualizes the scenes previously shown in the opening, yet the point of view of this rendition becomes uncertain. As Cross recounts his story, his voice-over follows the images, yet the camera cuts back to Hannah's mesmerized gaze, her apparent reverie, as she seems to retreat to a fantasy world. The last thing Cross says to his lover is "You like that?" which he then turns and asks Hannah, who dreamily responds "yes," comes to, and hastily replies "no." Cross's words, instead of being clinically regarded by the psychiatrist, become verbal titillation, stimulating what appears to be Hannah's visual subjectivity on screen. Cross ironically asks, "What are you afraid of?" but Hannah has already slipped; she has crossed the line from professional to personal involvement with her object of study.[16]

Later, while she takes a luxurious bubble bath at home, she begins to relive her experience with Cross, but this time instead of imagining the now-murdered woman within the scenario, she imagines herself. The film again visualizes the same series of events, down to the red dress the woman was wearing, but this time it is Hannah who wears the dress and appears to have the dominant role in the fantasy. At one point in the fantasy, she pulls a sharp spike on Cross, seemingly responding to the threat he produces in her by taking on the role of the aggressor. After Cross is released by the police, due to a lack of evidence, Hannah eventually sleeps with him, heedless of the dangers to her professional and personal life.

Similarly, in *Sexual Intent* (Kurt McCarley, 1994), the heroine eventually succumbs to a patient she is treating, despite his known history of misogyny and troubled relationships with women. The film further highlights the susceptibility of the therapist figure by having her be as easily deceived as all the other women seduced by the main character, John. The narrative focus of *Sexual Intent* oscillates between the story of Barbara, John's therapist, and the other women he systematically robs and cheats. For the first half of the film, Barbara studiously avoids John's advances, instead keeping her relationship with him on a professional level. At every turn he tries to break her resolve, and she finally drops him as a patient. He predictably believes this is because of her unprofessional feelings for him. Despite her knowledge of John's "misogyny, role-playing, and paranoia," her vulnerability as a single professional woman who is sexually unfulfilled proves too much for her self-control.

At first, Barbara's "unprofessional" nature reveals itself while she views female testimonials from her research on "sexual fantasy," during which she interviews women and records their responses on tape (a trope used repeatedly in soft-core television anthology series such as *Women: Stories of Passion* and *Red Shoe Diaries,* as well as in Zalman King's film *Shame, Shame, Shame*). As she watches one woman recounting her fantasy about being "forced" in an elevator, Barbara fantasizes herself into the scenario *with John as her seducer.*

While fantasy does not always mean an "acting out," her desires for John undermine her professional demeanor, especially when she knows firsthand about his pathology. After finding out about his arrest record, and even after he robs her, she still drives to help him when he calls.

Robert Burge's *The Dark Dancer* (1995) follows a formula like that of the other two thrillers, but it undermines the psychologist character by pathologizing her along with the male character/seducer. Dr. Margaret Stinson (Shannon Tweed) is both a published expert on female sexuality and a practicing psychologist, and inevitably, her sexual side is profoundly unfulfilled. She resolves this tension between her private and public lives by moonlighting some nights as Madame Ecstasy, an exotic dancer.[17] Within this extremely convoluted narrative emerges Ron, an undergraduate student in Margaret's human sexuality class, who insists he knows more about her subject matter than she does. She records in her notes later that day, "A young student made an observation about true love. I disagreed with him at first, but the more I think about it, I think he's right." Although Margaret is established as an expert in her field, a highly published author and college professor, her authority is easily undermined by her male student, which puts all of her expertise into question. The male character is represented as better at her job (more knowledgeable about female sexuality) than she is. This situation occurs in *Profile for Murder* as well when the male character, Cross, continually turns all questions and discussions toward Hannah. Even though she is supposedly the best in her field, according to her male colleagues, a man untrained in her profession is easily able to outmaneuver her psychologically (and the same can be said for Barbara in *Sexual Intent*).

Despite Margaret's knowledge of Ron's stalker tendencies, and the precariousness of her professional position (especially in relation to her moonlighting activities), she becomes involved with her student. Thus, within the countertransference thriller, the tensions between doctor and woman common to the therapeutic erotic thriller become more pronounced. Margaret is willing to risk losing her teaching position and destroy her private practice in order to fulfill herself sexually. She succumbs to Ron's persistent attentions and fulfills her inner needs by stripping. Similarly, Barbara's thesis, "A Clinical Study of Destructive, Co-dependent Female Pair Bonding Relationships with Men," is thrown away when she leaves to pick John up after he calls. In these examples, after the doctor's "fall from grace," where the heroine decides to focus on her sexual awakening to the detriment of her career, the films never really resolve themselves. Both *Profile for Murder* and *The Dark Dancer* end with the women becoming involved with police detectives on their respective cases, but the professional toll for "crossing the line" within the therapeutic relationship is never addressed.

This lack of resolution, relating to "unresolved" tensions within the erotic thriller, does not carry over when a man plays the role of psychologist/therapist.[18] In Gregory Hippolyte's *Body of Influence* (1994), the male character is surprisingly undeveloped, even though the film is supposedly focalized through him. Instead, as in the "bitch from hell" erotic thriller, the male character, Jonathan Brooks, suffers repeated humiliations and punishments for his transgressions, until he is stripped of all his power as a therapist and as a man. Like some classical film noirs, in *Body of Influence,* the male character recounts his experiences in voice-over. While this retrospective view posits a man's subjectivity, he clearly retells the narrative from a place of loss. Unlike the female therapist, who valiantly attempts to maintain her professionalism and objectivity, Jonathan eagerly sleeps with his clients. If a woman takes off her clothes in mid-session and climbs on top of him, he allows the scenario, taking this as one of the perks of the profession; he tells his clients to act their desires out as part of "the healing process." Unfortunately, he becomes involved with a seductive patient, Laura Nesbitt (soft-core regular Shannon Whirry), whom he mistakenly believes is suffering from multiple personality disorder.

The film follows Jonathan's deterioration scene by scene, as his voice-over reveals an increasingly delusional subjectivity. Laura starts trying to seduce him while in her "Lana" personality. Whereas before he watched his female patients act out, now he has sex with all of them, on videotape. His point of view is further splintered whenever Laura is in his office, confessing her secrets to him. The visuals never establish whether Laura is remembering her experiences or Jonathan is fantasizing about what those experiences might look like (a problem that also undermines Rebecca's authority in the *Indecent Behavior* series). Furthermore, there are moments when the film uses Laura's point of view. In one of the film's explicit sex scenes, Jonathan has sex with one of his patients—on camera. In another room, Jonathan's secretary and Laura watch the events unfold on a television monitor. The spectator watches the view from the monitor as well. Later, Jonathan arrives home to find Laura and his girlfriend watching the same tape. The male character suffers humiliation upon humiliation, until he is suitably punished for his disregard for the therapeutic relationship. What differentiates the male-lead countertransference thriller from the more common female-oriented narratives is both the character's pronounced mental instability and the film's lack of concern for his motivations or resolution (the film generally eschews any romantic coupling in its ending). The pleasures of the narrative are focused on the man "getting what he deserves."

The narrative structure of these films reveals a distrust of the psychiatric and psychological profession, while simultaneously promoting the importance and necessity of the therapeutic relationship and its divulging of secrets. Sexual healing, usually the heroine's, occurs through talking, yet the kind of talk involved, sexually titillating and unprofessional, threatens the careers of those who elicit the verbal exchange. Furthermore, the talk that occurs, forbidden in a professional setting, suggests the heroine's susceptibility to deception—a deception committed by her client in the course of his therapy. The sex scenes between doctor and patient in these films act as visual counterpoint to the verbal battle of the sexes. The countertransference thriller exploits the possibility of intimacy between analyst and analysand, something not so clearly marked in Foucault's version of the confessional. In the thriller's represented intimacy, the distinctions of power and authority are clearly gendered, as the heroine's search for sexual fulfillment allows for a simultaneous disempowerment within the public sphere.

PUBLIC SEX TALK: GENDERED SEDUCTION AND EXHIBITIONISM

Although most therapeutic discourses in the erotic thriller take place in private, clinical settings, the talk show thriller moves sex talk into the public sphere, usually involving a call-in radio audience. When sex therapy becomes a public medium, instead of residing in a private realm, the consumption of secrets and the exhibitionism of their telling collide. Deborah Lupton, in her analysis of the talk show, states, "The talk-show genre frequently uses the confession as a commodity, selling audiences the prurient pleasure of hearing about other people's intimate sex lives and feelings."[19] The public talk show in the erotic thriller is usually broadcast over the radio, and the show's outreach to a mass audience distinctly changes the confessional parameters of the therapeutic relationship. A three-way interchange often occurs, continually shifting power relations, between the doctor or "expert," the patient with the problem to be solved, and the public, which listens to the interchange on the radio. In turn, one or more listeners may call in and respond to what is said on the air, contributing to an unstable and unpredictable environment. Within this therapeutic dynamic, the expert's role becomes especially crucial, because the advice given to a patient with a question or problem is simultaneously judged as reliable and taken as advice by the listening audience.

This three-way interchange within the public therapeutic relationship places the therapist or expert in a very vulnerable position, especially if the show focuses on sex. The possibilities for "deceiving the doctor," who can communicate with patients only by phone call, becomes intensified by the voyeuristic and exhibitionistic aspects of disclosing "sex talk" on a mass scale. For the radio talk show, "Without a visual signifier that would locate the home audience within the apparatus of looking, talking becomes fetishized, a sort of verbal foreplay, explicit yet discreet, titillating."[20] In order to get ratings, the host-therapist has two choices: to maintain a professional demeanor and try to help those in need, or to contribute to the exploitation of the medium by using an on-air persona as seduction, "verbal foreplay." This distinction between the therapeutic and the pornographic (used for arousal) can also become blurred for the show's audience, as the show can become an exhibitionist performance space for sex. The erotic thriller, as a sexualized form of entertainment, exploits the medium's titillating capabilities. Yet, the role of expert and seducer is split across specifically gendered lines.

As previously established, women in the therapeutic erotic thriller usually struggle to maintain authority within their field; their expertise is frequently undermined by their simultaneous desire for sexual fulfillment. When the heroine is positioned as a talk show host, her ability to maneuver within the public sphere is based on her knowledge and wisdom in handling her patients/listeners and their problems. In *Sexual Response,* for instance, Dr. Eve Robertson (the ubiquitous Shannon Tweed) is a clinical psychologist and a published expert on sex and relationships. Her radio show, the eponymous *Sexual Response,* is very popular, and her work entails fielding calls about relationships, sex, and infidelity. While Eve poses as an expert on the air, her understanding of sexuality and relationships is based in theory. She may have a Ph.D., but the narrative reveals Eve's possession of book knowledge, not sexual experience. In an effort to maintain her authority, Eve does not allow her knowledge to cross into her personal life. She is married to a neglectful husband, Phillip, who alternates between verbally abusing and ignoring her, leaving Eve sexually unfulfilled. When she meets Edge, her love interest, she is celebrating her birthday at a bar with a coworker. Compared to her friend, Kate (Catherine Oxenberg), Eve is uptight around men and their attentions, coded as sexually repressed.[21] The narrative indicates the tension between Eve's sexual knowledge and sexual experience through the way her on-air advice mirrors the events in her own life. For instance, at the beginning of the film, a caller confides to Eve that she is thinking about cheating on her husband, because he is sexually distant. While Eve discourages her from the affair, the woman's husband calls and threatens to kill her if she strays from their marriage. Not only does this interchange reveal the three-way involvement of doctor, caller, and listener, but it also mirrors Eve's life. When she has an affair with Edge, her husband tries to kill her.

In another scene, a caller tells Eve that she's having "great sex," but that she is involved in an abusive relationship with her boyfriend and needs advice. Should she continue the relationship? Eve tells her to "buy a vibrator and get out of there"—sound advice, with a feminist tone toward abusive relationships and codependency. Yet, Eve's advice directly connects to her own life, for she continues to stay in her relationship with Phillip, who emotionally abuses her.[22]

Eve's position as a doctor, expert, and host of her own talk show is a significant accomplishment; yet, the film's trajectory undermines her authority by revealing her "expertise" as a masquerade. In the course of achieving sexual fulfillment outside of her marriage, Eve does gain sexual experience to match her theoretical knowledge. Still, this process of self-exploration proves treacherous. Her husband turns out to be a psychotic killer; her lover, Edge, is revealed as his vengeful, abandoned son; and her best friend is killed in the crossfire. While Eve still keeps her job in the narrative's resolution, she is severely punished for deceiving her audience by pretending to be a sex expert. In sexual terms, the only women with authority are those who actually have sexual experience (with sex workers as the true "experts" of the field).[23]

Not all DTV talk show erotic thrillers contain talk shows run by qualified female doctors or therapists. In Zalman King's *Women of the Night* (2000), the on-air sex talk is deliberately teasing and titillating, as the lead female character, Samantha, runs a late-night pirate radio show out of a specially equipped big rig. She and her crew are constantly on the move, on the run from her drug-dealing, murderous father, who supposedly killed her mother, her brother, and her lover. The motivation for Sam's late-night vocation is partially tied to her relationship with Mary (Sally Kellerman), a fellow late-night talk show host who was her father's former mistress, and partially connected to her desire for vengeance against her father. Often, both women's voices intermingle with each other, the camera cutting from Sam to Mary and back again, their voices equally sultry as they tell the stories of several women entangled in webs of desire. Sam's voice is the chief source of narration in this film, and she paints with her words images of opulence and seduction; the romantic mise-en-scène is visualized in flashes as she uses whispered descriptions to create the film's world.

As in many erotic thrillers, the film's "thriller" narrative is negligible, serving mainly as a backstory to the film's erotic sex scenes. The three main female characters whose stories are told—Charlotte, the law student; Molly, the comedienne; and Samantha, the heiress—are all in search of love and sexual fulfillment, which they encounter with Harley, Jack, and Sato, respectively. Each woman experiences sexual pleasure, but only Samantha, the heroine of the film, suffers tragically for her desires. As the group of lovers gathers in a cafe, Sato, trying to protect her, is shot dead by some of her father's men, and Samantha is literally struck blind in her despair. It is after this climactic shootout that Samantha enlists a crew to start her radio show, where she tells her story to those who will listen. The heroine's sexual desires are ultimately destroyed, and all she has left is the ability to taunt her father over the airwaves. In the very last moments of the film, the heroine's father catches up with her. He throws himself on a knife he hands her, claiming that he killed his family only to save them from suffering at the hands of his ruthless enemies. Samantha's experience as a talk show host comes to a conclusion as her story ostensibly ends.

Some films, such as Eric Gibson's *Bare Deception* (2000), are more overt about the titillating, exhibitionistic role that sex talk might take. In this film, Julia Collins (Tane' McClure) hosts a matchmaking show, *Talk Love,* supposedly for women to find love, romance, and the perfect mate. But the show really elicits discussion of physical attributes and sexual skills, not love, and casual sex hookups result. The women who call into the show seem disinterested in love, as they repeatedly disrobe while talking on-air and describing themselves. The men who call in are not visually shown in an equally exhibitionistic manner, even though they describe themselves in similar ways. While Julia's lover and producer, Christian, is obsessively interested in ratings, Julia herself is interested in "turning men on," and she uses her low, husky voice to lure them to her show (figure 7). Still, the success of her Los Angeles radio talk show must compensate for her sexual dissatisfaction with Christian, who participates in numerous extramarital activities with one of the radio station's managers and several of the women calling into *Talk Love.* (He uses false names and a voice-disguising device to call into the show, so that Julia will not recognize him.)

Figure 7. Julia Collins broadcasting on her radio show in *Bare Deception* (2000).

Inevitably, one of the "dates" that Julia sets up on *Talk Love* ends in murder, and the police are understandably suspicious of Christian. With her relationship falling apart, Julia seeks comfort with the chief detective on the case, Paul. In one scene, where she caresses the detective's card with her fingertips, she fantasizes about his "interrogating" her and seducing her. Their love scenes are styled in typical DTV fashion, with low lighting, soft music, and other trappings of romance. *Bare Deception* has a conflicted take on infidelity. Because of his stepping out on his relationship with Julia, Christian is represented as dumb and caddish, almost pathological in his need for daily fulfillment. Julia's scenes with Paul, however, imply a possible relationship in the making and emphasize the trust and friendship that develop between the two. Once Christian is arrested for murder, Julia is able to focus on her burgeoning feelings for Paul, as well as on soaring ratings, as *Talk Love* becomes the hottest radio show in Los Angeles. Still, in a perverse last-minute twist, the film clues the spectator into the fact that Julia has framed Christian in order to find sexual fulfillment and boost her ratings. She gets away with these crimes, which indicates, as in the "bitch-from-hell" erotic thriller, that lying, cheating bastards get what they deserve in the end.

Male characters, and male talk show hosts, perform quite a different function within the DTV talk show erotic thriller, where they frequently serve as seducers and objects of desire. In *Night Rhythms* (A. Gregory Hippolyte, 1992), the male protagonist, Nick West (Martin Hewitt), does not possess professional qualifications for his on-air, sex therapist role. Instead, he is qualified *because he is a man.* The film opens as flickering lights move over a woman's lingerie-clad body. The film reveals her in shadow, talking to Nick on the phone. The possible performative and exhibitionistic capabilities of the medium are exploited as Nick and his "patient" basically have phone sex on-air. Initially, the relationship between the two characters is therapeutic. The woman, Linda, complains to Nick that there's no passion or foreplay during sex with her husband. Yet, instead of suggesting some ways for the couple to resolve their problems, Nick huskily describes in detail what he would do to her, stimulating her fantasies and eventually bringing her to orgasm on-air.

The film produces a discrepancy in subject/object relations, especially in terms of aural-versus-visual titillation and objectification. While Nick seduces women with his voice, the spectator can see only his face and his lips as he talks. Visually, Nick's female callers are often displayed full-bodied, touching themselves and becoming aroused by his words (similar to the way female callers are displayed in *Bare Deception*). Women are objects for a visual gaze, yet Nick can never possess that gaze or fully interact with his clients; he is performing a service. Nick exists for the purpose of each woman's sexual gratification as an on-air sex worker. While he may be excited during his work, his placement on-air makes it impossible for him to achieve release. He has to live vicariously through orgasming women.

When Nick tries to cross the line beyond erotic object, he is duly punished. One of his regular callers, Honey, shows up at the studio. A notorious exhibitionist (like Nick), Honey convinces him to have sex with her. She "unwittingly" hits the "on-air" button, thereby broadcasting their sex across the air waves. After Nick leaves the room for a moment, he comes back to find Honey dead. The entire incident is recorded on an aural "snuff tape," and Nick goes on the run to prove his innocence. Phone sex is safe sex—noncommittal, where talk is fetishized. Whenever Nick becomes involved with actual bodies, his actions lead to murder.

Nevertheless, while Nick may be a master at verbal foreplay, not all of his listening audience appreciates his position as seducer of women. One caller, John, accuses him of being a "sexist hypocrite who has screwed-up broads crying on his shoulder just so he can go out and nail them." Another caller calls him a pervert, while another insists he's using the show as his own personal dating service. Nick's punishment for actual sex, as well as the animosity from other callers, indicates a prescriptive ideology toward the abuses of the therapeutic relationship. While Nick proves a useful tool for women's sexual stimulation, his negotiation of the talk show, frequently a female-oriented daytime genre, is critiqued within the film's narrative.

The titles of the characters' talk shows indicate how the films work along a gendered divide. Eve's daytime show is entitled *Sexual Response,* an homage to Masters and Johnson's landmark book, *Human Sexual Response.* Her show focuses on working through various sexual and relationship problems, based upon her professional credentials and expertise. While the film reveals Eve's lack of sexual experience, her serious interest in the therapeutic relationship exists throughout the narrative. Conversely, Nick's nighttime show is entitled *Talk to Me* and supports the use of talk as titillation and verbal foreplay. His female callers ask him to "talk to me," and he solves their problems with immediate sexual gratification.

All of the films categorized as therapeutic erotic thrillers initially establish the authority and power dynamic of the therapeutic relationship, then proceed to undermine the role of the doctor or expert who supposedly possesses a position of power. The films indicate that the therapeutic dynamic represents an unstable and changeable power relationship, one in which either role, of doctor or patient, can become manipulated for personal sexual satisfaction. For most of these narratives, the "problem" becomes how to produce and regulate normative female heterosexuality, with women serving as experts on the subject. Yet these same heroines are incapable of resolving their own problems and tensions: negotiating their public and private lives, finding love, and achieving sexual fulfillment. Both the narratives of the erotic thrillers and their related societal tensions remain largely unresolved.

SURVEILLANCE, SUBJECTIVITY, AND SOFT CORE: "YOU LIKE TO WATCH, DON'T YOU?"

oyeurism is a chief semantic element of the DTV (direct-to-video) erotic thriller genre.[1] Due to the genre's sexually focused subject matter, someone is always pleasurably (and often secretively) viewing another person as an object, whether within the diegetic film world or outside, through the eyes of the spectator. The erotic thriller narrativizes this voyeuristic theme in a variety of stylistic ways—through staging erotic photo shoots, by having sex therapists gaze through two-way mirrors at sex surrogates, by showing a woman's eye at a keyhole, and especially through the use of video surveillance.

With the advent of accessible and consumer-friendly technologies, sex and its spectatorship has become an increasingly mediated experience. With each new technological medium, from home video to the Internet, cell phones to virtual reality, and beyond, representations of sexuality have shifted and transformed. The intersection of sex and technology facilitates a performative, mediated understanding of sexuality, one that moves away from the natural and original to the postmodern realm of mutable boundaries and role-playing. Consumers develop a more intimate connection to the production of surveillance through technology, as both subjects and objects of a gaze. As Lili Berko explains in her work on surveillance and subjectivity:

> The combination of computer and communications technologies and their entry into the consumer marketplace has produced the possibility for each one of us to not only be the object of surveillance, but its subject as well. In this way, the postmodern panopticon moves beyond Bentham's model, which allowed individuals to exercise control only through a pro-

cess of "interiorization in which the individual becomes his own over-seer," to a postmodern model in which individuals enjoy the possibility of becoming the owners and operators of personal and professional seeing machines, mini-videographic systems, producing their own mini-panop-ticons as they go along, challenging the power of the official panoptic gaze of the invisible "other."[2]

Berko differentiates the postmodern panopticon from Bentham's model, referring to Michel Foucault's study of surveillance and the regulation of the individual in *Discipline and Punish: The Birth of the Prison*. In this book, Foucault explains how an idealized prison system, aiming to discipline and punish, would set up a surveillance complex that featured a central-ized viewing area from which guards would watch and survey the inmates. The building, or panopticon, was designed so that the prison inmates could never tell when the guards were looking, but were left with the impression of a continuous, unavoidable surveillance. As Foucault explains, "Each indi-vidual, in his place, is securely confined to a cell from which he is seen from the front by the supervisor; but the side walls prevent him from coming into contact with his companions. He is seen, but he does not see; he is the object of information, never the subject of communication."[3] After some time, the inmates would internalize this constant surveillance and regulate their own behavior, whether the guards were actually watching or not. Thus, the panopticon would "induce in the inmate a state of conscious and permanent visibility that assures the automatic functioning of power."[4]

Lili Berko suggests that within postmodernism, power relations shift be-cause of the consumer's increased accessibility to the means of surveillance. Furthermore, a state of constant visibility still exists, but the access to control of that visibility is changing. Subject-object relationships shift under the weight of a consumer-operated surveillance, and the idea of constant vis-ibility suggests a resistance to regulation through the performative. Berko states, "In this way, we come to perceive the surveilled as active participants in their own monitoring, performers on a mediated, postmodern stage."[5]

The accessibility of surveillance for consumption, and a performative in-teraction with this technology, is most apparent in the current popularity of amateur pornography, celebrity sex tapes (such as Pam Anderson's and Paris Hilton's), and the overwhelming presence of reality television. Industry research and the popular press indicate that amateur porn started to grow more than a decade ago, when video cameras became more affordable.[6] In

1983, the first amateur-porn mail-order house, Homegrown Video, was established. Truly "amateur" porn is represented by sex between nonprofessionals recorded with a home video camera, but variations on amateur porn include videos shot by professional photographers and videos that use a mixture of professional and amateur talent. Product lines such as "Mr. Peepers' Amateur Home Videos," "Neighborhood Watch," and "Real Deal Swingers" are examples of the growing market, as are sorority house video cams and "documentary" Web sites such as Bangbus.com.[7] Through amateur porn and the accessibility of nonintrusive home video camcorders and DV (digital video) cameras, including cell phones, there is an increasing mediation of human interaction, including sex. The awareness and acknowledgment of surveillance produces pleasures in performance and gives rise to exhibitionism.

Still, there are limits to technology's ability to simulate and stimulate the sex act. Amateur porn is predicated on the awareness of performance and voyeuristic pleasure. Yet, viewing any type of porn is still limited to stimulation through the scopic drive. Cybersex and virtual reality, which utilize more advanced computerized technology than the mere recording of an image, still only stimulate on a cerebral, fantasy level, instead of inducing a tactile, touch-based interaction. While technology can produce arousal, mediated sex always differentiates itself from the actual, bodily sensations of the sex act. Consumer technology has yet to produce the causal stimulation of directed body sensation through a visual apparatus. These technological limits are replicated in the erotic thriller through the continual reaffirmation of the difference between fantasy and reality, the virtual and the real.

In support of the genre's syntactical structure, the "surveillance" erotic thriller combines pleasure and danger. Films of this type display a playful voyeuristic curiosity accompanied by anxiety over the uses and abuses of the surveillance apparatus. While accessibility to technology places surveillance on a more performative stage, the access to and control over that technology still distributes power unevenly, usually along gendered lines. The pleasurable ability to capture a moment, sexual or otherwise, often turns dangerous for the heroine when the mediated act, recorded on tape, inevitably falls into the wrong hands. The flexibility of subject-object relations attributed to the use of surveillance equipment is controlled and regulated by the subject's or object's possession of the means of production. Thus, the DTV surveillance erotic thriller, through its thematic use of surveillance, both stimulates and critiques voyeurism and the gendered power relationships that ensue.

Within the surveillance erotic thriller, the narrative produces possibilities for voyeurism through the medium of technology; it frequently uses video surveillance cameras in a protective capacity, or as a form of self-discovery and/or analysis. Rodney McDonald's *Night Eyes 2* (1992) exemplifies the utilization of surveillance technology and the repercussions of its use. The film is a sequel to the incredibly popular *Night Eyes* (1990), which is recognized as the catalyst of the glut of erotic thrillers to follow. *Night Eyes 2* stars Andrew Stevens and Shannon Tweed, the Tom Cruise and Julia Roberts of the erotic thriller genre; their names on a box cover immediately raise expectations for the soft-core spectator. (See figure 8.) Will Griffith, played by Stevens, owns a security company called Night Eyes, which sets up high-tech surveillance systems for wealthy clients in the Beverly Hills area. When Marilyn (Tweed) and her politician husband, Hector, are shot at on arrival at their new home, they immediately solicit the assistance of Will and his surveillance system to protect them. Thus, the threat surrounding the home and domestic environment relates this film to other DTV erotic thrillers that utilize tropes of the gothic genre.

Following the formulaic elements of the DTV erotic thriller genre, Marilyn's marriage is sexually frustrating and emotionally unfulfilling, because her husband's political ambitions make him more interested in his wife's money than her sex drive. Marilyn develops an attraction to Will, whom she asks to serve as her personal bodyguard. Their involvement leads to infidelity, hot sex, and, inevitably, murder. The surveillance cameras perpetuate the pleasure/danger principle common to the erotic thriller's structure, for they serve a dual purpose: they both protect against intruders and provide safety through their constant presence, while they simultaneously project a controlling, malicious gaze that watches and regulates the sexuality contained within. The pleasures Marilyn may experience from being seen and desired by Will exist alongside the danger of being watched, of being caught in an act of transgression. The film's narrative therefore combines a playfulness regarding the thrill of exhibitionism with the dangerous surveillance that stimulates and regulates its expression.

Because the film serves as erotic entertainment, the narrative often playfully produces voyeuristic moments for stimulation. Certain scenes within *Night Eyes 2* not only purposefully produce opportunities for voyeuristic

Figure 8. Shannon Tweed, queen of erotic thrillers, in *Forbidden Sins* (1998).

pleasure, but also critique the role of the spectator, as well as the fixity of the object of a voyeuristic gaze along gendered lines. For instance, after an extended, "getting-to-know-you" montage, during which Will and Marilyn go tie shopping and laugh over lunch in the sunshine, they enter a bookstore. While the two casually look at books, they are always aware of their relationship and proximity to each other, eventually finding themselves alone behind a bookcase in the back of the store.

Unbeknownst to Marilyn and Will, a bespectacled "Peeping Tom" begins to spy on Marilyn from the other side of the bookshelf. Initially, Marilyn smiles at the man while reading a book, but suddenly, from his point of view, her eyes widen and she meets his gaze. As he furtively glances down at his book and then back to the display, Marilyn throws her head back and moans. The camera eventually pulls back from the tight closeups of the bookshelf to reveal Will at Marilyn's feet, caressing her legs and thighs. While Marilyn appears to be in the throes of ecstasy, the man misinterprets her repeated glance at him as an invitation. Yet once he develops the courage to step to the other side of the bookshelf, Marilyn (and Will) has disappeared.

The shopping trip and tie-buying episodes appear to fulfill stereotypical female pleasures, but the scene in the bookstore specifically remarks on sexual subjectivity within this film. Marilyn first notices the bespectacled male voyeur and then confronts his shy, nervous look with her own active, repeated gaze. Her pleasure comes not only from Will's secret caresses, but also from her interaction with the male voyeur. She enjoys his surveillance, while he furtively glances around him, fearful of the very structures that give her pleasure and allow his gaze. This scene critiques not only voyeurism but also soft-core spectatorship. Marilyn's act in the bookstore is a projected act, a performance of sex for an implied audience; within this scene she looks, looks back, and exchanges gazes with the voyeur instead of just receiving them.

The surveillance apparatus in *Night Eyes 2* perpetuates this experience, for the actors/characters are always performing before a camera—surveillance or otherwise. This performance is not merely sexual spectacle for a voyeuristic spectator, for "it is the structure of our seeing, not her nakedness, that must become apparent to us."[8] The presence of the surveillance cameras reminds the spectator of her own mediated gaze and how it is regulated within the text, where, according to the theorist Wheeler Winston Dixon, "every act of the surveilled personages is in fact a projected act, one which confronts the audience, an actor look that challenges and meets the gaze of the receptor."[9] When Marilyn confronts the gaze of the bookstore voyeur with her own look, she confronts the gaze of the spectator as well.

Significantly, Marilyn is not the only character regarded voyeuristically. The narrative takes great pains to construct Will Griffith, the Night Eyes security head and main object of desire, as a "sensitive" guy, who talks about his feelings, cares about a woman's pleasure, and willingly follows the female protagonist's lead. His character serves as counterpoint to the insensitive, unavailable, and nonsexual husband or boyfriend who refuses to fulfill the heroine's sexual and emotional desires. Furthermore, Will's position as male voyeur is constantly called into question; even though his gaze is periodically caught by the apparatus, he prefers unmediated acts with Marilyn rather than their simulation. Will thus serves a dual function as protector and sexual object; his shifting between these roles is marked by his relationship to the surveillance apparatus he installs. While his aim is to protect, the masculine barrier of surveillance is breached by evil forces. He is repeatedly caught by the cameras that he installs and thereby becomes the object of a gaze.

As with most erotic thrillers, *Night Eyes 2* does not stand up well under "reality testing." Although Will is hired to place surveillance equipment throughout Marilyn's home, he appears entirely forgetful that his every action is under surveillance. He is repeatedly caught on camera, often in situations of intimacy.[10] As Will falls for Marilyn, he loses his professional objectivity and becomes increasingly unaware of the power relations connected to his implanted technology. The first time Will is caught on camera, he rushes to Marilyn's aid as she develops a severe cramp in her leg while working out—he first witnesses her expression of pain in the monitoring booth. As he massages her upper thigh, he lifts his eyes to meet the gaze of the camera he has installed in the room. Later, they share a tender moment, and their first kiss, on the stairs. Afterwards, Will hastily remembers the surveillance apparatus and confiscates the tape that captured the moment.

Ultimately, Will loses complete control of the apparatus he has installed, as he becomes the object of a malicious and dangerous gaze. With Hector, Marilyn's husband, out of town, the couple decides to indulge their passions in a romanticized sex scene involving candles, firelight, champagne, raspberries, and lingerie, which culminates with sex performed on gym equipment.[11] Will even has the presence of mind to make sure the cameras in the room are turned off. Unfortunately though, dangerous elements that threaten the couple have control over the apparatus. As Will lets his guard down, they are caught on tape. Later, while Will is in the monitoring booth, he spies Hector's head of security, Luis, watching the tape of Will and Marilyn from the night before. The increased distance and mediation of the sex scene—a video monitor captures a spectator watching a tape of sex from a video monitor—signifies Will's powerlessness regarding the surveillance technology he had previously possessed and controlled.

While the production and installation of surveillance technology appears to reside in male-dominated terrain in *Night Eyes 2,* suggesting a gendered panoptic gaze, these structures of looking are continually rendered unreliable or penetrable. Will seems to have almost no control over the apparatus he installs. Whenever he moves from the subject of surveillance to the object of its gaze, he is rendered vulnerable and stripped of phallic power. Marilyn maintains mobility within the film's structure, capable of moving between subject and object positions with more ease than the male (just as the female spectator must do when negotiating the soft-core text). The film seems to present the voyeuristic male gaze as dangerous, but also as an unstable gaze that can be rendered powerless.

Inevitably, the illicit sex (since Marilyn is a married woman) is caught on tape, to be further manipulated and copied by whatever evil force threatens the couple—an evil husband or a jealous coworker of the female protagonist. Thus, the narrative suggests the dangers of relying on simulation, as the tape moves further away from the "evidence" of the woman's desire through its reproduction into something else: a punishment of the woman's pleasure and autonomy. Still, this critique is an indictment not of the woman's active sexuality, but of the apparatus that attempts to regulate it, capture it, and control it through technological manipulation. And yet this same apparatus of surveillance is replicated in the spectator's eye as she watches the story unfold on the television screen within the home; she watches and is simultaneously watched, trapped within a discursive system that situates female looking as pleasurable and dangerous.

The struggle over the control and experience of voyeuristic pleasure, and the power relations that relate to who looks and who is looked at, is interrogated within the narrative structure of *The Lipstick Camera* (Mike Bonifer, 1994). A voyeuristic gaze is introduced immediately, while the opening credits roll. The film begins with the pixillated screen of surveillance; a reproduced, heavily mediated image of a couple having sex plays on a television monitor. The grain and pixillation of the image indicate that it is a reproduced simulation of the act, and the spectator is experiencing someone else's voyeuristic gaze as the tape plays.[12] An angry woman's voice then comments, "You know what I feel when I see this? Nothing!" The camera pulls back to reveal the filming of the scene in which the video was playing, and a young woman packing to leave. There is no indication of who is holding the camera on her every movement, swerving after her, except for a man's voice stating, "I can't believe you're doing this."

This opening scene reveals a particular tension within the surveillance erotic thriller; frequently the male character's erotic stimulation and involvement with a woman, often the heroine, must be kept at a distance. Mediation must occur through some type of visual apparatus for contact to occur. As the scene ends, the surveilled woman replies, "Well, you're getting it on tape, aren't you?" implying that the male character's only relationship to truth or belief is through the recorded evidence of a video camera. The apparatus subsumes personal contact. The woman's last act is to come forward and bash the camera, turning the screen to black as she leaves.

This scene serves as a commentary on the gendered relationships to surveillance apparatus and technology throughout the rest of the film, which soon falls into the more standard, formulaic parameters of the DTV erotic thriller narrative. The film follows the life of Omy, a young woman enamored by the technological possibilities of video, who pursues her dream of becoming a political videographer, along the lines of her unwitting mentor, Flynn. She is first revealed as she composes a video letter to Flynn, hoping to work with him and learn from him. As the film progresses, she is frequently accompanied by her male friend and fellow technophile, Joule, who supplies her with the lipstick camera of the title.[13]

Omy visits Flynn's studio and asks if she can work with him, but he is condescending toward her interests in video technology and her access to surveillance apparatuses. She eventually follows him on an assignment to tape a woman having sex with her husband, a supposedly "secret camera" operation. While Flynn sets up surveillance, Omy secretly places the lipstick camera in an overhead light, setting off a chain of events that leads to several murders and to the endangerment of her own life. The catalyst for these events is her use and possession of state-of-the-art surveillance technology, which implies that when a woman possesses the voyeuristic gaze or controls surveillance technology, she cannot go unpunished.

Still, *The Lipstick Camera* presents all the male characters' relationships to surveillance and technology as obsessive and even more deadly. The initial images during the film's credits turn out to reveal Flynn repeatedly and obsessively watching recordings of his own ex-girlfriend. When Omy later spies on Flynn through one of his windows, she watches the evolution of their relationship, from their first moments of courtship to his proposal of marriage, also caught on tape. Flynn cannot have any experience with a woman without mediation. Later, when Omy and Flynn eventually have sex, he puts a continuous-loop fireplace image on his large-screen television, simulating sex by firelight. For Flynn, the actual sex act can lead only to his true source of pleasure, the voyeuristic study of its simulation.

Similarly, Omy's friend Joule is "addicted" to the apparatus, to the point where even the clothes he wears have cameras attached, so that his view, retrospectively, is always a mediated one. In a sense, these characters rely solely on visual technology to see. They are almost completely separated from their material bodies, preferring the distance and safety of the mediated image over actual interaction. Joule is in love with Omy, but he can never tell her in person, managing only to record these words on a videotape to her. He is killed before he can bring his fantasies out from his virtual world.

Although Omy shares with these men a fascination for video technology and surveillance, she begins to discover that the use of videotape as evidence—whether of love, truth, or guilt—is suspect, especially for such a manipulatable medium. The "truth" of a video record is always qualified by the possibilities of performance for an apparatus. Ultimately, Omy's use of surveillance technology implicates her in a series of deaths, but it also saves her life. While watching the tape left by the lipstick camera, she sees Flynn have sex with his client and kill her, recording a snuff film. This murder is not his first, since the narrative crosscuts between Omy voyeuristically watching this scene and Flynn watching the tapes of his ex, only this time, the tape ends with her murder as well. *The Lipstick Camera* suggests that male voyeurism, especially pushed to extremes, is pathological. While Omy reacts in horror to what she sees, Flynn is titillated. Yet, in the end, the only way to stop him is to make him the object of surveillance and no longer its subject.

In their final confrontation, Omy turns a camera on Flynn and records his confession just as the police come to her rescue. She has not left the realm of surveillance unaffected. Omy sells Flynn's story to the press and makes a profit from her footage. She finally takes control of the surveillance apparatus for her own purposes, but not without severe punishment meted out for its acquisition—the loss of her best friend, Joule. *The Lipstick Camera* provides a warning to those fascinated by voyeurism and its pleasures. The film's resolution implies that all those who abuse the power of surveillance, regardless of gender, must recognize that the same apparatus can be turned against them and render them the objects, not the subjects, of a sadistic voyeuristic gaze.

In numerous DTV erotic films, women do have control of the camera, but they sublimate their voyeuristic desires into making a documentary, creating an art project, or using the camera as a tool for a scientific study of voyeurism. For instance, in both *Bare Witness* (Kelley Cauthen, 2002) and *Visions of Passion* (Randall St. George, 2003), female characters attempting to make documentaries mistakenly record people involved in scandals and/or committing crimes. In *Bare Witness,* Julie uses her call-girl rendezvous as material for her documentary; but when she unwittingly records an assassination order, her voyeuristic interests lead to her death. The rest of the erotic thriller's narrative revolves around her best friend, Carly (Angie Everhart), who teams up with Detective Killian (Daniel Baldwin) to find the tape, foil the assassination, and catch her killer. Of course, a romantic and sexual relationship develops between them as well. In *Visions of Passion,* Jeannie mistakenly captures her neighbor, Alice, another call girl, having sex with a married senator. A male coworker, who helps her edit the documentary, sees this footage, steals it, and leaks the footage to the press in an effort to blackmail the senator for money. His selfish act succeeds in destroying the relationship, both personal and intimate, that grows between Jeannie and

Alice. In both films, female characters who possess and wield surveillance technologies do not understand the dangers that voyeuristic pursuits can bring; both Carly and Jeannie experience sexual satisfaction, but these pleasures are countered by the perils surveillance technology reaps.

Maura, in Zalman King's *Shame, Shame, Shame* (1997), develops an art project that takes videotaped confessions of partially clothed and nude subjects, capturing them as they divulge their sexual fantasies. Her work attempts to discover "which fantasies are taboo, and why we often feel shame and guilt for them," but this project is only a cover for her own journey of self-discovery. In numerous therapy sessions, Maura tries to understand why she repeatedly turns down marriage proposals from her boyfriend, McCarthy (Costas Mandylor). Her therapist believes that Maura's fear of intimacy has connections to something she voyeuristically saw during her childhood. As Maura obsessively tapes all of her subjects, she becomes caught up in their stories and proceeds to act out their fantasies with McCarthy. For instance, in one scene she asks Callie, a stripper, to perform for the camera. Callie flirts with the camera, dances sinuously, and talks about the power and control she feels as a stripper; she then proceeds to tell the story of how she lost her virginity at sixteen, carefully choosing words that heighten the erotic charge of her narrative. Maura, moved by Callie's sexual assertiveness, later plays her fantasy on her video monitors and mimics her words, wanting to become her. In another instance, she tapes her friend Sadie's story of seduction and then uses the identical story during an intimate love scene with McCarthy. Only when Maura comes to terms with her shameful feelings about her past—in which she watched her mother having sex with a neighborhood teenager, was caught, and therein destroyed their once close relationship—can she work through her troubled intimacy with McCarthy and make a more permanent commitment; here, technology functions as a therapeutic tool.

In *Voyeur Confessions* (Tom Lazarus, 2001), Lisa Morrison sets out to study voyeurism as part of a research project she undertakes at a lab. The film opens with a high overhead shot of a couple making love next to a swimming pool; the sounds of sex are muted, as if someone is watching from behind a closed window. As the camera pulls away from the couple having sex, the film reveals Lisa watching from her window, as her subjectivity guides the camera's point of view. While the film makes clear that Lisa already has voyeuristic inclinations, she remains oblivious to her own desires, firmly sublimating them into her scientific study. In the process of interviewing three admitted voyeurs (all men) who agree to participate in her study, she herself becomes

Figure 9. Lisa watches a ménage à trois in *Voyeur Confessions* (2001).

more obsessed with watching. She tapes each subject in a medium head shot, using video technology as a study tool rather than an outlet for her desires. Yet she becomes titillated by the stories that David, Christopher, and Steven tell, as she is visually thrust into their subjective points of view while they narrate their voyeuristic encounters. Eventually she is compelled to greater and greater voyeuristic acts of her own, from using a camera and binoculars on the apartments nearby, to capturing a ménage à trois next door with a high-powered telescope (figure 9).

Initially, Lisa insists that only men suffer from these overwhelming voyeuristic desires; but in the end, when she is almost caught by a police officer as she spies on someone from the safety of her car, she must accept her voyeurism "addiction." After a title announcing "one year later," Lisa turns the camera on herself as she confesses her own problems with voyeurism, firmly demolishing the idea that voyeurs are always male. In the end, Lisa finds the right balance between the titillation of watching and the use of the camera as a therapeutic tool. She feels it is a better rush to be "in a loving relationship" and she chooses to leave behind the addictive attractions of mediated voyeurism. In all of these DTV erotic thrillers, technology plays a dual role: the camera captures sexual performances that are used to titillate the heroine (and also the spectator), providing an outlet for the heroine's sexual curiosity, while it also represents a potentially dangerous tool, which when overused or abused, could prove destructive.

AMATEUR PORN AND EXHIBITIONISM

Some DTV erotic thrillers, in the course of building their suspense narratives, focus on the danger that technology might fall into hostile hands, or that the pleasure of voyeurism might become obsessive as a fetishized substitution for physical contact. Other films tend to emphasize the positive uses of surveillance equipment, reflecting a contemporaneous interest in producing homemade sexual entertainment, and the "healthy" and "natural" characteristics emphasized in the marketing of amateur porn. As Amateur Home Video claims, "These are real folks just having fun in front of the camera, for everyone to see. . . . Is that the girl next door? How about that guy? Didn't you just see him at the supermarket?"[14] A cover from Home Maid videos suggests, "Perhaps after viewing, you will be tempted to contribute your own version. . . . Each new position is bound to excite you and inspire you and yours."[15] In the *Animal Instincts* series of DTV erotic thrillers, the films take on an instructional tone, suggesting, especially in the original *Animal Instincts* (A. Gregory Hippolyte, 1992), that amateur porn can work therapeutically to solve a couple's marital problems and spice up their sex life.

When reality-tested, the film's narrative reveals a taste for voyeurism that is specifically gendered as male, yet the resolution of that narrative produces a structure that is ideologically utopian. *Animal Instincts* suggests that women can achieve pleasure through exhibitionism and that, even taken to extremes, this performance of sex for a camera is without repercussions. The film is largely the recollections of a woman, Joanna Cole (Shannon Whirry), who confesses to an offscreen female interviewer the secrets that have placed her in the news and made her a celebrity. The elements of these interview scenes, including the words of Joanna and the soft voice of the female listener, suggest the workings of a therapeutic relationship. Joanna divulges sexual intimacies to this woman and represents herself as the married, sexually unsatisfied wife common to the erotic thriller genre. Her goal, it would seem, is sexual fulfillment, but her husband is perpetually distant, worried about providing her with material possessions rather than with love and affection. The quest for sexual pleasure is exacerbated by the prescribed antidepressant medication Joanna takes, which supposedly *increases* her sexual desire.[16] Joanna eventually discloses that she and her husband learned how to use video technology to resolve their sex problems: Joanna had sex with other men while her husband, David, watched these liaisons on a television monitor in another room.

Again, *Animal Instincts* emphasizes a supposed male need to have sex mediated in order to fulfill some desperate voyeuristic desire. From the opening moments of the film onward, David is constantly drawn to the televisual apparatus. This frustrates Joanna at first, but she eventually caters to his interest. After they have sex, David immediately turns on the television, to which Joanna replies, "I'm still here, David." In another scene, after Joanna tries on numerous lingerie ensembles, she approaches David in a seductive, sheer teddy. He is so engrossed in the television that he barely turns to look at her. Later, after Joanna discovers that he "likes to watch," they set up a camera in their bedroom. In a room down the hall, he manipulates the camera, zooming in and out on his wife, who is again dressed in revealing lingerie. This time, though, because of the physical distancing of the camera lens, he is turned on, seemingly noticing for the first time that Joanna is sexy and desirable.

As Joanna begins to prostitute herself with strange men, her sex life with David grows more and more exciting and intimate for both of them. Joanna tells her listener that "they accepted each other for who they really are" (a voyeur and an exhibitionist). She even comments on the instructional benefits of the sex she has with other men. The first time she sleeps with another man, she and David have sex immediately afterwards. He then asks her what was different about her interaction with another man. Joanna uses this moment to teach David about how to be a better lover, for the other man was "unselfish"; he was only interested in making her feel good. This "sexual-empowerment" attitude toward infidelity is a repeated theme within all these films. Later, she explains that she and David started watching the tapes together. Here the film again shifts from regarding taped pornography as strictly voyeuristic to the idea that videos carry an instructive message. The tapes could instigate role-playing and increased communication between the couple. As Joanna explains, "I would be the woman on the screen. He would be the man, or whoever . . . And that way, we could share the benefits of our education."

While the heroine suggests the possibilities for video surveillance to open up sex as performance and to produce shifting and changeable gender roles, the film's subject/object relationships belie these supposedly progressive capabilities. Significantly, David is *never* caught on their home camera, and never regarded voyeuristically by his wife, even though he is objectified by the camera during his nude scenes. He seems never to be completely comfortable as an object of desire.

This film can also be read as containing strong homosexual undertones. The spectator rarely experiences David's subjectivity, since the film's narrative is focalized and visualized through its heroine, but there are a few fragments that would suggest David's penchant for men.[17] His relationship with his partner, Rod (they are both cops), reveals his first fascination with voyeurism, when he spies Rod kissing a woman in a topless club. His desire is further spurred when he spots another male colleague having sex with a prostitute in a room at the precinct house. Later, as Joanna tries to get his attention in her sheer teddy, David is consumed with flashbacks and images of these scenes. Eventually, Rod, masquerading as a doctor, has sex with Joanna while David watches in another room. The encounter does not bother David at all. In fact, he asks Rod to recount the details when they are on duty the next day. The film never makes clear whom David is identifying with during the sex act, and who is his object of desire.

Throughout the film's narrative, David maintains a vendetta against a local crime boss, Lamberti, known for finding innocent girls and turning them into prostitutes—an ironic subplot, considering that David does the same thing to his wife, Joanna. In the convoluted suspense plot that accompanies the sex scenes, David eventually blackmails someone in power in order to influence local politics. His plan backfires, the couple is caught, and the nefarious mayoral candidate, Fletcher Ross (Jan-Michael Vincent) is forced to withdraw from the race. Still, Joanna and David are never punished for their involvement in prostitution and extortion. Their defense attorney addresses the press and informs reporters (and the film's spectators) that Joanna, suffering from nymphomania induced by her prescribed medication, experienced therapy through these tapes under the close supervision of her loving husband. The use of a camera became David's way of "assessing his wife's condition." The film even implies that the couple should be seen as heroes for handling their marital problems in this proactive and instructive way. Ideologically, the film appears to support male voyeurism by shifting the blame to Joanna's exhibitionistic needs, even though those needs were drug induced. Still, this is the assessment of a male character, and the real storyteller, the one who structures the narrative, has not finished her confession.

The camera reveals gift baskets and flowers being delivered to their house as Joanna and David are now seen as heroes and celebrities. The camera pulls back to reveal finally an attractive blond female journalist, apparently interviewing Joanna for the "true" story. When asked about her new popularity, Joanna replies, "I think it fulfills a need. I think a lot of people would like to experience my story firsthand, but they can't, or they won't, so the more details they hear, the more real the experience becomes for them." Again, Joanna argues that her tale of utilizing amateur porn "to save her marriage" fulfills an instructional need, this time for the people who would vicariously experience the details of her story through media representation. In fact, she is actually giving a video interview as she concludes her tale by saying "Hi" to her mom and dad, thereby expressing her exhibitionistic pride and pleasure in telling her story on camera. Unlike many of the other surveillance thrillers that explore the complicated power dynamics surrounding voyeurism and the possession of surveillance apparatuses, *Animal Instincts* appears to validate the use of video technology as a marital aid. The protagonists are regarded as heroes, and their "punishment" is a trip to Barbados, where they will continue to work out their marital difficulties "on the beach."[18]

VIRTUAL REALITY, SEXUAL FANTASY, AND THE LIMITS OF TECHNOLOGY

As a film genre, direct-to-video erotic thrillers focus on the visual as a means to sexual arousal. The motif of video technology and surveillance legitimizes voyeurism, as the repeated use of cameras self-reflexively comments on characters in the act of looking. However, not all technology creates the visual stimuli suitable for representation in the erotic thriller; the act of typing is rarely erotic. Cybersex through Internet chat rooms has not become a plotline of the genre. Instead, the possibilities of a technology that can incorporate fantasy into its structure are thematized in the genre's use of virtual reality (VR) technology. Films such as *Virtual Encounters* (Cybil Richards, 1996), *Virtual Encounters 2* (Cybil Richards, 1998), *Forbidden Passions* (also titled *Cyberella,* Jackie Garth, 1996), and *Cyberotica* (John Kain, 1996) each contain heroines who experiment with the pleasures and limitations of this underdeveloped technology.

Under the technology's current standards, VR participants can experience three-dimensional worlds, interacting within this environment through the use of a headset and a directional glove. Still, this three-dimensional world has little verisimilitude as a one-to-one correlate to reality, since technology has not developed far enough to make the VR world appear unmediated by its technology. One has difficulty suspending disbelief with the weighty head-

and-body gear necessary for simulated experiences. A mainstream film such as Kathryn Bigelow's *Strange Days* (1996) takes place at the cusp of the millennium and imagines a tactile technology; yet, the ability to transcend one's body and feel someone else's sensations does not yet exist. Neither has VR become a mass-consumed product, accessible to a wide variety of people.

Erotic thrillers that utilize VR technology take place in a future in which technology has lost its limitations, and the differences between the real and virtual worlds are barely distinguishable. When a character enters a VR world, his or her representation is vivid and fully formed, instead of emitting a cyberglow or appearing as computerized and technological, an image first popularized in Brett Leonard's mainstream theatrical film *The Lawnmower Man* (1992) and reiterated in Barry Levinson's *Disclosure* (1994). Furthermore, in these DTV erotic thrillers, technology is advanced enough to simulate not only a visual world, but bodily sensation as well. Within the VR world of the erotic thriller, senses are stimulated beyond mere sight and sound, as technology literally becomes a "body genre." With these new capabilities for sensation, sex—the focus of the narrative—becomes achievable through completely technological means. Still, even with these advanced capabilities, VR erotic thrillers ideologically construct a fantasy world that is differentiated from the actual physical world of contact and interaction. Virtual reality serves both as a means to arousal and an instructional tool. Any abuse or excessive reliance on technology is actively discouraged in these films.

The VR erotic thriller still follows many of the formulaic imperatives of the genre, as the heroine who enters the VR world does so in search of sexual empowerment and personal growth. As with the use of amateur porn in *Animal Instincts*, VR thrillers focus less on the dangerous thrills of new technology and more on VR's use as an instructional tool and a way to enhance personal relationships outside the VR world. Entry into the virtual domain stems from a dissatisfaction with the actual.

In *Forbidden Passions* (Jackie Garth, 1996), for example, the heroine's explicit goal is to learn a lesson, even though the narrative keeps her trapped within the world of virtual reality. As the film begins, Mara, the film's heroine, is preparing for a romantic rendezvous. Dressed in filmy lingerie, she chills some wine, lights the candles, and stokes the fire in the fireplace. Time goes by, and her "date" never arrives until she has fallen asleep, therefore situating her as the frustrated, neglected woman in her relationship. Once Steven arrives, they have sex, but he quickly gets dressed to leave. This scene establishes Mara's codependency problems and unfortunate focus on pleasing her partner over herself. Steven informs her that he has been transferred and that he was planning on leaving without telling her. When Mara suggests that she would be willing to accompany him, he tells her that she is "smothering him" but that he will miss the sex, thus situating his character as selfish, untrustworthy, and devious. He implores her to "work on herself," implying that she focus on her burgeoning career as a freelance VR programmer, and finally leaves her. In despair, she turns to a constructed VR program, Dreamworlds, for peace and solace.

While she is experiencing this virtual world, one of the candles burning in her apartment topples over, setting the actual world on fire. Mara dies from a real fire while in the virtual world, trapping her in a virtual purgatory. In order to move on to a "higher plane," she must become a VR angel; she must help others through the medium of VR in order to learn a valuable lesson she had never learned while alive and in the actual world. The film then structures each sex scene as a step toward reaching that goal.

Mara's relationship to those she helps in the actual world thematizes the conflicts involved between fantasy and reality, as well as the way point of view and subjectivity function within the VR realm. She accesses individuals through their respective VR programs. For instance, her first encounter is with a frustrated painter who is seeking inspiration through his Virtual Paint interface. When she appears to him, he comments on how lifelike she appears, and he says he did not realize the capabilities of the technology he possesses. Similarly, in another episode, Brent, a young hacker, attempts to configure his "dream woman," Sandy, in the virtual world and find the courage, virtually, to ask her out on a date. When Mara emerges within his program to help him, he also continually comments on how lifelike she appears and how impossible she is in terms of VR's technological capabilities.

Mara's strange and unwarranted appearance within their virtual worlds emphasizes the splintering and shifting points of view in the narrative and raises questions about cinematic subjectivity. The film is primarily focalized through Mara's character. The narrative's trajectory follows her disappointment in her romantic life, her death, and her pursuit of her goal: learning her lesson. She even consults with a mysterious female mentor after each cyber-interaction and expresses her thoughts and feelings as if she were in a therapeutic relationship. Yet VR technology functions through the subjective power of the person who utilizes it. When Brent dons his headgear and enters his VR program, the spectator supposedly experiences his subjective sensations, experiences, and point of view. Thus, Mara represents a gendered struggle over subjectivity in relation to technology. While she has a supernatural ability within each VR program to understand each character's problem and possesses the power to create visual stimuli for each person beyond his or her own means, she still resides in a virtual world enabled by a technological apparatus. This discrepancy in subjectivity hinges on the difference between the actual and the virtual, reality and fantasy. Each character perceives her as a technological manifestation of his or her own subjectivity and not as an actual prescient being. When the characters take off their headgear and leave the virtual world, Mara disappears, left alone in virtual reality. She has no existence beyond being an enabler for their fantasies. This representation clashes with her role as subjective heroine, a character who provides the narrative causality and emotional identification for the film.

Mara's role as technological enabler contradicts the lessons she must learn: to act for herself and to experience sexual pleasure on her own terms. Her mentor therapeutically evaluates her codependency problems. In one scene, she enters the virtual world of Amy, a lesbian dancer who uses a Virtual Dancer program because she suffers from stage fright. Mara enters the woman's virtual world and creates a virtual audience, so that Amy can know what it feels like to dance for a crowd and overcome her fear. Her problem is resolved quickly, and immediately after, she propositions Mara, who is clearly uncomfortable with her first lesbian encounter, virtual or otherwise. In this example, Mara no longer has control subjectively in the virtual world, as Amy seduces her. The scene never establishes a clear mode of identification or point of view, because Mara is subjectively experiencing sex with a woman, yet this fantasy is based on Amy's desires, not Mara's; Mara's lack of control is represented by her discomfort and shy hesitancy. This subjective slippage also brings into question the means by which to fulfill Mara's goal. Her lesson is to learn to be self-sufficient and focus on her own needs and desires, instead of someone else's. The narrative helps support "do-me" feminism's ideological drive toward sexual empowerment. Mara's specific conflict is expressed in a conversation she has with her therapeutic mentor after her encounter with Amy:

Mentor: What you did with Amy. Did you want it?
Mara: She wanted it.
Mentor: I know. But you—did you want it?
Mara: I'm supposed to please people. To help them. That's what you said.
Mentor: Helping and pleasing people are not one and the same.

This exchange indicates that Mara's goal is centered on sexual pleasure, but recognition of her codependency enables her finally to leave the virtual purgatory in which she resides.

Mara's problem appears to be an inability to think or act for herself, for she is dependent on the happiness of others in constructing her self-identity. Yet the film reveals Mara's real problem as a failure to distinguish fantasy from reality, or to negotiate the differences between the virtual and actual worlds. Mara dies within her Dreamworlds program, but she is unaware she exists on a different plane, despite her unfamiliar surroundings, until her mentor figure explains her circumstances. Still, Mara cannot accept that she can no longer interact in reality, and she continually tries to cross this technological divide. After she inspires the painter, she informs him that she'll be with him forever, but he is eager to get back to his painting. Similarly, once Brent feels he has enough confidence to ask his friend Sandy out on a date, he no longer needs Mara's assistance and prefers to act outside of VR. While technology fulfills the fantasies of the people Mara assists, VR serves only as a catalyst, a causal agent, for what happens in the outside world. In contrast, Mara frustratingly tries to affect lives outside her virtual realm and finds herself unable to negotiate or understand the boundary between the two domains.

When Mara learns her therapeutic lesson regarding codependency, she simultaneously understands the differences between fantasy and reality. Her last assistance scenario involves her helping the object of a former high-school crush, Bob, to overcome his own codependent tendencies. In Bob's virtual program, he sits in a bar, inactive, until Mara, posing as a waitress, talks to him. The virtual bar was a business venture he shared with his girlfriend, who recently severed their relationship. Now, he feels he has no future, and he tells Mara how much he needed his girlfriend. Mara, working in a therapeutic manner, finally absorbs her lesson. She informs him that "love has to be on equal terms" and that he should now go into business for himself. In the process of helping Bob, she takes the place of her own mentor and teaches the lesson she has learned. In the same instance, she tells Bob good-bye, instead of clinging to a fantasy realm that has given her sexual fulfillment and emotional growth. Even though Bob would like her to stay, Mara moves on, recognizing the difference between fantasy and reality, virtual and lived experiences.

In *Forbidden Passions*, virtual reality serves as an instructive tool for everyone who uses it, but no one ever develops a dependency on the technology's virtual fantasies, despite their sensational and lifelike realism. Cybil Richards's *Virtual Encounters* (1996) also represents virtual reality as an idealized, utopian technology that only assists the heroine, through fantasy, to recognize her underlying sexual drives. Here virtual reality is more explicitly instructive, as the heroine's journey is one that is extremely common in the erotic thriller genre: she must move from sexual inexperience to sexual knowledge and fulfillment.

Amy, a successful businesswoman, is newly involved with a man, Michael. The film opens with the two sharing a romantic Saturday night—complete with wine, candles, and a roaring fire. As the two start to kiss, Amy stops their intimacy and tells Michael she is "not ready" and needs "to work a few things out in my head." Later, her secretary, Maggie, remarks on her inhibitions. She buys Amy some lingerie for her birthday. Amy, preoccupied with her career, has completely forgotten what day it is. A package arrives from Michael; he gives her a membership to Virtual Encounters, an exclusive club he wants her to partake in while he is out of town. Again, as in Gary Delfiner's *Teach Me* (1997), a membership to Virtual Encounters becomes Amy's course of instruction, as the mysterious other world is a virtual-reality playground, where the heroine experiences a variety of different sexual interludes.

Amy is greeted by a digital, disembodied voice named Rob, who serves as her guide and mentor within the virtual realm. Significantly, in every experience Amy has within VR, Rob is ever present, summoned merely by her voicing a question or addressing him directly.[19] Rob is accessible at all times, implying that he is always watching, the perpetual voyeur to her sexual discoveries. He is also gendered as male, which makes his constant surveillance discomfiting. He appears as a regulatory figure who constructs appropriate female heterosexuality during each of Amy's encounters. Rob also partially controls the images that Amy experiences, as well as the speed at which she gains her "education." Initially, Amy's first two encounters are merely voyeuristic; she watches other people having sex in front of her. Only after she has experienced this "virtual foreplay" is she allowed to become a virtual participant.

Virtual Encounters is the only one of these films that encourages the dissolution of gender boundaries, and it thereby suggests the *constructed* quality of gender through its utopian outlook on VR technology. Within this erotic thriller, VR has again evolved, this time through the invention of a body-sensitive skin suit, to permit the actual physical experience of bodily sensations. This new technology allows Amy to fulfill fantasies provided by Virtual Encounters software and the melding of her own imagination. In one scene, she inhabits the body of an exotic dancer and actually feels a man's hands on her skin. In another moment, she participates in a threesome, inhabiting another woman's body.

Virtual-reality technology inscribes gender mutability in another scene in which Amy inhabits the body of a man. Within the scenario, she cannot stop touching herself, curious and fascinated by the physical sensations of having a penis. She is actually able to have sex with a woman from a man's point of view. This use of VR technology hints at a possible multitude of identifications, similar to the gender masquerade and performance that occurs in chat rooms and in cyberspace. The difference lies in the ability to possess the sensations of different organs and their uses, a way to destabilize gender identity through the dissolution of biodetermined sexuality.

Following this out-of-body experience, Amy states, "I think I could really get hooked on this," implying a possible dependency on the fantasy life that she experiences within the virtual world. Rob is quick to point out, "Nothing beats the real thing" and "what you learn in a virtual encounter can only serve to heighten your reality." Keeping fantasy and reality distinct from one another is the recurrent concern of the VR thriller. This film is ideologically utopian, for the narrative implies that VR serves as a causal agent for actions in the actual world, but the technology is used only with the best intentions.

Amy's virtual education culminates in a ménage à trois with two men in which she inhabits her own body within the scenario. She comes back to the actual world forever changed. When Michael returns from his trip, he stops by her office, where the woman once uncomfortable with the intimacy of kissing has now turned into a sexual virago who attacks him as soon as he walks in.[20] He suggestively observes, "I guess you've had your virtual encounter." While this change in Amy's behavior occurs under the guise of self-empowerment and "do-it-for-yourself" rhetoric, Michael's involvement raises the question of who really benefits from her virtual encounters. As in *Teach Me*, the male character serves as the instigator to the woman's acquisition of sexual experience, qualifying how much she is able to attribute to her own sexual agency. Amy appears to get in touch with her sexual side, but Michael also gets the nympho he always dreamed of, a woman who cannot even wait until they leave her office. While Amy experiences sex through her own virtual, subjective experience, the technology she uses is not only male-driven (through her mentor, Rob), but also male-induced (through the birthday gift from Michael).

Women's relation to sexually explicit technology within the erotic thriller is unstable and therefore supports the genre's pleasure/danger narrative paradigm. The genre oscillates between a glorification and fascination with sexually oriented technology's voyeuristic and instructional possibilities and a pervasive techno-anxiety surrounding the equipment's possible abuse and manipulation. The surveillance erotic thriller reveals this anxiety through the frequent thematic reiteration of the difference between simulation and actuality. William Bogard astutely explains the anxiety that surrounds the overuse and dependency on technology for erotic stimulation: "Who needs 'real' sex anymore. . . . Sex *is* the display, and like all virtual technologies, cybersex is about making the (physical) display disappear, leaving just 'sex itself,' the 'real thing,' behind. Of course, sex 'itself,' 'real' sex, is already long dead by this time, a mere residue of its digitized surrogate."[21]

The representation of surveillance and cyber-technology in the DTV erotic thriller, as both an enabler of arousal and an instructional tool, presents a distinct paradox in relation to the consumption of mediated sex. While the reiteration of technology as a means to *enhance* reality indicates anxiety over its use as a substitution for "the real thing," the validation of these technologies in the erotic thriller's narrative creates the possibilities of consumption necessary to keeping the genre alive. The consumption of the erotic thriller is all about the use of mediated sex (on videotape or DVD) to stimulate arousal and serve as an instructional tool. Through the erotic thriller's ideological representation of technology, the genre suggests that technology is useful and helpful but should not be overly relied on as a way of negotiating sexuality and sexual pleasure. Furthermore, considering the representations of gender involved in these surveillance thrillers, women have the most to lose from an abuse of technology, and so they must remain vigilant in distinguishing fantasy from reality. Their possession of the technology of surveillance, however beneficial to their own self-empowerment and growth, is always accompanied by danger.

CONCLUSION:
WHOSE PORN IS IT? THE CASE OF
WOMEN: STORIES OF PASSION

A man and woman stumble playfully outside a shop for adult books and toys. The man hesitates as the woman boldly takes him by the hand, leading him into this traditionally male enclave. Her narrative voice-over recounts, "I always wanted to go into a real porn shop. They were like some dark fantasy that I as a woman wasn't allowed to partake of." So begins Angela's initial sexual adventure in "Kat Tails," an episode of the erotic series *Women: Stories of Passion,* which premiered in 1997 and a decade later was still showing late at night on Showtime Women, part of the Showtime Cable Network. Angela's approach toward the titillating yet transgressive world of porn is similar to the heroine's adventure into the forbidden world of stripping and prostitution in the erotic thriller. Each type of erotic entertainment stimulates through the fantasy of vicarious experience, and all of these venues are stereotypically seen as culturally constructed for the pleasure of heterosexual men. This exploration of supposedly unfamiliar, male-dominated territory suggests a quasi-reclamation of sexually explicit material for a female-gendered audience, as popular feminist rhetoric insists that women become responsible for their own sexual agency and empowerment.

While the majority of this book has focused on the direct-to-video erotic thriller, the television series *Women: Stories of Passion* provides an excellent case study of the role of female authorship in relation to erotic entertainment. The series, broadcast in twenty-six-minute episodes, proves significant to the recent pursuit of a female-gendered audience, for it is produced, written, and directed exclusively by women, for women. Yet despite its female-gendered production crew, this erotic anthology series does not differ significantly from other forms of contemporary soft-core film and television, such as Zalman King's *Red Shoe Diaries* series. Ultimately, these market-driven vehicles, which are targeted specifically at heterosexual female audiences, reveal much about the cultural roles women are supposed to take on, and how those roles formulate what women may desire.

If the force of Angela's curiosity is indicative of women's changing relationship to sexual materials such as porn, the possibilities for a female-driven erotic series appear promising. Finally, women display *their* fantasies, tell sexual stories in *their* voice, and show the workings of desire through *their* eyes. A female orientation implies a certain authenticity to the sexual materials represented; yet "authentic" experiences are subjective and implicated by cultural pressures. Elisa Rothstein, the creator of the series *Women: Stories of Passion,* claims, "This is the first time on television that this genre has been tackled from a woman's perspective."[1] Rothstein dismisses the soft core directed by and toward men (referring specifically to Showtime's own *Red Shoe Diaries* series) and says that the makers of *Women* set out to make a product distinctly different.

Although the goals of the series superficially suggest groundbreaking changes in the erotic realm, questions and contradictions arise regarding female authorship, feminist filmmaking practice, definitions surrounding "women's erotica," and the production and regulation of female heterosexual desire. Would soft core's aesthetic and visual practices be transformed under the influence of women, or was this simply male-oriented porn "in a dress"?[2] The question therefore looms: Whose porn is it, anyway?

FEMALE AUTHORSHIP AND FEMINISM

Female authorship's efficacy in creating difference within an established soft-core genre raises issues within feminism and film criticism. Celebrating the purported difference in something created by and for women suggests a level of essentialism, wherein women desire differently because they are intrinsically different from men and require different forms of entertainment for stimulation. While the construction of gender—along with identity-related issues of class, race, age, sexual orientation, and ethnicity—contributes to different levels of experience, feminist research simply has not proven that women make different films from men simply because they are *women.* As Judith Mayne points out in her work on Dorothy Arzner, "feminist film critics simply do not have the body of evidence to suggest how and in what ways female-authored cinema would be substantially different from cinema directed and created by men."[3]

An author's intentions are only one layer to the many meanings produced by a text through marketing, textual practices, exhibition space, and audience reception. Because of this varied circulation of meanings, and also due to the dearth of women directors in film and television, auteur studies have not generally pervaded feminist film theory. Intentionality can also be influenced under specific industrial filmmaking circumstances. *Women: Stories of Passion* is a large-scale film production bankrolled by Playboy, a company with a long history of producing male sexual entertainment. Nonetheless, the gendered social subjectivity of the film's authors should not be completely dismissed, especially in relation to work that explores a sexual terrain. When many of the key players involved in a film—director, writer, producer, director of photography, set designer, gaffer, and so on—are women, a group that has not had a longstanding foothold within the mainstream film industry, the stated gender goals of the series, to differentiate itself from male-oriented entertainment, become crucial to the film's interpretation. Yet women's access to the means of production, again, is only one aspect in the production and reception of sexual materials.

The canon of work previously and currently produced by men within the industry remains important to any reworking of the erotic soft-core genre. Feminist film practice responds by attempting to dismantle hierarchies erupting around gender, a practice that stands in opposition, committed to difference. However, this focused opposition serves to substantiate the male canon as well, as work from the margins tends to define the center, and vice versa. Still, power relates to access, and pop feminism is about accessibility. As Naomi Wolf states, "If you don't like your group's image in the media, decide on another image and seize control of the means of producing it."[4] Thus, the women filmmakers who contributed to *Women: Stories of Passion* set out to respond directly to erotica currently available on cable. Elisa Rothstein insists, "This was going to be my opportunity to set the record straight."[5]

Most of the filmmakers involved in the series were familiar with theories of gender representation instilled by the cinematic apparatus, and they knew the techniques utilized to highlight the generic objectification of women within both hard and soft pornographic representations. Nancy Rommelman, one of the writers involved with the series, describes the passion behind redressing erotica that she and others "felt had been harmful and heinous to women. . . . Now [we] were going to rectify the situation."[6] Still, in the face of a male-oriented film industry, headed in part by male executives at Playboy Entertainment (despite Christie Hefner's role as CEO of Playboy), and immersed within a culture in which women represented the traditional object of desire, how would a group of intrepid women filmmakers significantly change the state of soft core as it currently exists?

In part, these female filmmakers felt compelled to subvert the traditional subject/object relations familiar to sexual entertainment, in which men were positioned as subjects looking at female objects; but to switch the viewing positions in this binary arrangement does not immediately equalize uneven gender power dynamics. Although primary storytelling within *Women* is focalized through a series of female voice-over narratives, this technique already exists in Zalman King's *Red Shoe Diaries*.[7] Rothstein differentiates her series from this male-directed one by pointing to what she perceives as King's inherently voyeuristic camera.[8] She claims, "I don't think women in general tend to view men as voyeuristically as men view women."[9] Still, do women not participate as extensively in voyeurism because they cannot, or because they are not frequently given the opportunity?

The "problem" of voyeurism for women has always been a fundamental component of early feminist film criticism and Freudian psychoanalysis. The feminist film theorists Laura Mulvey and Mary Ann Doane define male-oriented cinema as voyeuristic; in landmark essays, they suggest that both Freudian theory and socialized gender imbalances attest to the "impossibility" of women's experiencing visual pleasure through voyeurism.[10] Yet, if early feminist film psychoanalysis is followed, denying women any access to a scopophilic drive also seems to deny them the experience of certain forms of narrative pleasure. Female spectatorship suddenly becomes indescribable within a woman-oriented erotic series, even though the entire genre focuses upon the displayed nudity of male and female bodies. According to Rothstein, there are no pleasures for women in the acquisition of a voyeuristic gaze. Again, she posits that women intrinsically desire differently. How exactly would women look at men differently without objectifying them through an active fantasmatic process? Within a sexually explicit series, a voyeuristic gaze, useful when viewing other people as objects, would appear to be a necessary component to the visual pleasures displayed.

Theoretically, feminist aesthetics have been associated with the idea of "counter-cinema," a filmmaking practice that attempts to destroy the system of narrative pleasure that creates unequal gender representations within the cinema. Beginning with the work of Laura Mulvey and Claire Johnston, the way visual media frames the gendered human body has been crucial to feminist film theory.[11] Reacting against the "men act, women appear" standard supposedly enforced by the cinematic apparatus, feminist filmmakers have historically used disruptive, non-narrative forms or avant-garde techniques to dismantle the machinations of narrative pleasure.[12] Yet, limiting feminist filmmaking to an oppositional, difference-oriented practice creates a "politically correct" filmmaking agenda similar to the policing of "correct" desires that erupted during and after the 1982 Barnard conference. As Jane Gaines explains, "One might say that counter-cinema's politically correct aesthetics was the formal equivalent of egalitarian sexual relations. Upholding feminist principles right down the line, it refused 'male power trips' and espoused utopian ideals, especially in its advocacy of a cinema without seduction."[13]

A cinema "without seduction" becomes a problem when dealing with sexual entertainment, for its very purpose is to turn on, arouse, and stimulate its viewers. Again, the conflict occurs within soft core's generic structure, where narrative realism provides a necessary component for the identification involved with visual pleasure. The same point of view, eyeline match, shot–reverse shot, and gaze/object structures that create male point of view and gendered looking are utilized to create identification for the female spectator.

Adele Bertei-Checci's *Women: Stories of Passion* episode "City of Men" specifically thematizes the dilemma that arises from erotic entertainment produced and directed by women. The episode's heroine, Anna, lives in a futuristic society in which men and women live in separate cities and meet once a year for a mating ritual. The only artistic medium available to the citizens of this new totalitarian regime is pornographic films; Anna is the official pornographer of the City of Women. Still, while she is behind the camera, in control of the apparatus and objectifying her male model, the shadow of another camera is always present, watching her and her assistant with a persistent erotic charge. The film opens with Anna and her female assistant, Pascal, choosing a man for their latest erotic collaboration. Seated at a cafe in the City of Men, they actively regard the various men present, judging by their appearance and attitude whether they are suitable objects of desire. Men glance up and look away, vulnerable to the women's assessing looks. The women finally choose a man, Joseph, based on his "defiant" and "menacing" qualities, as he aggressively meets their gaze with his own.

Anna brings Joseph to their studio and orders him to undress and pose for her camera, telling him to crawl across the bed slowly and sensuously touch himself. While Anna orchestrates the scene for her camera and her eye, the point of view occasionally shifts to Joseph, as he looks over at Pascal. Anna orders him to look at Pascal, to stimulate his own voyeuristic desire by watching her with his gaze.[14]

While this episode demonstrates the pleasure of looking, for both the male and female characters, the camera does not objectify male and female bodies equally. Pascal's body is shown in tight closeup, the camera moving over her, stopping to ogle her breasts or her hands as she pleasures herself. Joseph's body is seen in a master shot, where a static camera never explores the surfaces of his body or any signs of his apparent pleasure (via erection). Furthermore, to stimulate Joseph, Pascal's body must become his object of desire, circumventing his passive eroticism; *his* voyeuristic pleasure must be taken into account. Despite the film's women-directed production, soft core's conventions of sexual explicitness and body display are unchanged. Does the problem lie with an inability to break from established filmmaking codes? Nancy Rommelman comments, "It was just that the form didn't want to accept something new. It just kept sliding back to the same old thing."[15] The question still remains: what would "something new" or "different" entail?

If the porn industry is evolving to embrace a female audience as part of the "couple's market," then certain aesthetic practices *could* be transformed in response to changes in industrial concerns. But these changes are constituted by cultural conceptions of male and female desire. The changes are most clearly seen in the soft-core erotic series and the erotic thriller, in the excessive use of glamorous, romanticized mise-en-scène and in the importance placed on narrative combined with the sex scenes. These changes are also occurring in other forms of adult entertainment. Hetta Eisenberg and Kelly Holland, female executives working for Playgirl TV, a pay-per-view channel that appeals to heterosexual female viewers, came to similar conclusions when they surveyed women by phone as to how they liked their erotic entertainment. Art direction was of utmost importance. As Holland explains, "Women were telling us they were really into lingerie, and it has to be at least Victoria's Secret, but better you have Prada."[16] Mark Graff, the founder of Playgirl TV, elaborates, "From the headboards to shoes to his haircut, her haircut, everything that was in the room was being closely examined—whether or not her nails were done, whether or not the bedspread was pretty."[17]

Significantly, the male body is becoming more evident as a voyeuristic object of desire within shifting subject/object relations. Susan Faludi explains this phenomenon in terms of the changing face of the hard-core porn market: "Suddenly, in the 1980s and 1990s, ornamental occupations [for men] became the employment oases. It was like having consigned the Indians to a barren desert, then discovering oil on the reservation. In the rush to stake a claim in territory long ceded to women . . . [suddenly we] have entered a land of mirrors and a million flickering screens, a realm where manhood is displayed, not demonstrated."[18]

Indeed, third-wave feminists Leslie Heywood and Shari L. Dworkin posit that American culture is moving toward equally commodifying the bodies of women and men: "For better and for worse, male and female bodies are in a process of resignification. It is a profoundly important historical development that men now have their body projects, too, for that changes the whole critical framework. Guys aren't against us, they are with us—we are all 'women' in the sense of being judged by appearances."[19] Still, these aesthetic changes are not immediate, and they often elicit complaints regarding a growing "feminization of porn." According to Heywood and Dworkin, one porn producer "fears that the industry, with the rise of cable-ready, stylized filmmaking, is falling prey to 'the feminization of Hollywood.' He explains, 'Even this business is losing its masculine fibre. We're being absorbed into the mainstream, which terrifies me.' Already, the X-rated shelves are overrun with . . . 'coffee-table porn,' the prettified MTV-style adult videos produced for the so-called couples' market."[20]

Both erotic thrillers and erotic anthologies represent women actively looking at and desiring men, and sexual materials display more and more of an objectified male body in an attempt to seduce the female component of the "couple," or to lure single women used to ogling men on shows such as *Sex and the City.*

Nevertheless, the display of the male body within a soft-core, R-rated genre has its limitations, ones strictly enforced by both ratings codes and the many male executive producers who create these standards. "The double standard is alive and well," exclaims Rothstein in relation to the series' attempts to distribute frontal nudity evenly between the sexes.[21] While the preponderance of female nudity in soft-core films comments specifically on the heterosexual male viewer who "looks" while the female "appears," the lack of equally revealing male nudity within a "woman-oriented" series tends to suggest (and perhaps mistakenly assume) that female spectators do not enjoy looking at naked men. Adele Bertei-Checci describes the way these standards were enforced within her own series episode: "I was told we could have soft-penis shots on cable. . . . So in 'City of Men,' I had what I thought was this very tasteful, two-second shot of a penis. I mean, the actor was covered in rose petals, and they still made me cut it. Which I thought was kind of ironic. We're asked to supply a lot of female nudity, but none of men. What does that say about women's erotica? That we only want to look at other women?"[22]

According to Dick Rosetti, president of production for Playboy in the late 90s, the company's research proved that "women are interested in looking at butts, chests, all kinds of things, but penises are not a priority."[23] Richard Bencivengo, the company's executive vice president of production at that time, elaborates on Playboy's position and puts some of the blame on the male executives at Showtime. He claims, "We try in the stuff that runs on Playboy to put as much male frontal nudity as we can in there. The problem is that once you get into the sex act, we believe that seeing a flaccid penis is like saying 'this is simulated sex'—breaking the fourth wall. We don't want to see a bunch of erect penises running around, because we have a standard that says no erect penises. So once you get into the nitty gritty, we shy away from seeing the penis."[24]

The lack of male frontal nudity in *Women: Stories of Passion,* and in softcore representations in general, problematically presupposes inherent differences between what visually stimulates men and women, but it also further solidifies the unsubstantiated belief that women want narrative whereas men want bodies.[25] In fact, Playgirl TV is running into similar problems. As Susan Dominus explains,

> The filmmakers [at Playgirl TV] still say they have a few aesthetic choices to work out, including the display of male genitals. In those initial phone surveys, *Playgirl* readers said they wanted to see as many as possible. But as Ms. Holland herself admits, the preferences of the female *Playgirl* reader may not represent the average American woman's tastes. "I have to take women at face value when they say they want to see more penises," she says. "But I factor in, how much of that is just because they want their MTV, so to speak—their right to media and their right to those sexual images? It's sort of an expression of their process of sexual liberation. It's like those rowdy women you see at a male strip club—it's almost like they're acting out some male construct of what sexual desire is supposed to look like. You have to balance what they really want with what they feel socially compelled to say."[26]

How does one determine what women "really want," especially if these choices are defined by their opposition to men's erotic desires? *Both* heterosexual female and male viewers may be "socially compelled" to make choices based upon contemporary American understandings of femininity and masculinity. This dichotomy between male and female ways of desiring is sustained by the makers of *Women: Stories of Passion.* As Nancy Rommelman suggests, the problem with typical adult films directed by men lies in their "put-the-peg-in-the-hole sensibility," suggesting that this sensibility is specifically attributable to male, not female, desire.[27]

Candida Royalle, a porn producer and director, also posits that women have a different approach toward sex, with women maintaining a more "circuitous," romantic orientation rather than the more "goal-oriented" male approach.[28] She prides herself on making films that "have plots and focus on the erotic, showing 'genuine heat' between the screen lovers, many of whom are partnered in real life."[29] Royalle is quick to denounce mainstream hard-core porn films aimed at heterosexual male viewers: "They all have at least one girl-on-girl scene, fellatio, cunnilingus, anal sex, double penetration and group sex. The camera angles and the way it's shot—they have to show things as grotesque and graphically as possible. . . . Cunnilingus looks like open-heart surgery. The 'money shot' is always the external 'come shot'—it's like your typical bad sex—no imagination and it's always over when the man comes."[30]

If hard-core pornography, as Linda Williams has carefully argued, presupposes genital closeups, an exploration of anatomical depth, and the requisite goal of the money shot—all characteristics aimed at heterosexual men—then, following the belief that women "desire differently," anything "women-oriented" would necessitate a divergence from these goals.[31]

An R-rated mainstream erotic series that exhibits similarities to porn's episodic structure remains distinct from X-rated films, not only through its aesthetic practices, but also through a deeper focus on narrative and storytelling. This shift also emphasizes a different site of arousal, away from the corporeal and toward the cerebral. Yet evidence to substantiate that women are (or are not) turned on by male frontal nudity, or any other specific series of images, is not readily available.

PORN, EMPOWERMENT, AND THE REGULATION OF DESIRE

What exactly constitutes erotica for women? Both Elisa Rothstein and Nancy Rommelman emphasize "the totality of the sexual experience" as a trait exclusive to women's erotica.[32] Whereas, for women, "Sex [isn't] about getting laid, [it's] about the glance that made you decide you want to sleep with her, the chafe of his beard on your breast"; or as Rothstein explains, it involves "an attention to detail. It's not just about the act, but the things that go into it."[33] This elaborate setting of desire is a characteristic found in both the *Women* series and erotic thrillers. Rothstein also refers to an "emotional involvement" necessary for the turn-on; as she suggests, "women tend to identify with the woman in the story. So they really want to know about who she is, and what her thoughts and feelings are."[34] Still, within a twenty-six-minute timeframe, structured by a genre that relies heavily on the sex number as a narrative principle, a spectator's emotional involvement in the narrative is limited. Ironically, within women's erotica it is supposedly the narrative that seduces, and yet within feminist film theory and practice, that very seduction is regarded with suspicion.

While women-centered works can never be regarded as feminist strictly because of their subject matter, the question of what constitutes feminist film erotica has remained a burning issue long after the publicized furor of the sex wars in the 1980s. Mainstream sexual entertainment, whether it is produced by women filmmakers or not, does not stand up well under the sharp edge of a feminist critique; for not only do most erotic films sustain gender imbalances within their visual practices, but the films also substantiate strains of "compulsory heterosexuality" anathema to some of the earliest struggles within the feminist movement.[35] Jane Gaines stipulates that "feminist heterosexuality" remains dangerously undertheorized, because female heterosexual identity always constitutes a certain "sleeping-with-the-enemy" reaction.[36] Yet, lesbian porn does not always formulate the route to "true" feminism, just as lesbian representations within heterosexual hardcore and soft-core porn do not always implicitly stimulate only the male heterosexual viewer.

This contention regarding the implied audience for "girl-on-girl" sex scenes has swirled around the Showtime Original Series *The L Word*, a drama that centers on the lives of lesbians living in Los Angeles, since its premiere in 2004. Despite the predominance of a female-gendered, lesbian crew—consisting of creator and writer Ilene Chaiken, writer/director Rose Troche, director Lisa Cholodenko, and writer Guinivere Turner—the show has been accused of pandering largely to a heterosexual male audience by playing "into another stereotype—and male fantasy—of the lipstick lesbian," existing mainly as "visual candy for men."[37]

Much of the uproar relates to the show's persistence, in both the first and second seasons, in having straight characters as both placeholders and voyeurs. In the first season's pilot, Jenny (Mia Kirshner) moves into her boyfriend Tim's apartment in West Hollywood, which adjoins the home of Bette and Tina, the lesbian power couple at the core of *The L Word*'s social milieu. While in her backyard, Jenny spies the show's lesbian lothario, Shane, fooling around with another woman in Bette and Tina's pool next door. The scene is shot from a distance, behind a fence, to emphasize Jenny's subjective, desiring gaze. Later that evening, Jenny has sex with Tim and uses her earlier voyeuristic experience as verbal titillation, describing in detail what she saw earlier that day. The sex scenes that Jenny and Tim share are just as explicit as the scenes between women, with the soft lighting and shadowed bodies typical of contemporary soft-core filmmaking; also, over the course of the season, Jenny becomes attracted to Marina (Karina Lombard), embarks on a lesbian affair, and engages in steamy encounters, demolishing her heterosexual relationship in the process.[38] Similarly, in the second season, Jenny and Shane, now roommates, invite a straight male filmmaker, Mark, to live in their guesthouse, unwittingly giving him access to their rooms, where he hides lipstick cameras and clandestinely films their sexual and romantic experiences. Mark is often shown watching the footage he has taped, shot in black-and-white from distant, overhead angles.

While *The L Word* has become quite popular with some lesbians (as attested to by fan sites such as afterellen.com), other lesbian and non-lesbian viewers take issue with the aesthetic choices the show makes. Tavia Nyong'o remarks, "In the typical pornographic video, long bouts of sex are interspersed with half-assed efforts at plot continuity. This situation is reversed in *The L Word* and *Queer as Folk,* in which long bouts of plot continuity are interspersed with half-assed sex that lacks even the mild frisson that the 'lace and bodypaint' erotica available on the same cable channel arouses."[39]

Ironically, *The L Word* does share aesthetic similarities with the "lace and bodypaint" erotica to which Nyong'o refers, particularly in the way the series creates a mise-en-scène of desire through detailed and lavish art direction and costuming. Perhaps because of these choices, the show garners a significant straight female audience, known as "Sapphosexuals: straight women with a twinge of curiosity, a natural penchant for flirting with their female friends, and a high dose of emotional frustration with the crop of narcissistic metrosexual males who perennially fail the Prince Charming test."[40] Ilene Chaiken comments that the show's appeal to straight women coexists with a certain "bi-curious phenomenon. . . . Women are a lot more sexually fluid than men." But even though lesbian-identified women are behind the show's production, the series still uses soft-core conventions familiar to Showtime's usual audience of erotic-programming viewers.

Does seizing control of the "means of production" necessarily create feminist work? "Some feminist women understand the importance of creating our own sexual material," according to Candida Royalle. "You can't be fully empowered without being sexually empowered."[41] Even so, the materials and circumstances that constitute "empowerment" are growing and changing, and what was empowering in the 1970s is now sometimes seen as outdated. If one combines the narrative tensions in the DTV erotic thriller with the popular-culture rhetoric espousing empowerment, then to be a heterosexual woman *empowered* in contemporary culture is to be a high-priced call girl, stripper, or dominatrix (or at least to have their skills and experiences).[42] As Melinda Gallagher, a founder of the New York City–based sex party Cake explains, "Cake is the result of everything feminism has built up to so far. . . . It's being played out by the new generation of women and we're just giving them a stage."[43] The cultural evolution of "do-me" feminism suggests that popular feminist rhetoric can produce changes in what types of sexual desires are seen as appropriate or inappropriate, and what forms are defined as feminist. Yet Wendy Kaminer asks, "Who holds the copyright on feminism?"[44] A close analysis of erotic thrillers, some of which are directed by women, reveals that the films' narratives and visual practices support some feminist tenets, but they could not be defined as specifically feminist in aim, or as examples of counter-cinema. To create sexual material of one's own does not automatically imply an intrinsic course to empowerment, no matter what the intention.

Nancy Rommelman pinpoints the problem behind the best feminist intentions. She explains, "We, by doing this series, were told we were taking control of something. . . . I think there were a lot of feminists involved in the production who wanted to get back at all the patronizing and bad erotica that was demeaning to women. . . . Now they were going to do it right. But what is right?"[45] The regulation and construction of normative female heterosexuality, and the appropriateness of that constructed desire based on contemporary and constantly changing feminist discourses, may very well conflict with novel attempts to produce stimulating erotic entertainment. While *Women: Stories of Passion* may exhibit the influence of feminism through a cadre of women who possess the means of production, structurally and narratively, erotic entertainment continues to defy any standardized system of feminist film practice based on an opposition to masculinist aesthetics. Furthermore, female-produced-and-directed sexual materials have failed to transform the aesthetic practices that currently codify soft-core porn, a genre that has already evolved to aim at seducing female spectators.

Only within the last fifteen years have women emerged as mainstream creative forces inside the adult film industry. The popularity of women's erotic fiction is also a fairly recent development. Susie Bright recalls "begging, screaming, [and] hounding people for stories" for the first *Herotica* book.[46] Changes within the market involving couple's porn, whereby hardcore continues to grow more mainstream, will allow certain types of erotica to become accessible and acceptable. In this sense, *Women: Stories of Passion* and soft-core erotic thrillers do break some *new ground,* not only through increasing the quantity of female-authored products, but also by adding to the variety of sexual discourses already available.

Still, the DTV erotic thriller appears to fill a niche for the female market by addressing women who seemingly like their sex with a little narrative that is romanticized, aesthetically pleasing, and focused on relationships, with semi-explicit imagery. These aesthetic qualities do not necessarily speak to all heterosexual women, but they do replicate some of the images and representations of female heterosexuality and femininity that exist within contemporary U.S. culture.

The problem remains that in a market-driven economy, in which sexuality is represented by and through commodities, an authentic relationship to sexual desire outside of market influences becomes suspect. Women who "desire differently" and thus produce alternative materials (which is not the case in the soft core discussed) may have less to do with the different desires between genders, and more to do with the maintenance of that difference to establish and reiterate social norms. Instead, in looking at the erotic thriller and female-oriented sexual representations and materials, the focus might shift, from whether women have a more authentic relationship to their desires, to how those desires are produced and constructed through different circulating ideas about sexuality, femininity, and feminism. Through the tracing of patterns within a variety of cultural products geared toward female consumers (films, television, magazines, novels, clothes, luxury goods), one can eventually uncover the persistent representations and ideologies that construct gendered power relations in the United States.

NOTES

INTRODUCTION

1. Cake's philosophy and ideals are expressed on its Web site at http://www.cakenyc.com.

2. Much of the statistical evidence given here has been taken from Cake's Web site and from Nancy Jo Sales's exploration of the phenomenon in "Girls, Interrupted."

3. Quoted in Sales, "Girls, Interrupted," 117.

4. Class description from http://www.crunch.com.

5. Quoted in Lehmann-Haupt, "How to Talk Dirty and Influence People," 62.

6. Eva Illouz makes a similar argument about the construction of femininity in relation to romance, and how romance is translated into commodified forms that are consumed by women within popular culture. See Illouz, *Consuming the Romantic Utopia*.

7. An example of this cultural imperative in popular culture is John Gray's popular "Men Are from Mars, Women Are from Venus" self-help series. His many books, tapes, films, and lectures all pivot on a crucial understanding of the *differences* between the genders. For a detailed study of his self-help oeuvre in relation to sexual materials in the home, see Juffer, *At Home with Pornography*.

8. See Faludi, *Backlash*.

9. The phrase "pleasure and danger" refers to the 1982 Barnard College conference of the same title. Documentation of this conference and its controversies is in Vance, *Pleasure and Danger*.

10. See Wing and Marrone, "Seven Days to Even Better Sex"; Kemp, "Are You Having All the Orgasms You Can?"; Taylor and Sharkey, "8 Pleasure Maxing Positions"; and Formichelli, "The Better-Orgasm Diet!"

11. I hesitate to define rigidly the terms "feminist film criticism" and "feminist film" based on feminism's ever-evolving borders and definitions. My methodological approach toward feminist film criticism combines psychoanalysis, a Foucauldian approach to power relations and the circulation of discourses, and a detailed cultural analysis of film texts and cultural products that participate in the construction of contemporary femininity.

12. See Wexman, *Creating the Couple*.

13. The difficulty of tracking accurate viewing demographics is twofold, for there is not only relative anonymity in video store rentals, but extreme anonymity in cable

and satellite viewing. For more on this, see Kleinhans, "The Change from Film to Video Pornography."

14. Porn has undeniably become a hot topic in academe, with classes on sexual representation being taught in universities across the country. For an early discussion of the trend see Lord, "Pornutopia." Another useful resource is Williams, *Porn Studies.*

15. The following anthologies are excellent resources for third-wave feminist writings on sexuality: Damsky, *Sex and Single Girls;* Johnson, *Jane Sexes It Up;* Maglin and Perry, *"Bad Girls" "Good Girls";* and Nagle, *Whores and Other Feminists.*

16. I use the word "deviant" as in deviating from a monogamous, heterosexual, pro-reproductive, family-value-oriented attitude toward sexuality and sexual practices. This deviation may include sex for money—prostitution—exotic dancing, bondage and S/M, swinging, wife swapping, group sex, and gay/lesbian/bisexual sex.

17. I use these phrases within the text to distinguish the different types of films that deal with therapy and analysis.

CHAPTER 1: PLEASURES AND DANGERS

1. Williams, *Hard Core,* 154.
2. Naremore, *More than Night,* 162.
3. Williams, *Hard Core,* 126.
4. Tudor, "Genre," 6–7.
5. Rick Altman explains the different aspects of these approaches in "A Semantic/Syntactic Approach to Film Genre."
6. Buscombe, "Idea of Genre in the American Cinema," 21.
7. R. Altman, "Semantic/Syntactic Approach to Film Genre," 30.
8. Williams, *Hard Core,* 130–52.
9. Jameson, *Postmodernism,* 18.
10. Ibid., 15–20.
11. Ibid.
12. Hutcheon, *Theory of Parody,* 107.
13. Ibid., 110.
14. Ibid., 8.
15. *Illicit Dreams* is discussed in more detail in chapter 3.
16. Hutcheon, *Theory of Parody,* 94.
17. On the "woman's film" see Doane, *Desire to Desire.* E. Ann Kaplan writes on film noir in *Women in Film Noir;* Linda Williams dissects hard-core pornography in *Hard Core;* and Tania Modleski explores Harlequin romances and soap operas in *Loving with a Vengeance.*
18. My understanding of the repetitive performances of gender stems from Butler's *Gender Trouble.*
19. Doane, *Desire to Desire,* 1.

20. For a more detailed discussion of "body genres" see Williams, "Film Bodies" and *Hard Core;* Clover, *Men, Women, and Chain Saws;* Sobchack, *Carnal Thoughts;* and Martin, "Never Laugh at a Man with His Pants Down."

21. Kurinasky, "Personal File: Sex."

22. Williams, *Hard Core,* 7.

23. *Wild Orchid 2* was briefly released in theaters, but it achieved more success on home video. The film was released on a digitally remastered DVD in 2005.

24. Williams, *Hard Core,* 73.

25. Ibid., 50.

26. Grosz, *Volatile Bodies,* 35–36.

27. Ibid., 35.

28. See Mulvey, "Visual Pleasure and Narrative Cinema."

29. See Williams, *Hard Core.*

30. Andrew Blake, a director of hard-core porn, produces films heavy on exotic setting and high production aesthetics. Films such as *House of Dreams* (1990) or *Desire* (1991) are episodic, without a narrative to connect them to soft-core's romanticized elements. Also, bodies are represented with distinctly hard-core aesthetics (penetration, genital closeups). Still, because of the films' crossover appeal as art porn, they are featured in female sex catalogs such as *Good Vibrations* and *Eve's Garden.* For more on Blake, see Bright, "The Pussy Shot."

31. In the hard-core film *Dickheads* (Midnight Video, 1993), when one of the female leads has sex at a neighbor's house, the living room there is identical to her own.

32. Stoller and Levine, *Coming Attractions,* 26.

33. Schor, *Reading the Detail,* 4.

34. Elsaesser, "Tales of Sound and Fury," 62.

35. Doane, *Femmes Fatales,* 25–26.

36. Ibid., 44–75.

37. Ebert, "Melodrama Helps Wilt *Wild Orchid II.*"

38. Kehr, "*Wild Orchid II* More Romance than Erotica."

39. Guthmann, "'Venus' Has Lots of Steam but Little Heat."

40. See Modleski, *Loving with a Vengeance;* White, *Tele-Advising;* and Rapping, *Movie of the Week.*

41. See Williams, *Hard Core;* Modleski, *Loving with a Vengeance.*

42. Unrated versions of many DTV soft-core erotic thrillers are available. While marketing a film as "unrated" may allow for more female frontal nudity, these films are markedly less explicit than hard-core porn.

43. Dyer, "Entertainment and Utopia," 222.

44. Malek, "Mad, Bad, and Dangerous to Know," 75.

45. The focus on narrative differentiates soft core from hard core in this instance. Hard core's explicit goal is not the resolution of a narrative.

46. Snitow, "Mass Market Romance," 250.

47. Cowie, "Fantasia," 88.

48. Seidel, "Judge Me by the Joy I Bring," 165.

49. Cowie, "Fantasia," 79.

50. Rapping, *Movie of the Week*, 108.

51. Whereas Cowie's analysis exhibits some problems in its logic of visual plea-sure as constantly mobile (and not addressing gendered social positioning and the continual performance of that gender), she establishes the importance of setting in eliciting and constructing identification through fantasy.

52. Cowie, "Fantasia," 87.

53. Laura Kipnis recounts the "policing" of fantasy within the Daniel DePew case, in which a man was imprisoned for voicing fantasies of pedophilia. See Kipnis, *Bound and Gagged.*

54. Stern, "Body as Evidence."

55. Clair, "Sweet Subversions," 69.

56. Krentz, *Dangerous Men and Adventurous Women*, 7.

57. Cowie, "Fantasia," 88.

58. Thurston, *Romance Revolution*, 154.

59. Chapter 4 will delve more deeply into this aspect of the erotic thriller.

60. Thurston, *Romance Revolution*, 154.

61. Doane explains in *The Desire to Desire* that Hollywood, during the war, was attempting to cultivate a large female audience and systematically created its own new genre. See Doane, *Desire to Desire*, 3–4.

62. Haskell, *From Reverence to Rape*, 163.

63. Ibid.

64. Ibid., 168.

65. Carman, "Steamy Sex at Bottom of *Lake*" (first quote); Inman, "Movie Review: *Wild Orchid*," 22S (second quote).

66. Williams, *Hard Core*, 130.

67. Mulvey, "Visual Pleasure and Narrative Cinema," 62.

68. Marchetti, "Ethnicity, the Cinema, and Cultural Studies," 287.

69. The "masquerade" is a psychoanalytic term introduced by Joan Riviere that describes the process by which a woman wears a mask of excessive femininity to as-suage male anxieties regarding her threatening power. In "Film and the Masquerade: Theorizing the Female Spectator," Mary Ann Doane states that representations of excessive femininity on screen can provide the proper distance female spectators require in order not to overidentify with female characters masochistically or narcis-sistically.

70. The idea of the male "gaze" was introduced in the 1970s by the theorist Laura Mulvey, who posited that men are active, voyeuristic subjects who use an aggressive

gaze to possess the passive, female objects common to Hollywood cinema. This aggressive gaze circumvents the threat women pose as sexually different (without a penis/phallus), their very presence on screen implying castration. See Mulvey, "Visual Pleasure and Narrative Cinema."

71. Carman, "Steamy Sex at Bottom of *Lake*" (first quote); Weistein, "King Takes Erotic Fare to Showtime" (second quote); Epstein, "Interview with Zalman King" (third quote). In the Epstein interview, King expresses understandable dissatisfaction with the term "soft core," as it is used to ghettoize his work. Still, throughout this book, I use "soft core" as a technical term, not a derisive criticism, for I believe that he has shaped the entire soft-core oeuvre, from anthology series to erotic thriller.

72. *Red Shoe Diaries* episodes are still occasionally broadcast late at night on Showtime Beyond, part of the Showtime Cable Network.

73. "Showtime Networks Teams Up with Cybergrrl and FanciFull."

74. Epstein, "Interview with Zalman King."

75. Armstrong, "Zalman King" (King quote); Fienberg, "Zalman King Delivers Heat" (King on female empowerment).

76. Epstein, "Interview with Zalman King."

77. A more detailed analysis of the erotic thriller's relationship to feminism and feminist discourses will be undertaken in chapter 2.

78. King films such as *Business for Pleasure* and *Women of the Night* do contain suspense narratives that combine female sexual desires with their concurrent dangers.

79. A male narrator is atypical of the erotic thriller or erotic anthology series. Initially Jake provided the narrative connection from feature film to episodic series; now David Duchovny (who plays Jake) has become a significant object of desire for mainstream audiences thanks to the Fox series *The X-Files*.

80. Berger, *Ways of Seeing*, 46.

81. Images of women looking at women are common to the structure of fashion advertising. See Fuss, "Fashion and the Homospectatorial Look."

82. Coward, *Female Desires*, 229. Some theorists have recently argued that the United States has become an "equal opportunity exploitation culture," where men's bodies are objectified as frequently as women's bodies. See Heywood and Dworkin, *Built to Win*.

83. Doane, *Femmes Fatales*, 22.

84. See Mulvey, "Visual Pleasure and Narrative Cinema."

85. Cowie, "Fantasia," 56.

86. Webster, "The Forbidden," 391.

87. This scenario contributes to the instructive, "how-to" quality characteristic of soft-core erotic thrillers. Often, the heroine is naïve, and her pursuit of sexual adventure and knowledge becomes the narrative's goal, helping to construct her

sexual identity. In the meantime, through identifying with the heroine, the spectator witnesses different sexual techniques, all for the purpose of enhancing sexual
abilities. These fantasy scenarios maintain a playful quality, allowing the spectator to
vicariously experience "forbidden" sexual acts or taboos and perhaps later to utilize
them in the bedroom through role-playing.

88. Silverman, "*Histoire d'O*," 326.

89. As I will explain further in chapter 3, the emasculated man is often represented
concurrently with the female acquisition or use of sexual power.

90. Foucault, *History of Sexuality*, 61.

91. Ibid.

92. Haskell, "Rape Fantasy," 85.

93. This is similar to the cat-and-mouse toying that occurs in *Basic Instinct* (1992).

94. The two main female characters on *Chromiumblue.com,* Vivian and Maria,
combine a seductive femininity with the freedoms and desires typical of men. Vivian loves driving a motorcycle *fast,* and at one point she saves a man in distress—a
gigolo guilty of seducing another man's wife. Maria also likes to drive fast—a fitting
desire for a chauffeur—and is attracted to violence as well. She knocks out one man
in a fight and is essential in springing Vivian from jail, styled as a leather-wearing,
bad-ass action chick.

95. Armstrong, "Zalman King."

96. Recycled material is quite common in Zalman King's films. Car-crash footage
from *Business for Pleasure* recurs in *Women of the Night* (2000). A scene of a black
stripper walking atop a narrow bar in *Shame, Shame, Shame* (1997) is repeated in
Business for Pleasure. Footage of the Christ statue and carnival in Rio is reused in
Wild Orchid, some *Red Shoe Diaries* episodes, and *Women of the Night.*

97. Quoted in Jemielity, "Stroke on the Water."

98. Epstein, "Interview with Zalman King."

99. Ibid.

CHAPTER 2: HOW TO BE A GOOD FEMALE HETEROSEXUAL

1. Linda Williams borrows the phrase "education of desire" from Andrew Ross.
Williams, *Hard Core,* 264.

2. Friend, "Yes: Feminist Women," 48.

3. Many feminist critics suggest that the term "sex wars" was coined during the
1982 Pleasure and Danger conference at Barnard College. While there is no complete
history of this period, there are several significant anthologies that provide writings
outlining some of the arguments within feminism at the time. See Vance, *Pleasure
and Danger;* Lederer, *Take Back the Night;* Ellis et al., *Caught Looking;* and Snitow et
al., *Powers of Desire.*

4. Two examples of the mainstream press's handling of the "sex wars" are "The War

against Pornography" and Stengel, "Sex Busters." Both articles emphasize the role of antipornography feminism as the prominent feminist position, entirely one-sided information.

5. Friend, "Yes: Feminist Women," 48.

6. Pat Califia is now a transgendered activist, known as Patrick Califia in academic and activist circles.

7. Rapping, "Women Are from Venus."

8. Pollitt, "Subject to Debate: Gender Wars"; Shalit, "Canny and Lacy"; and Leveen, "Sex and the Scholarly Girl," 628.

9. Leveen, "Sex and the Scholarly Girl," 631.

10. Friend, "Yes: Feminist Women," 50.

11. Henry, *Not My Mother's Sister*, 110.

12. Damsky, *Sex and Single Girls*, xiii.

13. Bellafante, "Feminism," 55.

14. Kaminer, "Whither Feminism?"

15. Ibid.

16. Friend, "Yes: Feminist Women," 50.

17. Ibid., 52.

18. Baumgardner and Richards, *Manifesta*, 136.

19. Ibid., 139.

20. Wolf, *Fire with Fire*, 93.

21. Orr, "Charting the Currents," 42–43.

22. Pollitt, "Subject to Debate: Gender Wars."

23. Pollitt, "Subject to Debate: Dead Again?" 10.

24. Sandra Gilbert, quoted in Leveen, "Sex and the Scholarly Girl," 627.

25. Quoted in Kaminer, "Whither Feminism?"

26. Ibid.

27. Schultz, "Great Sexpectations."

28. Wolf, *Fire with Fire*, 88.

29. Kaplan, quoted in Shattuc, *Talking Cure*, 124.

30. Baumgardner and Richards, *Manifesta*, 161.

31. Shattuc, *Talking Cure*, 27–28.

32. See Kemp, "Six Best Sex Positions"; Childerhose, "Toys in Babeland"; McCafferty, "Take Your Climax to the Max"; Kalish, "46 Things to Do to a Naked Man"; Bakos, "3 Steps to Your Best Orgasm Ever"; and Goins and Stephens, "Blab Your Way to Better Sex."

33. Rapping, "Women Are from Venus." In recent years, magazines such as *Men's Health* and *Maxim* have brought men's concerns about sex and relationships to the forefront.

34. Kleinplatz, "'Educational' Sex Videos."

35. Quoted in Miller, "Stores Shy Away."

36. Ibid.

37. This is a scene immortalized in the soft-core classic *Nine ½ Weeks* (Adrian Lyne, 1986) and used in *The First Nine ½ Weeks* (Alex Wright, 1998).

38. Karbo, "Sex Ed for Grownups."

39. Eberwein, "Sex Instruction Videos," 40. Also see Eberwein, *Sex Ed.*

40. The films that use these scenarios are too numerous to list here, but they include *Virtual Encounters* (Cybil Richards, 1996), *Carnal Crimes* (A. Gregory Hippolyte, 1990), *Secret Games 3* (A. Gregory Hippolyte, 1994), *Lap Dancing* (Mike Sedan, 1995), *Striking Resemblance* (Kelley Cauthen, 1997), *Sexual Predator* (Robert Angelo, 2001), and *Visions of Passion* (Randall St. George, 2003).

41. Liebensen, "Hot Property." Erotic painting sessions are also numerous, in films ranging from Andrew Blake's *House of Dreams* to *Forbidden Passions* (Jackie Garth, 1996).

42. Wurtzel, *Bitch*, 23.

43. Paglia, *Vamps and Tramps*, ix.

44. Wolf, *Fire with Fire*, 229.

45. Wolf, *Promiscuities*, xvii.

46. Johnson, *Jane Sexes It Up*, 2.

47. Wolf, *Promiscuities*, xxii.

48. Paglia, *Vamps and Tramps*, ix.

49. Wolf, *Fire with Fire*, 231.

50. Paglia, *Sex, Art, and American Culture*, 11.

51. Quoted from "Criminal," the first track of Fiona Apple's 1997 album, *Tidal*.

52. This idea is discussed in Eberwein, "Sex Instruction Videos," 37; Eberwein, *Sex Ed*; and White, *Tele-Advising*.

53. Langton, "Nice Girls Undress for Success: Strippers." The title of the article exemplifies the tendency for nice girls in the 1990s to be "bad," and suggests that this idea can be both fantasy (through reading the article) and reality to women.

54. Ibid.

55. Hefner, "Why Erotic Material May Be Healthy for You."

56. M. Altman, "Everything They Always Wanted You to Know," 115.

CHAPTER 3: THE SUBJECT OF PASSION, THE OBJECT OF MURDER

1. Attributing a reflexive methodology to film genre formations proves inadequate. My understanding of genre follows the "dialectical thinking" of Jameson in *The Political Unconscious*. For further discussion on the way culture impacts genre, see Grant's edited anthology *The Film Genre Reader*.

2. Jameson, *Political Unconscious*, 140–41.

3. Diane Waldman provides a substantive discussion of the female gothic's rela-

tionship to the historical situation of women in the forties. See Waldman, "'At Last I Can Tell It to Someone!'"

4. See Doane, "Paranoia and the Specular," in her *Desire to Desire,* 123–54.

5. Ibid., 125.

6. Jameson, *Political Unconscious,* 145.

7. Several critics have commented on the most recent fictional examples of this genre, which faded from popular women's fiction during the 1980s. See Modleski, *Loving with a Vengeance;* Holland and Sherman, "Gothic Possibilities"; and Russ, "Somebody's Trying to Kill Me."

8. Ellis, *Contested Castle,* ix–x.

9. Ibid., ix.

10. Ibid., x.

11. Ibid., x–xi.

12. Ibid., 3.

13. Waldman, "'At Last I Can Tell It to Someone!'" 30.

14. Ibid.

15. Gallafent, "Black Satin."

16. Robert Eberwein discussed this typical opening of the genre in "The Erotic Thriller," paper presented at the Society for Film Studies Conference in New York City, March 1995.

17. Doane, "The 'Woman's Film,'" 288.

18. For Christine and her husband, this period was ironically before Richard was passed over for tenure by the university.

19. Doane, *Desire to Desire,* 135.

20. The situation with Jack is another indication that marriage represents danger and dread in the erotic thriller.

21. Carol Clover explains the masochistic engagement of the *male* spectator with the "final girl" of the slasher films, pointing out that identification can occur across gender boundaries. While this is also possible within the erotic thriller (as well as all genres), the graphic violence exhibited in the slasher film and the romantic elements of the DTV erotic thriller would tend to align those films with a specific gendered address. Clover's astute analysis does reveal the possibilities of masochistic pleasure for either gender. See Clover, *Men, Women, and Chain Saws.*

22. Freud's essay on the uncanny explores a subject's intellectual uncertainty and subsequent anxiety regarding reality testing and the unknown. He attributes instances of the uncanny to repression and psychological explanation, but concentrates on male subjectivity and the Oedipus complex as his models. Still, the undercutting of *female* subjectivity within the gothic genre also involves the subject's apparent intellectual uncertainty, and the narrative frequently links this to the uncanny. See Freud, "The 'Uncanny,'" 217–52.

23. Freud relates these frightening recurring elements to the uncanny. Freud, "The 'Uncanny,'" 241.

24. Smith, "Film Noir, the Female Gothic, and *Deception.*"

25. Doane, "The 'Woman's Film,'" 288.

26. The mainstream theatrical thriller *Blue Steel* (Kathryn Bigelow, 1990) provides a contemporary Hollywood example. While Meagan (Jamie Lee Curtis) remains a tough cop, she subsequently cannot get a date. She becomes unwittingly involved with a vicious serial killer, who terrorizes her after she discovers his guilt (he rapes her, kills her best friend). She is simultaneously subject and object, pursuer and victim, and can survive only by destroying her initial love object through violence.

27. This scene distinctly echoes one in *Basic Instinct,* another neo-noir. While Detective Nick Curran (Michael Douglas) happens to be picking up his suspect, Catherine Trammell (Sharon Stone), for questioning, he catches a glimpse of her naked, changing clothes in another room. This exhibitionistic tease is characteristic of the femme fatale and reveals itself through the "fatal man" as well.

28. Critical work on the femme fatale in film is extensive. Some of the best work can be found in the revised edition of Kaplan's *Women in Film Noir.*

29. Doane, *Femmes Fatales,* 2.

30. The femme fatale's implicit goal, to prove that watching porn is "okay," reveals the influence of feminist discourses on the genre, as well as the push by popular culture for women to embrace their sexuality. The destruction of the sex-crazed male characters also implies their apparent harmlessness to women—they can always be overpowered. The narrative clearly displays the workings of utopian fantasy.

31. The film connects to mainstream Hollywood by replicating some of the plot elements of *Fatal Attraction* (Adrian Lyne, 1987), yet it diverges by giving the "female psychopath" more power and narrative control—and ending quite differently. For a rereading of the "bitch from hell," see Jermyn, "Rereading the Bitches from Hell."

32. Jim Wynorski, who directed *Body Chemistry 3* and *4,* takes scenes directly from the former and places them into the latter, literally repeating generic elements.

33. Cowie, "Fantasia," 79.

34. In *Body Chemistry 4,* the spectator witnesses Claire's machinations to their fullest extent. Through her subjective gaze, we see her setting up each character, and her duplicity in several scenes is often accompanied by a smirk of amusement as she plays with Simon Marshall, her lawyer and pawn. By privileging the psychopath more in the fourth film, the genre indicates where narrative pleasure lies: with the active female character.

35. Three other significant theatrical feature films that also represent this crucial relationship between the emasculated man and the new femme fatale are *The Last Seduction* (John Dahl, 1994), *Romeo Is Bleeding* (Peter Medak, 1993), and *The Hot Spot* (Dennis Hopper, 1990).

1. The terms "transference" and "countertransference" are taken from Freudian theory and refer directly to the growth of a relationship between analyst and analysand. During transference, the release of unconscious wishes and repressed desires are precipitated by the patient's growing intimacy and dependent relationship with his or her doctor. Further, countertransference occurs when the analyst's own unconscious wishes and desires are drawn forward and played out through the doctor's relationship with the patient. For more detailed definitions of these terms, see Laplanche and Pontalis, *Language of Psychoanalysis,* 92–93 and 455–62.

2. Foucault, *History of Sexuality,* 61.

3. M. Altman, "Everything They Always Wanted You to Know," 122.

4. For the purpose of this analysis, I will focus on three texts by feminist theorists that utilize Foucault's paradigm: Shattuc, *Talking Cure,* in relation to television talk shows; White, *Tele-Advising,* regarding a wide variety of television formats; and Williams, *Hard Core,* through her discussion of pornography.

5. Foucault, *History of Sexuality,* 62.

6. Shattuc, *Talking Cure,* 115.

7. Rebecca's sex work connects her to the "sex workers"—call girls, exotic dancers, and strippers—in erotic thrillers manifesting instructional discourses. These women are "experts" as well.

8. While Rebecca's Extremis conviction is useful for connecting the three films, her punishment for repeatedly experimenting with a drug that cures erectile dysfunction is both ironic and prescient in the wake of Viagara's introduction only a few years later.

9. Janet Walker explores the relations between psychiatry and women in post–World War II cinema in *Couching Resistance,* 125.

10. These concepts are discussed at length in Mulvey's "Visual Pleasure and Narrative Cinema" and in Doane's "Film and the Masquerade."

11. See Doane, *Desire to Desire,* 57. Doane, like Walker, focuses on films of the 1940s and 1950s, for this was the period when Freud and psychoanalysis were most visibly apparent in Hollywood cinema.

12. White, *Tele-Advising,* 178.

13. Walker, *Couching Resistance,* 123.

14. Ibid., 45.

15. Ibid., 23.

16. One of the few female-protagonist-driven mainstream theatrical thrillers to deal with these issues in a similar way is *Whispers in the Dark* (Cameron Crowe, 1992).

17. For this chapter's purposes, *The Dark Dancer*'s analysis is limited to the loss of authority and vulnerability of the therapist. Yet, there is a killer involved who slashes exotic dancers and prostitutes, and Margaret's boyfriend, who feels that she works

too hard and does not pay him enough attention, regularly cheats on her. Margaret's pathology stems from a traumatic moment in her past. Her mother, who was an exotic dancer, ends up slashing her boyfriend with a butcher knife, when she arrives home to find him having sex with her teenage daughter (Margaret).

18. A mainstream theatrical version of the countertransference erotic thriller with a male protagonist is *Color of Night* (Richard Rush, 1994). Ironically, since Bruce Willis is in the lead therapist role, the film ends up containing more action film tropes than explorations of the main character's sexuality and psyche.

19. Lupton, "Talking about Sex," 48.

20. Banks and Zimmerman, "Dr. Ruth Westheimer," 65.

21. Catherine Oxenberg, like the soft-core regular Morgan Fairchild, is known for her role on a nighttime soap opera—in her case, *Dynasty*.

22. A similar setup occurs in *Sexual Intent* (1994), where Barbara's videotaped testimonials act as a Greek chorus to the events unfolding within the rest of the narrative. Whenever an event occurs within the plot, the "videotaped confessions" of Barbara's patients mirror that event through similar commentary.

23. Adam Simon's *Body Chemistry 2* veers from this paradigm. In this film, Claire Archer is a radio talk show host who maintains her authority and has a great deal of sexual experience to sustain her sexual knowledge. Still, while Claire may be an "expert" in her profession, she is also a cold-blooded killer, qualifying her expertise within the public sphere.

CHAPTER 5: SURVEILLANCE, SUBJECTIVITY, AND SOFT CORE

1. This fascination was expressed in the phrase "You Like to Watch, Don't You?" which was the tagline on the movie poster for *Sliver* (Phillip Noyce, 1993), a mainstream theatrical erotic thriller about surveillance. While the press called the film an "erotic thriller," the film's large budget and well-known stars, Sharon Stone, William Baldwin, and Tom Berenger, as well as the film's theatrical run, disqualify it for consideration within this particular genre study. Because the *Night Eyes* and *Animal Instincts* series began before the film's release, one could infer that *Sliver* was made in an attempt to cash in on DTV erotic thrillers' popularity.

2. Berko, "Surveying the Surveilled."

3. Foucault, *Discipline and Punish,* 200.

4. Ibid., 201.

5. Berko, 64.

6. See Mano, "'I'm Ready for My Come Shot Now, Dear.'" Some other sources for this information include Mueller, "Porn Biz Awash in Amateur Efforts"; Judith Gaines, "Home-video Sex Sells"; and Kuipers, "Sex, Home, and Videotape; Homemade Erotica."

7. Judith Gaines, "Home-video Sex Sells," 1.

8. Fred See, "Something Reflective," 169. In this article, See analyzes the film *Rising Sun* (1995).

9. Dixon, *It Looks at You,* 51.

10. These lapses in judgment could relate to the infrequent roles male characters play as objects of a gaze. He just does not imagine himself being looked at.

11. All of these elements, except the gym equipment, are stereotypical character-istics of the soft-core sex mise-en-scène.

12. The film's opening, self-reflexive structure and relationship to voyeurism are similar to those of Michael Powell's *Peeping Tom* (1960).

13. Although not quite as small as a lipstick, a lipstick camera is small enough to be concealed anywhere, making it a highly effective piece of surveillance equipment.

14. Quoted in Judith Gaines, "Home-video Sex Sells," 1.

15. Ibid.

16. Ironically, one of the known side effects of many antidepressants is sexual dysfunction and a substantial decrease in sexual desire. This increase in sex drive is another example of the utopian aspects of the film's narrative (and convenient for a film focusing on sex scenes).

17. Thomas Waugh sees similar possibilities in his analysis of the American stag film. See Waugh, "Homosociality in the Classic American Stag Film."

18. While most sequels in a particular erotic thriller series merely repackage the same plot again and again, the *Animal Instincts* series does transform itself with each version. *Animal Instincts 2* (A. Gregory Hippolyte, 1994) treats male voyeurism as much more pathological, as Joanna, now single, tries to have a "normal" life but slips back into her exhibitionistic ways. Yet, in *Animal Instincts 3* (A. Gregory Hip-polyte, 1995), Joanna is unapologetically exhibitionistic. She has now managed to turn her performances into a career and is writing another bestselling book about her adventures.

19. An omniscient observer and mentor figure also appears in *Forbidden Passions,* but she exists only when Mara is not interacting with another character.

20. Amy's changed attitude suggests there can be negative consequences of a causal connection between technology and sexual behavior. If a trip through VR can cause the sexually inhibited to become aggressive, influenced through representa-tion, then the power of images to induce behavior supports one of the greatest fears about pornography—that the representation of violent images against women has a causal connection to sexual abuse and violence against women in the actual world.

21. Quoted in Dery, "Robocopulation," 211.

CONCLUSION

1. Rothstein, interview.

2. Rommelman, unpublished essay.

3. Mayne, *Woman at the Keyhole,* 93.

4. Wolf, *Fire with Fire,* 95. Wolf's statement does not take into account that "choosing" one's image is also a produced and mediated experience.

5. Rothstein, interview.

6. Rommelman, interview.

7. The most significant difference between the two series is that *Red Shoes* has Jake (David Duchovny) as a bracketing narrator, while *Women* introduces each episode with a female interviewer (Elisa Rothstein).

8. Rothstein, interview. Rothstein, along with King's wife, Patricia Louisianna Knopp, wrote the screenplay for the King-directed *Delta of Venus* (1995). In her interview, Rothstein commented on the film, stating that "from a purely visual perspective, I thought he turned a movie about a woman's awakening into a voyeuristic male fantasy."

9. Rothstein, interview.

10. See Mulvey, "Visual Pleasure and Narrative Cinema," and Doane, "Film and the Masquerade."

11. The landmark "counter-cinema" articles referred to are Johnston, "Women's Cinema as Counter-Cinema," and Mulvey, "Visual Pleasure and Narrative Cinema."

12. The idea that "men act" while "women appear" initially comes from John Berger's analysis of gendered representation in painting. See Berger, *Ways of Seeing.*

13. Jane Gaines, "Feminist Heterosexuality and Its Politically Incorrect Pleasures," 22. Gaines published an article of the same title in *Critical Inquiry* 21, no. 2 (Winter 1995): 382–410.

14. In this futuristic society, the regulation of sexuality is produced by an enforced distance between the sexes, substantiated through their residence within different cities. They are allowed to look at each other, but are forbidden to act on that desire physically except during the mating season.

15. Rommelman, interview.

16. Quoted in Dominus, "What Women Want to Watch," 1.

17. Ibid.

18. Faludi, "Money Shot."

19. Heywood and Dworkin, *Built to Win,* 129.

20. Ibid.

21. Rothstein, interview.

22. Rommelman, unpublished essay. Playboy would not allow me access to any of its demographic research and analysis.

23. Ibid.

24. Bencivengo, interview.

25. In a 1994 study that compared women's sexual and emotional responses to

male- and female-produced erotica, the authors found that "a woman-made film might be more sexually exciting for women when considering subjective responses, but not when genital responses are considered." Laran et al., "Women's Sexual and Emotional Responses to Male and Female-produced Erotica," 167.

26. Dominus, "What Women Want to Watch."

27. Rommelman, interview.

28. Quoted in Beale, "Her Blue Heaven."

29. Quoted in Barnard, "Action!"

30. Quoted in "Sex on Film for Girls."

31. See Williams, *Hard Core.*

32. Rothstein, interview.

33. Rommelman, unpublished essay (first quote), and Rothstein, interview (second quote).

34. Rothstein, interview.

35. The term "compulsory heterosexuality" is defined in Rich, "Compulsory Heterosexuality and Lesbian Existence."

36. Jane Gaines, "Feminist Heterosexuality and Its Politically Incorrect Pleasures."

37. Stanley, "TV Weekend." Stanley further comments, "*The L Word* conveniently fits in with a trend currently preoccupying magazines, afternoon talk shows and parents' meetings: young women, including high-school students, who experiment with bisexuality both for a sense of female empowerment and as a way to seduce men."

38. Eve Kosofsky Sedgwick describes Jenny's first voyeuristic experience in detail in "'The L Word.'" She elaborates, "I will be relieved when the writers decide they have sufficiently interpellated straight viewers and can leave behind the lachrymose plot of Jenny's Choice."

39. Nyongo'o, "Queer TV," 104.

40. Amad, "Sapphosex in the City."

41. Quoted in Beale, "Her Blue Heaven."

42. Utilizing these qualifications, Jenna Jameson, the former stripper, porn star, bestselling author, and CEO of ClubJenna.com epitomizes the empowered, sexually experienced, and liberated woman.

43. Quoted in Hill, "Manhattan's Women Find Power in Sex."

44. Kaminer, "Feminism's Third Wave."

45. Rommelman, interview.

46. Quoted in Rockett, "Some Like It Hot." *Herotica* is a series of collected erotic stories written by female authors.

WORKS CITED

Altman, Meryl. "Everything They Always Wanted You to Know: The Ideology of Popular Sex Literature." In Vance, *Pleasure and Danger,* 115–30.

Altman, Rick. "A Semantic/Syntactic Approach to Film Genre." In Grant, *Film Genre Reader,* 26–39.

Amad, Shazia. "Sapphosex in the City." *Toronto Star,* March 6, 2005. http://web.lexis-nexis.com.proxy.library.emory.edu/Universe (accessed August 18, 2005).

Armstrong, Rod. "Zalman King: The Sultan of Soft-Core Speaks." Reel.com Web site. http://www.reel.com/reel.asp?node=features/interviews/king (accessed May 30, 2005).

Bakos, Susan Crain. "3 Steps to Your Best Orgasm Ever." *Redbook,* February 2005, 62.

Banks, Jane, and Patricia Zimmerman. "Dr. Ruth Westheimer: Talking Sex as a Technology of Power." *Journal of Film and Video* 45, no. 2–3 (Summer–Fall 1993): 60–71.

Barnard, Linda. "Action! The Ins and Outs of the Porn Film Industry." *Toronto Sun,* August 25, 2001, 43. http://web.lexis-nexis.com.proxy.library.emory.edu/universe (accessed August 18, 2005).

Baumgardner, Jennifer, and Amy Richards. *Manifesta: Young Women, Feminism, and the Future.* New York: Farrar, Straus, and Giroux, 2004.

Beale, Lewis. "Her Blue Heaven." *New York Daily News,* October 20, 1993, 41.

Bellafante, Ginia. "Feminism: It's All about Me!" *Time,* June 29, 1998, 54–61.

Bencivengo, Richard. Interview by author. Tape recording. Chicago, May 9, 1997.

Berger, John. *Ways of Seeing.* London: British Broadcasting Corporation, 1972.

Berko, Lili. "Surveying the Surveilled: Video, Space, and Subjectivity." *Quarterly Review of Film and Video* 14, no. 1–2 (1992): 63.

Blanchard, Keith. "Your Husband's Most Secret Sex Wish: Manually Stimulating a Man to Orgasm." *Redbook,* April 1, 1999, 128–31.

Bright, Susie. "The Pussy Shot: An Interview with Andrew Blake." In *Susie Bright's Sexwise,* 80–87. San Francisco: Cleis Press, 1995.

Buscombe, Edward. "The Idea of Genre in the American Cinema." In Grant, *Film Genre Reader,* 11–25.

Butler, Judith. *Gender Trouble.* New York: Routledge, 1990.

Cake. http://www.cakenyc.com (accessed September 9, 2003).

Carman, John. "Steamy Sex at Bottom of *Lake.*" *San Francisco Chronicle,* February 26, 1993, D1.

Childerhose, Buffy. "Toys in Babeland." *Chatelaine,* March 1, 1999, 94–96.

Clair, Daphne. "Sweet Subversions." In Krentz, *Dangerous Men and Adventurous Women,* 61–72.

Clover, Carol J. *Men, Women, and Chain Saws: Gender in the Modern Horror Film.* Princeton: Princeton University Press, 1992.

Coward, Rosalind. *Female Desires: How They Are Sought, Bought, and Packaged.* New York: Grove Press, 1985.

Cowie, Elizabeth. "Fantasia." *m/f* 9 (1984): 71–105.

Crunch Fitness. http://www.crunch.com (accessed September 9, 2003).

Damsky, Lee, ed. *Sex and Single Girls: Straight and Queer Women on Sexuality.* Toronto: Seal Press, 2000.

Dery, Mark. "Robocopulation: Sex Times Technology Equals the Future." *Escape Velocity.* New York: Grove Press, 1996.

Dixon, Wheeler Winston. *It Looks at You: The Returned Gaze of the Cinema.* Albany: State University of New York Press, 1995.

Doane, Mary Ann. *The Desire to Desire: The Woman's Film of the 1940s.* Bloomington: Indiana University Press, 1987.

———. *Femmes Fatales: Feminism, Film Theory, Psychoanalysis.* New York: Routledge, 1991.

———. "Film and the Masquerade: Theorizing the Female Spectator." In *Issues in Feminist Film Criticism,* edited by Patricia Erens, 41–57. Bloomington: Indiana University Press, 1990.

———. "The Woman's Film." In Gledhill, *Home Is Where the Heart Is,* 283–98.

Dominus, Susan. "What Women Want to Watch." *New York Times,* April 29, 2004, Arts and Leisure, 1. http://web.lexis-nexis.com.proxy.library.emory.edu/universe (accessed August 18, 2005).

Dyer, Richard. "Entertainment and Utopia." In *Movies and Methods: Volume II,* edited by Bill Nichols, 220–32. Berkeley: University of California Press, 1985.

Ebert, Roger. "Melodrama Helps Wilt *Wild Orchid II.*" *Chicago Sun-Times,* May 8, 1992, 43.

Eberwein, Robert. "The Erotic Thriller." Paper presented at the Society for Cinema Studies Conference, New York City, March 1995.

———. *Sex Ed: Film, Video, and the Framework of Desire.* New Brunswick, N.J.: Rutgers University Press, 1999.

———. "Sex Instruction Videos: One Finger on the Pause Button." *Jump Cut* 41 (1996): 36–41.

Ellis, Kate, et al., eds. *Caught Looking: Feminism, Pornography, Censorship.* East Haven, Conn.: LongRiver Books, 1992.

Ellis, Kate Ferguson. *The Contested Castle: Gothic Novels and the Subversion of Domestic Ideology.* Urbana: University of Illinois Press, 1989.

Elsaesser, Thomas. "Tales of Sound and Fury: Observations on the Family Melodrama." In Gledhill, *Home Is Where the Heart Is,* 43–69.

Epstein, Daniel Robert. "Interview with Zalman King." http://suicidegirls.com, January 6, 2004 (accessed May 30, 2005).

Faludi, Susan. *Backlash: The Undeclared War against American Women.* New York: Doubleday, 1991.

———. "The Money Shot." *New Yorker,* October 30, 1995, 68.

Fienberg, Daniel. "Zalman King Delivers Heat for Bravo's *Forty Deuce.*" Zap 2it.com, April 5, 2005. http://tv.zap2it.com/tveditorial/tve-main/1,1002,271 %7C94556%7C1%7C,00.html (accessed August 1, 2006).

Formachelli, Linda. "The Better-Orgasm Diet." *Redbook,* May 2000. http://www .proquest.umi.com (accessed August 5, 2005).

Foucault, Michel. *The Birth of the Clinic.* 1973. Translated by A. M. Sheridan Smith. New York: Vintage, 1994.

———. *The History of Sexuality: Volume 1, An Introduction.* 1978. Translated by Alan Sheridan. New York: Vintage, 1990.

———. "Panopticism." In *Discipline and Punish: The Birth of the Prison,* 195–228. Translated by Alan Sheridan. New York: Vintage, 1979.

Freud, Sigmund. "The 'Uncanny.'" In *The Standard Edition of the Complete Psychological Works of Sigmund Freud,* vol. 17, 217–52. Edited by James Strachey. London, 1955.

Friday, Nancy. *Women on Top: How Real Life Has Changed Women's Sexual Fantasies.* New York: Simon and Schuster, 1991.

Friend, Tad. "Yes: Feminist Women Who Like Sex." *Esquire,* February 1994, 48–54.

Fuss, Diana. "Fashion and the Homospectatorial Look." *Critical Inquiry* 18, no. 4 (Summer 1992): 713–37.

Gaines, Jane. "Feminist Heterosexuality and Its Politically Incorrect Pleasures." Paper presented at the Society for Cinema Studies conference, New York City, March 1995.

———. "Feminist Heterosexuality and Its Politically Incorrect Pleasures." *Critical Inquiry* 21, no. 2 (Winter 1995). http://ejournals.ebsco.com.proxy.library.emory .edu/direct.asp?direct=true&db=aph&an=9504213255.

Gaines, Judith. "Home-video Sex Sells; Unwilling Stars Cry Foul." *Boston Globe,* May 17, 1992, Metro/Region, 1.

Gallafent, Ed. "Black Satin: Fantasy, Murder and the Couple in *Gaslight* and *Rebecca.*" *Screen* 29, no. 3 (Summer 1988): 94.

Gledhill, Christine, ed. *Home Is Where the Heart Is: Studies in Melodrama and the Woman's Film.* London: British Film Institute, 1987.

Goins, Liesa, and Betsey Stephens. "Blab Your Way to Better Sex." *Cosmopolitan,* August 2000, 133–34.

Grant, Barry Keith, ed. *The Film Genre Reader.* Austin: University of Texas Press, 1993.

Grosz, Elizabeth. *Volatile Bodies: Towards a Corporeal Feminism.* Bloomington: Indiana University Press, 1994.

Guthman, Edward. "'Venus' Has Lots of Steam but Little Heat." *San Francisco Chronicle,* November 17, 1995, C3. http://web.lexis-nexis.com/proxy.library.emory .edu/universe (accessed July 24, 2005).

Gutmann, Stephanie. "What a Video Can Teach You about Sex." *Cosmopolitan,* July 1996, 80.

Haskell, Molly. *From Reverence to Rape.* 2nd ed. Chicago: University of Chicago Press, 1987.

———. "Rape Fantasy: The 2,000–Year-Old Misunderstanding." *Ms.,* November 1976, 84–96.

Hefner, Christie. "Why Erotic Material May Be Healthy for You." *Cosmopolitan,* November 1997, 64.

Henry, Astrid. *Not My Mother's Sister: Generational Conflict and Third-Wave Feminism.* Bloomington: Indiana University Press, 2004.

Heywood, Leslie, and Shari L. Dworkin. *Built to Win: The Female Athlete as Cultural Icon.* Minneapolis: University of Minnesota Press, 2003.

Hill, Amelia. "Manhattan's Women Find Power in Sex," *London Observer,* June 17, 2001, 19. http://web.lexis-nexis.com.proxy.library.emory.edu/universe (accessed August 1, 2006).

Holland, Norman N., and Leona F. Sherman. "Gothic Possibilities." *New Literary History* 8 (Winter 1977): 279–94.

Hutcheon, Linda. *A Theory of Parody.* New York: Methuen, 1985.

Illouz, Eva. *Consuming the Romantic Utopia: Love and the Cultural Contradictions of Capitalism.* Berkeley: University of California Press, 1997.

Inman, David. "Movie Review: *Wild Orchid.*" *Courier Journal,* April 23, 1990, 22S.

Jameson, Fredric. *The Cultural Logic of Late Capitalism.* Durham: Duke University Press, 1991.

———. *The Political Unconscious: Narrative as a Socially Symbolic Act.* Ithaca, N.Y.: Cornell University Press, 1981.

Jemielity, Sam. "Stroke on the Water: Erotic Auteur Zalman King of *Red Shoe Diaries* Renown Sets Sail on A Sea of Love." http://www.playboy.com/arts-entertainment /features/chromiumblue (accessed August 3, 2006).

Jermyn, Deborah. "Rereading the Bitches from Hell: A Feminist Appropriation of the Female Psychopath." *Screen* 37, no. 3 (August 1996): 251–67.

Johnson, Merri Lisa, ed. *Jane Sexes It Up: True Confessions of Feminist Desire.* New York: Thunder's Mouth Press, 2002.

Johnston, Claire. "Women's Cinema as Counter-Cinema." In *Feminist Film Theory,* edited by Annette Kuhn, 133–43. London: Routledge, 1983.

Juffer, Jane. *At Home with Pornography: Women, Sex, and Everyday Life.* New York: New York University Press, 1998.

Kalish, Nancy. "46 Things to Do to a Naked Man." *Redbook,* July 1998, 84–87.

Kaminer, Wendy. "Feminism's Third Wave: What Do Young Women Want." *New York Times,* June 4, 1995, late ed., sect. 7, 3.

———. "Whither Feminism? Feminism's Identity Crisis." *Current* 359 (January 1994): 4.

Kaplan, E. Ann, ed. *Women in Film Noir.* Rev. ed. London: British Film Institute, 1998.

Karbo, Karen. "Sex Ed for Grownups: Can You Learn to Be a Better Lover by Watching How-to Tapes?" *Redbook,* November 1993, 62.

Kehr, David. "*Wild Orchid II* More Romance than Erotica." *Chicago Tribune,* May 8, 1992, D2.

Kemp, Kristen. "Are You Having All the Orgasms You Can?" *Marie Claire,* January 2004, 146–48. http://www.proquest.umi.com (accessed August 5, 2005).

———. "The Six Best Sex Positions." *Cosmopolitan,* April 1, 1999, 208–11.

Kipnis, Laura. *Bound and Gagged: Pornography and the Politics of Fantasy in America.* New York: Grove Press, 1996.

Kleinhans, Chuck. "The Change from Film to Video Pornography: Implications for Analysis." In Lehman, *Pornography.*

Kleinplatz, Peggy J. "'Educational' Sex Videos: What Are They Teaching?" *Canadian Journal of Human Sexuality* 6, no. 1 (Spring 1997): 39.

Krentz, Jayne Ann, ed. *Dangerous Men and Adventurous Women: Romance Writers on the Appeal of the Romance.* Philadelphia: University of Pennsylvania Press, 1992.

Kuipers, Dean. "Sex, Home, and Videotape; Homemade Erotica." *Playboy,* November 1995, 114+.

Kurinasky, Dr. Judy. "Personal File: Sex." *Newsday,* April 18, 1995, B17.

Langton, James. "Nice Girls Undress for Success: Strippers." *Cosmopolitan,* July 1996, 98.

Laplanche, J., and J. B. Pontalis. *The Language of Psychoanalysis.* Translated by Donald Nicholson Smith. New York: Norton, 1973.

Laran, Ellen, et al. "Women's Sexual and Emotional Responses to Male and Female-produced Erotica." *Archives of Sexual Behavior* 23, no. 2 (April 1994): 153–69.

Lederer, Laura, ed. *Take Back the Night: Women on Pornography.* New York: William Morrow, 1980.

Lehman, Peter, ed. *Pornography: Film and Culture.* New Brunswick, N.J.: Rutgers University Press, 2006.

Lehmann-Haupt, Rachel. "How to Talk Dirty and Influence People: The Selling of the Female Orgasm. *Paper Magazine,* January 1999, 61–65.

Leveen, Lois. "Sex and the Scholarly Girl: Plugging the Feminist Gender Gap." *Women's Studies* 25, no. 6 (1996): 619–35.

Liebensen, Donald. "Hot Property: Shannon Tweed Has Become Video's Queen of the Erotic Thriller." *Chicago Tribune,* April 7, 1994, Tempo, 3.

Lord, M. G. "Pornutopia: How Feminist Scholars Learned to Love Dirty Pictures." *Lingua Franca,* April–May 1997, 40–48.

Lupton, Deborah. "Talking about Sex: Sexology, Sexual Difference, and Confessional Talk Shows." *Genders* 20 (Fall 1994): 45–65.

Maglin, Nan Bauer, and Donna Perry, eds. *"Bad Girls" "Good Girls": Women, Sex, and Power in the Nineties.* New Brunswick, N.J.: Rutgers University Press, 1994.

Malek, Doreen Owens. "Mad, Bad, and Dangerous to Know: The Hero as Challenge." In Krentz, *Dangerous Men and Adventurous Women,* 73–80.

Mano, Keith D. "'I'm Ready for My Come Shot Now, Dear': Amateur Porn Puts the Sin Back into Sincere." *Playboy,* August 1996, 80.

Marchetti, Gina. "Ethnicity, the Cinema, and Cultural Studies." In *Unspeakable Images: Ethnicity and the American Cinema,* edited by Lester D. Friedman, 277–307. Urbana: University of Illinois Press, 1991.

Martin, Nina K. "Never Laugh at a Man with His Pants Down: The Affective Dynamics of Comedy and Porn." In Lehman, *Pornography,* 189–205.

Mayne, Judith. *The Woman at the Keyhole: Feminism and Women's Cinema.* Bloomington: Indiana University Press, 1990.

McCafferty, Megan Fitzmorris. "Take Your Climax to the Max." *Cosmopolitan,* February 1, 1999, 154–55.

Miller, Trudy. "Stores Shy Away From Better-sex Vids: Tape Content Limits Retail Exposure." *Billboard,* April 24, 1993, 49–50.

Modleski, Tania. *Loving with a Vengeance: Mass Produced Fantasies for Women.* New York: Methuen, 1984.

Mueller, Mark. "Porn Biz Awash in Amateur Efforts." *Boston Herald,* January 16, 1996, 2nd ed., 6.

Mulvey, Laura. "Visual Pleasure and Narrative Cinema." In *Feminism and Film Theory,* edited by Constance Penley, 57–68. New York: Routledge, 1988.

Nagle, Jill, ed. *Whores and Other Feminists.* New York: Routledge, 1997.

Naremore, James. *More than Night: Film Noir in Its Contexts.* Berkeley: University of California Press, 1998.

Nyongo'o, Tavia. "Queer TV: A Comment." *GLQ: A Journal of Lesbian and Gay Studies* 11, no. 1 (2005): 103–5.

Orr, Catherine M. "Charting the Currents of the Third Wave." *Hypatia—A Journal of Feminist Philosophy* 12, no. 3 (1997): 37–45.

Paglia, Camille. *Sex, Art, and American Culture.* New York: Vintage, 1992.

———. *Vamps and Tramps: New Essays.* New York: Vintage, 1994.

Pollitt, Katha. "Subject to Debate: Dead Again?" *Nation,* July 13, 1998, 10–11.

———. "Subject to Debate: Gender Wars." *Nation,* March 21, 1994, 369.

Rapping, Elayne. *The Movie of the Week: Private Stories, Public Events.* Minneapolis: University of Minnesota Press, 1992.

———. "Women Are from Venus, Men Are from Mars." *Progressive* 58, no. 5 (May 1994): 40.

Rich, Adrienne. "Compulsory Heterosexuality and Lesbian Existence." In Snitow et al., *Powers of Desire,* 177–204.

Rockett, Eve. "Some Like It Hot." *Chatelaine,* May 1996, 75.

Rommelman, Nancy. Interview by author. Tape recording. Chicago, May 5, 1997.

———. Unpublished essay on *Women: Stories of Passion.* May 1996. Author's collection, Chicago.

Rothstein, Elisa. Interview by author. Tape recording. Chicago, May 4, 1997.

Russ, Joanna. "Somebody's Trying to Kill Me and I Think It's My Husband: The Modern Gothic." *Journal of Popular Culture* 6, no. 4 (Spring 1973): 666–91.

Sales, Nancy Jo. "Girls, Uninterrupted." *Vanity Fair,* September 2002, 114–19.

Schor, Naomi. *Reading the Detail: Aesthetics and the Feminine.* New York: Methuen, 1987.

Schultz, Connie. "Great Sexpectations: Contradictions in Glut of Information on Bedroom Behavior Can Cause Couples Stress When Reality Doesn't Match Up." *Cleveland Plain Dealer,* January 25, 1998, Arts and Living, 13.

Sedgwick, Eve Kosofsky. "'The L Word': Novelty in Normalcy." *Chronicle of Higher Education* 50, no. 19 (Janury 16, 2004). http://web25.epnet.com/Delivery (accessed August 18, 2005).

See, Fred G. "Something Reflective: Technology and Visual Pleasure." *Journal of Popular Film and Television* 22, no. 4 (Winter 1995): 162–71.

Seidel, Kathleen Gilles. "Judge Me by the Joy I Bring." In Krentz, *Dangerous Men and Adventurous Women,* 159–79.

"Sex on Film for Girls." http://www.kband.com/bluprnt/000391.html (accessed August 21, 2005).

Shalit, Ruth. "Canny and Lacy." *New Republic,* April 6, 1998, 32.

Shattuc, Jane M. *The Talking Cure: TV Talk Shows and Women.* New York: Routledge, 1997.

"Showtime Networks Teams Up with Cybergrrl and FanciFull in Honor of Its Red Shoe Diaries Interactive Site Launch." *Business Wire,* March 7, 2000. http://web.lexis-nexis.proxy.library.emory.edu/universe (accessed July 24, 2005).

Silverman, Kaja. "*Histoire d'O:* The Construction of a Female Subject." In Snitow et al., *Powers of Desire,* 320–49.

Smith, Murray. "Film Noir, the Female Gothic, and Deception." *Wide Angle* 10, no. 1 (1988): 67.

Snitow, Ann Barr. "Mass Market Romance: Pornography for Women Is Different." In Snitow et al., *Powers of Desire,* 245–63.

Snitow, Ann Barr, et al., eds. *Powers of Desire: The Politics of Sexuality.* New York: Monthly Review Press, 1983.

Sobchack, Vivian. *Carnal Thoughts: Embodiment and Moving Image Culture.* Berkeley: University of California Press, 2004.

Stanley, Alessandra. "TV Weekend: Women Having Sex, Hoping Men Tune In." *New York Times,* January 16, 2004, E1. http://web.lexis-nexis.com.proxy.library.emory .edu/universe (accessed August 5, 2005).

Stengel, Richard. "Sex Busters." *Time,* July 21, 1986, 12–21.

Stern, Leslie. "The Body as Evidence." *Screen* 23, no. 5 (Nov./Dec. 1982): 55.

Stoller, Robert J., and I. S. Levine. *Coming Attractions: The Making of an X-Rated Video.* New Haven: Yale University Press, 1993.

Taylor, Emma, and Lorelei Sharkey. "8 Pleasure Maxing Positions." *Cosmopolitan,* February 2005, 130–33. http://www.proquest.umi.com (accessed August 5, 2005).

Thurston, Carol. *The Romance Revolution: Erotic Novels for Women and the Quest for a New Sexual Identity.* Urbana: University of Illinois Press, 1987.

Tudor, Andrew. "Genre." In Grant, *Film Genre Reader,* 3–10.

Vachon, Anne. "Multiple O's: Why One Orgasm Is Never Enough." *Cosmopolitan,* July 1998, 154–57.

Vance, Carole S., ed. *Pleasure and Danger: Exploring Female Sexuality.* London: Pandora Press, 1992.

Waldman, Diane. "'At Last I Can Tell It to Someone!': Feminine Point of View and Subjectivity in the Gothic Romance Film of the 1940's." *Cinema Journal* 23, no. 2 (Winter 1983): 29–40.

Walker, Janet. *Couching Resistance: Women, Film, and Psychoanalytic Psychiatry.* Minneapolis: University of Minnesota Press, 1993.

"The War against Pornography." *Newsweek,* March 18, 1985, 58–67.

Waugh, Thomas. "Homosociality in the Classic American Stag Film: Off-Screen, On-Screen." In Williams, *Porn Studies,* 127–41.

Webster, Paula. "The Forbidden: Eroticism and Taboo." In Vance, *Pleasure and Danger,* 385–98.

Weistein, Steve. "King Takes Erotic Fare to Showtime." *Los Angeles Times,* June 13, 1992, F14.

Wexman, Virginia Wright. *Creating the Couple: Love, Marriage, and Hollywood Performance.* Princeton: Princeton University Press, 1993.

White, Mimi. *Tele-Advising: Therapeutic Discourse in American Television.* Chapel Hill: University of North Carolina Press, 1992.

Williams, Linda. "Film Bodies: Gender, Genre, Excess." *Film Quarterly* 44, no. 4 (Summer 1991): 2–13.

———. *Hard Core: Power, Pleasure, and the "Frenzy of the Visible."* Berkeley: University of California Press, 1989.

———, ed. *Porn Studies.* Durham: Duke University Press, 2004.

Wing, L. L., and Stefanie Marrone. "Seven Days to Even Better Sex." *Redbook,* January 2002, 68–71. http://proquest.umi.com (accessed August 5, 2005).

Wolf, Naomi. *Fire with Fire: The New Female Power and How to Use It.* New York: Fawcett Columbine, 1994.

———. *Promiscuities: The Secret Struggle for Womanhood.* New York: Fawcett Columbine, 1997.

Wurtzel, Elizabeth. *Bitch: In Praise of Difficult Women.* New York: Doubleday, 1998.

INDEX

Abercrombie, Ian, 50
abuser narrative, 89–90
adultery. *See* infidelity
aesthetics: affected by women, 158, 163–65, 169; eroticized, 67, 81; of erotic thriller, 30–31, 34, 40–41, 55–56; feminist, 158–60, 168–69; gendered, 25, 165, 169; narrative and, 91–92
AIDS, 60
Altice, Summer, 50
Altman, Meryl, 77, 111
Altman, Rick, 17
Angelo, Robert, 31, 36, 71
Animal Instincts, 146–50
Animal Instincts series, 6, 17, 37, 146
antifeminists, 63
Arcangeli, Domi, 50

bad girls, 3–4, 8–9, 68–69, 71–72, 76–77, 108, 119
Baldwin, Daniel, 143
Bare Deception, 130–32
Bare Witness, 143–44
Barrymore, Drew, 70
Basic Instinct, 15, 16, 26, 99, 107
Bauer, Stephen, 41
Baumgardner, Jennifer, 62
Berger, John, 42
Bellafante, Ginia, 61
Bencivengo, Richard, 164
Bentham, Jeremy, 134–35
Berko, Lili, 134–35
Bertei-Checci, Adele, 161, 163
Bigelow, Kathryn, 150
blackmail, 88, 143, 148
Bodily Harm, 94, 96, 99
Body Chemistry, 102–4, 106
Body Chemistry 2, 103, 106
Body Chemistry 3, 103–6

Body Chemistry 4, 103, 106
Body Chemistry series, 6, 17, 33–34, 94, 101, 103, 106–7
Body Heat, 19
Body of Evidence, 16, 68
Body of Influence, 126–27
Bogard, William, 156
bondage, 44, 53, 58, 63, 106, 117
Bonifer, Mike, 141
Bright, Susie, 169
Brolin, James, 121
Brolly, Shane, 50
Bryant, Gay, 64
Burge, Robert, 30, 71, 122, 125
Buscombe, Edward, 16
Business for Pleasure, 38, 52

Califia, Pat, 59
Campion, Jane, 16
Capital Crimes, 71, 83
Cauthen, Kelley, 31, 33, 115, 143
celebrity sex tapes, 135
Chaiken, Ilene, 166–68
Cholodenko, Lisa, 166
Chromiumblue.com, 30, 38–39, 50–55
cinematography, 17–18, 23–25, 28, 31, 33–34, 45, 48, 52, 95, 113–14. *See also* filmic techniques
Clair, Daphne, 32
class, 26, 64, 82–83
Club Cake, 1–2, 168
codependency, 57, 74, 150–53
Cold Sweat, 68
Cole, Kenneth, 30
Color of Night, 15
confession: and discourse, 111–13, 119, 127; sexual, 34, 47, 113–14, 116–17, 144; and surveillance, 143
consumerism: and erotic thriller, 6–7, 16–17,

30–31, 39; sexual, 2, 16–17, 34–35, 68, 77; and surveillance, 134–36; and women, 6, 10–11, 30, 42, 63–64, 68

Cosmopolitan, 3, 42, 77

costuming: in erotic thriller, 17, 25, 27, 30–31, 41; and femininity, 25, 27, 30; and gender identification, 45–46, 53–54; in gothic film, 82; lingerie as, 27, 30, 46, 57–58, 147–48, 150, 162

counter-cinema, 161, 168

countertransference thriller, 9, 110, 122–27, 181n1

Cowie, Elizabeth, 30, 31, 104

Criminal Passion, 94–99

cross-dressing, 46, 53–54

Cukor, George, 27, 85

Culp, Annette, 50

Cyberella, 149

Cyberotica, 149

cybersex, 136, 149

The Dark Dancer, 30–31, 71, 75, 122, 125

date rape, 60

Dead Sexy, 36, 72, 94, 96, 99

Deception, 94

Deck, James, 1, 31, 83, 94

Deitch, Donna, 95

Delfiner, Gary, 57, 58, 154

Delta of Venus, 28, 38, 39

Desire, 94

Dietrich, Marlene, 27

direct-to-video, 14–15

Disclosure, 150

Dixon, Wheeler W., 139

Doane, Mary Ann: on the female spectator, 21, 27, 118; and feminist film criticism, 20, 80, 160; on heroines, 88, 94; on femme fatale, 100

domesticity: dangerous, 82–85; ideology of, 82–83; traditional, 90–92

Dominus, Susan, 164

Double Indemnity, 101

Douglas, Michael, 107

Dragonwyk, 89, 91

dreams, 91–92, 113

drugs, 53, 115, 121, 147–48, 183n16

Duke, Randolph, 30

Dworkin, Andrea, 59

Dworkin, Shari L., 163

Dyer, Richard, 29

Ebert, Roger, 27–28

Eberwein, Robert, 67

Edel, Ulrich, 16, 68

Eisenberg, Hetta, 162

Eisenman, Rafael, 38

Ellis, Kate F., 82–83

Elsaesser, Thomas, 26

Emmanuelle, 22, 26

empowerment: changing, 168; female, 64–65, 68, 74–75; and infidelity, 147–48; to male benefit, 155; sexual, 1–2, 39–40, 56, 64–65, 69–72, 77, 121, 150, 152; and stripping, 1–2, 144, 168

Erotic Confessions, 38

erotic dancing. *See* exotic dancing

erotic thriller: aesthetic qualities of, 30–31, 34, 40–41, 55–56, 81, 91; appeal of, 4, 26–31, 33–35, 56; audience for, 5–8, 10, 14, 16–17, 20–21, 81, 157–58, 169; budgets of, 14–16, 26, 107; and class, 26; compared to female gothic films, 6, 18, 20, 26, 79–80; compared to gaslight films, 83–85; compared to gothic films, 27 81, 83–91, 93–94, 137; compared to hard-core pornography, 5, 8, 14–15, 18, 28–29, 33–36, 38; compared to melodrama, 18, 20–21, 26, 80; compared to musicals, 18, 37; compared to noir, 18, 79–81, 89, 93–94, 99–102, 107, 122–23; compared to romance novels, 5, 18, 20, 27–29, 34–35, 41, 43; compared to sexual instruction videos, 67, 71–73; compared to soap opera, 18, 21; and consumerism, 6–7, 16–17, 30–31, 39; critics of, 27–28, 36; defining of, 2–5, 8, 14–17; development of, 22–23, 38–39, 79–81, 83; and DVDs, 14–15; and erotic taboos, 44–45; erotic tension in, 33–34; escapism of, 29, 31, 49–50; and explicit sex, 15, 23, 34, 54; and feminism, 3–4, 7, 39–40, 100, 168–69, 180n30; and feminist discourse, 7, 58–59, 63, 70, 74, 108; as film genre, 8–10, 13–15, 18–21, 55–56, 156, 160, 182n1; gendered nature of, 6, 8, 13, 20–21, 24, 30–31, 41; genre conventions of, 75, 80–82, 137; and heterosexual representation, 8, 13–14, 17–18, 24; humor

in, 53–55; influence of, 68, 166–69; as
instructional, 1, 9, 57–58, 67–68, 71–76,
146–51, 154–56, 175n87; ironic sensibility
of, 104; marketing of, 14–16, 26, 55, 137,
158, 162–63, 169; moralistic judgments
in, 35–36, 48–49, 120–21; narrative tropes
of, 67, 79, 91–92, 94, 124; and nudity, 14,
23, 42, 97, 163–64; performers in, 14–15
(*see also individual actors*); and popular
culture, 6–8, 10–11, 59, 63, 67–68; and
pornography, 8, 161–62; and problem
of love, 6, 35–36, 40–41, 48–49, 54–55;
production values of, 25–26, 55–56, 67;
and race, 49–50; reality testing of, 139–40,
146; romance in, 17–18, 28–30, 50–52, 54,
169; sequels to, 17, 33–34, 71, 102, 121, 137,
183n18; and social tensions, 101–6, 111–16;
suspense in, 14, 18–19, 27, 29–30, 33, 79,
81–82, 87–88; technology in, 134–37,
140–46, 149–50, 153; types of, 9–10, 110;
use of fantasy in, 91, 93; use of fear and
anxiety in, 91–93; and women directors,
157–65. *See also* countertransference
thriller; fantasy; female detective thriller;
filmic techniques; mise-en-scène; narrative structure; pornography; sex scenes;
sex therapist thriller; surveillance thriller;
talk show thriller; therapeutic thriller;
virtual reality thriller
erotica for women, 165–69
eroticism, 23–24, 26–28, 33–34, 37, 39
Esquire, 59, 77
Everhart, Angie, 14, 31, 143
exhibitionism: in modern media, 127, 132,
136–37, 148; narrative uses of, 43, 71, 74,
98, 110; as women's power, 70
exotic dancing: and empowerment, 1–2,
75–76, 144, 168; as instructional, 155; male,
87; as masquerade, 31, 44; and women's
sexuality 1–3, 44–45, 71–74, 125, 157, 178n53

Fairchild, Morgan, 104–5
Faludi, Susan, 3, 162–63
fantasy: and danger, 93; gendered, 157–58;
men's efforts to control, 49, 50–51, 66, 132;
romantic, 32–33, 52, 66–67; sexual, 27–35,
39–40, 43–47, 53–54, 70–71, 131; taboo, 144;
and technology, 136, 144, 149–52, 154–55;

and therapy, 113, 122 24, 126; uses of,
31–33, 75–77; voyeuristic, 73–74
Fatal Attraction, 16
female authorship, 10, 157–59, 161–62
female detective thriller, 94–99, 101
female identity, constructed, 64–65, 67
female-in-jeopardy film (fem-jep), 89, 103
female sexual desire: and autonomy, 48–49;
changes in, 168–69; constructed, 10–11,
68; dangerous, 94, 97, 100; as hindrance,
94–96; and male nudity, 163–65; as motivation, 57–58, 88, 90; repressed, 91; in
women's films, 160, 162
female sexuality: active, 69–70; awakening,
55–56, 81; dangerous, 18; in films, 23–25,
79–82; frustrated, 84–85; and identity,
13–14, 41–42, 70; learned, 57–58, 64–66,
71–73; as limitation, 38; malleable, 69–70;
and the market, 10–11; in noir, 101–2;
normative, 8–9, 62; regulated, 67–68; tension within, 6–8; undermining authority,
95–96, 125
femininity: attitudes toward, 2–3; contemporary, 6, 11, 165; contradictory nature of,
17; normative, 61–63, 70; and ornamentation, 26; standards of, 4, 7–8; unstable, 80
feminism: academic, 63; and aesthetics, 160–
61; and class, 64; contested, 59–63, 68–69;
"do-me," 59–63, 65, 69, 74, 76, 77, 111, 152,
168; and eroticism, 10, 39–40, 160–61,
163, 166–69; and female power, 100, 107;
pop, 3–4, 9, 17, 58, 63, 68–70, 77, 108, 159;
and popular culture, 3–4, 8, 13–14, 61–64,
69, 107–8; and pornography, 158–65; and
race, 62; rhetoric of, 63–64, 69, 129; and
romantic novels, 32; and sexuality, 58–60,
157, 168–69; theoretical, 7, 22; third-wave,
7, 58, 60–63, 69, 163; and understanding
the erotic thriller, 3–5
feminist film criticism, 4, 10, 20–21, 28, 100,
158–61, 166, 171n11
femme fatale: in film noir, 80, 93–94; narrative role of, 79–81, 106–8; new, 89, 99–107
Field, Genevieve, 2
filmic techniques: camera work, 23–24, 28,
33, 45, 48–49, 95, 113–14, 161, 165; film
within film, 106, 126, 141, 182n22; focus
of, 23–25, 31, 106, 109, 116; lighting, 23–24,

28, 33, 52, 131; music, 24, 40, 52, 87; in sex
scenes, 23, 26, 28; sound and image, 34,
40, 91–92, 109, 129–30, 132, 141; visual
counterpoint, 127. *See also* mise-en-scène
film noir: as genre, 9, 18, 19, 79–81, 93–94,
122–23, 126; new, neo-, or erotic, 89,
99–104, 107–8
film theory: feminist, 20–21, 28; psychoana-
lytic, 37, 42, 116
Fiorentino, Linda, 96
Flashdance, 68
Forbidden Passions, 58, 74, 149–53
Forbidden Sins, 71, 94, 138
Forty Deuce, 39
Foucauldian analysis, 10, 22
Foucault, Michel, 47, 111, 127, 135. *See also*
Foucauldian analysis
fourth wall, 73, 118
Freud, Sigmund, 32
Freudian analysis, 10, 21, 43, 111–12, 120, 160
Friday, Nancy, 70
Friend, Tad, 59–60, 62, 77

Gaines, Jane, 161, 166
Gallafent, Ed, 84–85
Gallagher, Melinda, 2, 168
Garrett, Tay, 48
Garth, Jackie, 58, 149, 150
Gaslight, 27, 84–85, 89, 91
gaslighting, 82–85, 89
gaze: active, 139; clinical, 113, 118–19, 122;
constrained, 38, 49–50, 73; desiring, 167;
female, 44, 85, 116–17, 180n34; fluctuating,
42, 98; gendered, 132, 138, 140, 160–62;
male, 116, 174n70; malicious, 137, 140, 143;
and sexual desire, 47–48, 55, 86, 88; and
surveillance, 134–35, 140; unstable, 140;
voyeuristic, 4, 10, 43–45, 97–98, 141–43,
160
gender: distinctions of, 14, 34–35, 158–59,
164–66, 169; and power relations, 135–36;
representations of, 156, 159–61, 169,
174n69; social construction of, 2–3, 18, 20,
154–55, 168–69. *See also* gender identity;
gender roles
gender identity: conflicting, 114; and feminism, 60–61; normative, 10–11; and sexuality, 13–14, 111

gender roles: adversarial, 122; conflicting,
110, 114, 121; constructed, 11, 54, 61–62, 112;
dangerous, 90–91; dissolution of, 154–55;
persistence of, 79–80, 127; and sexuality,
10, 22, 69–70; shifting of, 91, 95–97, 101–4,
147–48; and technology, 135–36, 141–42;
and therapy, 133; traditional, 90–92;
unclear, 94; unstable, 80, 82–86, 92–93,
99–100
genres: body, 150; comparative, 9, 15–18, 20–
21, 26–28, 79–80, 83–85; conventions, 55;
and gender, 8, 20–21, 26–28, 35, 56, 80–81;
methodologies, 16–21; new, 18–20, 134–36,
149–50; reusable, 79–81
Gibson, Eric, 130
Girard, Michael Paul, 1
Glamour, 3, 64
gothic film: female, 9, 18, 20, 26, 79–80, 83,
101; as genre, 27, 82–85, 89, 93–95, 137. *See
also* neo-gothic film
Goursand, Anne, 33
Graff, Mark, 162
Greico, Richard, 15, 31
Grosz, Elizabeth, 24
Gustaff, Carlo, 109
Guthmann, Edward, 28

Harvey, Gail, 68
Haskell, Molly, 35, 47–48
Hefner, Christie, 77, 160
heterosexuality: constructed, 62, 64, 67,
70–71, 76–77, 111, 168; and female identity, 2–4, 7–8, 11, 30, 44, 56, 65, 107–8; and
male identity, 22, 71; normative, 13–14,
38, 40–41, 44, 46–47, 50, 58, 67; problems
of, 113; regulated, 133, 154, 158, 166; undermined, 107; unstable, 14, 17–18, 24, 45–46,
49, 59, 76
Heywood, Leslie, 163
Hilton, Paris, 135
Henriksen, Lance, 123
Hewitt, Martin, 132
Heywood, Leslie, 163
Hippolyte, A. Gregory, 71, 126, 132, 146
Hitchcock, Alfred, 27, 83, 86, 95, 120, 122
Holland, Kelly, 162, 164
home: as dangerous, 82–85, 88–89, 93, 106;
invasion of, by woman, 106; as symbol of

domesticity, 92, 106; woman as protector
of, 83, 90
homme fatale, 94, 122
homosexuality, 60–61, 148. *See also* lesbianism
hooks, bell, 59–60
How to Make Love to the Same Person Forever, 66
Hudson, Gary, 113
Hunter, Rachel, 14, 31
husbands: abusive, 90–91, 128; distant, 146;
homicidal, 18, 79–80, 82, 85, 87, 89, 93, 129;
paternalistic, 83–84
Hutcheon, Linda, 19–20

ideology: and feminism, 61–62, 69–70; and
film, 16, 19–20, 79–80, 120, 156; and gender, 11, 84, 168–69; and sexuality, 64–65,
71, 111, 133, 152
Illicit Confessions, 1
Illicit Dreams, 20, 27, 83, 89–93
Indecent Behavior 1, 36, 113–17, 119–21
Indecent Behavior 2, 109–110, 112, 118, 121
Indecent Behavior 3, 115, 117–20, 122
Indecent Behavior series, 6, 17, 116–17, 122, 126
infidelity: contradictory nature of, 121;
and murder, 89, 94, 102, 106–7, 129, 137;
as path to sexual fulfillment, 13, 44–46,
84, 86, 90–94, 147–48; punishment for,
100–104; and suicide, 96; on tape, 140–41,
143–44; as theme of erotic thriller, 35, 117,
120, 130; as therapeutic, 147–48
In the Cut, 16
Intimate Obsession, 83

Jackson, Janet, 15, 61
Jaeckin, Just, 22
Jameson, Fredric, 19, 80–81
Jameson, Jenna, 61
Jeffery, Doug, 14–15, 118
Johnson, Merri Lisa, 69
Johnston, Claire, 160

Kaige, Chen, 16
Kain, John, 149
Kaminer, Wendy, 61, 168
Kane, Ivan, 39
Kaplan, E. Ann, 20, 64
Kasdan, Lawrence, 19

Keating, Dominic, 50
Keene, Karlyn, 61
Kehr, David, 27–28
Killing Me Softly, 16
King, Zalman: aesthetics of, 52–54; cinematic style of, 24, 30, 39–40, 42, 50, 55,
160; critics on, 27–28; influence of, 8, 23,
38–39, 50, 158; films directed by, 23, 27, 28,
58, 124, 129, 144
Kirshner, Mia, 167
Kiss of Fire, 1, 76
Kleinhans, Chuck, 6
Kleinplatz, Peggy, 66
Knop, Patricia Louisianna, 38
Krabbé, Jeroen, 52
Krentz, Jayne Ann, 33

Lady in Blue, 1
Lake Consequence, 38, 50
Lang, Fritz, 27, 83
Langton, James, 75
Lanoff, Lawrence, 36, 113
Lap Dancing, 1, 2, 71–76
The Last Seduction, 14
The Lawnmower Man, 150
Lazarus, Tom, 58, 144
Lemmo, James, 96
Leonard, Brett, 150
lesbianism, 44–47, 53, 58, 59, 61, 166–68
Leveen, Lois, 60
Levinson, Barry, 150
Liebensen, Donald, 68
The Lipstick Camera, 141–43
Lombard, Karina, 167
love and sex: incompatiblity of, 85–87,
89–90, 93, 120–21; not confused with one
another, 97, 113, 130; tension between, 6,
55, 101
Love Street, 38
Lupton, Deborah, 127
The L Word, 166–67
Lyne, Adrian, 16, 38, 68

MacKinnon, Catharine, 59
Madonna, 70
Maher, Bill, 63
male: abusive, 74, 90–91; domineering,
85; emasculated, 85–86, 102–3, 140; hu-

miliated, 100, 102–8, 126–27, 131; negative views of, 102–3, 151; nudity, problem of, 163–65; as pawn, 81, 102–3; as rescuer, 88–89, 98; sensitive, 92, 139; sexuality, 83–84, 102; as talk show host, 132–33
Mandylor, Costas, 42, 144
Mankiewicz, Frank, 89
Marchetti, Gina, 37
marriage: boredom of, 29, 44; as confining, 90–92; contradictory nature of, 121; as dangerous, 6, 13, 86, 88–89, 94; dismantling of, 102–3, 106–8; as dysfunctional, 85–87, 93, 96, 120, 132, 146–48; and murder, 9, 18, 79–80, 82, 85, 101; negative images of, 13, 120–21, 128–29; saved by porn, 148–49; and sex, 3–4, 84, 90, 104, 137; and sexual fantasies, 41, 43–47; as unhappy, 18, 35, 83–84, 113. *See also* adultery
masculinity: aesthetics of, 165, 169; contemporary, 165; and identity, 90–91; and porn, 21–22; undermining of, 95–97, 100–101, 139
masochism, 89, 93
McCarley, Kurt, 122, 124
McClure, Tane', 72, 130
McComass, Lorissa, 72
McDonald, Rodney, 137
melodrama, 18, 20, 21, 26, 80, 107
Meyer, Russ, 26
mise-en-scène: of desire, 6, 25–27, 29–31, 66, 118; importance of, 8, 30, 166–67; romantic, 130, 140, 150, 154, 162
Modleski, Tania, 20, 28
Moore, Demi, 75
motherhood, 86
Mundhra, Jag, 27, 85
Mulvey, Laura, 25, 37, 160
murder: framed for, 87–89, 99, 121, 131–132; getting away with, 103–4, 106, 107; within marriage, 9, 18, 79–80, 82, 94, 101, 129; narrative use of, 36, 96–99, 113, 123, 130; as punishment of female authority, 115–17, 120, 142; as resolution, 85, 90, 93; and voyeurism, 143; by women, 101–4, 107
musicals, 18, 37

Nagel, Jens, 50
Nagle, Jim, 66

Naremore, James, 15
narrative power, shifting of, 100–102
narrative structure: ambiguity and conflict within, 13–14, 18, 46–47, 89; art direction in, 162, 167–68; as convoluted, 148; as discourse, 13, 38, 47–49, 58; as gendered, 24, 30, 34–35, 50, 80–81, 136; genre conventions of, 6, 9–10, 30, 52, 56, 71–72, 81, 83–86; ideology of, 79–80, 120, 152, 156; and narrative tension, 33–35, 40, 168; and omniscient narration, 49, 89, 93, 95, 99; and portrayal of sex, 23–25, 28, 33, 136, 165–66; as restricted, 98, 100–101; semantic elements of, 17–18, 20, 25–26, 29–30, 34–36, 40; and spectacle, 24–25, 36–37, 50, 139; unreal, 29, 139–40, 146; unresolved, 133; use of realism in, 161–62; and use of voice-over, 35, 40, 43, 47–49, 51, 53, 95, 109, 126; visual strategies of, 42–43, 5–46, 48, 52, 97–98; voyeurism of, 134, 149. *See also* filmic techniques
neo-gothic film, 80, 82–85, 90
Night Eyes series, 6, 17, 27, 31, 137
Night Eyes 2, 83, 137–41, 140
Night Eyes 3, 25, 36
Nightfire, 83
Night Rhythms, 132–33
Nin, Anaïs, 28
Nine ½ Weeks, 38, 67
nymphomania, 26, 87, 148, 155
Nyong'o, Tavia, 167

objectification: in erotic thriller, 24–25, 37–38, 42, 94, 132, 162–63; of female bodies, 5, 34, 98, 159–60; of male bodies, 6, 48–49, 87, 97, 102, 139, 148, 161–63; traditional, 10, 22
101 Ways to Excite Your Lover, 66–67
orgasms: better, 58, 64–65; on-air, 132; as women's responsibility, 70
Orr, Catherine, 63
Out of the Past, 101
Oxenberg, Catherine, 128

Pacula, Joanna, 52
Paglia, Camille, 62, 63, 68–70, 108
panopticon, 134–35, 140
Pendulum, 31, 94

Personals 2, 33, 58
Pescia, Lisa, 102
Peterson, Kristine, 102
Playboy, 22, 71, 77, 159, 164
Playboy channel, 22, 66–67
Playgirl, 162, 164
pleasure/danger principle: as genre conven-
    tion, 4, 8, 18, 36, 40, 81, 95, 136–37; and
    technology, 141–44, 156; in therapeutic
    thriller, 10, 110; and troubled subjectivity,
    10, 88, 91
Poison Ivy 2, 33
Pollitt, Katha, 60, 63
popular culture: and female identity, 64–65,
    168; and feminism, 62–63, 69–70; and
    images of women, 8–9, 107; and self-help,
    112; and sexuality, 6–8, 11, 42, 59, 61–62,
    64–65, 68, 77–78; and therapy, 122
pornography: amateur, 135–36, 146–49;
    changing, 162–63; characteristics of, 23,
    128, 165, 167, 165; couples market for, 5,
    162–63, 169; and feminism, 7, 59–60, 70,
    163, 165; feminization of, 163; and gender,
    5, 157–58, 162; hard-core compared to
    soft-core, 8, 13–16, 21–26, 28–29, 33–36, 38,
    50, 71; lesbian, 166; male reaction to, 102;
    scholarship regarding, 5, 21–22, 165; soft-
    core, defined, 2, 8, 17, 175n71; types of, 71,
    163–66. *See also* erotic thriller
postfeminism, 2, 14, 60–62
The Postman Always Rings Twice, 48
postmodernism, 18–19, 81, 134–35
Prior, Erica, 50
Profile for Murder, 122–25
promiscuous friends, 87, 89, 92–93, 120–21
prostitution, 44, 70, 71, 74–75, 113, 119, 143,
    148, 157
Psycho, 95, 120
psychoanalysis: conflicted view of, 126–27,
    132; and detachment, 117–18, 128; influ-
    ence of, on film, 32, 122, 160; lack of de-
    tachment within, 115–16, 118–21, 124–26,
    132–33; and power relations, 110–13; ses-
    sions of, in films, 109–110, 116–19, 123–24,
    144; and technology, 144, 146; tensions of,
    113–18, 121–22, 133

Queer as Folk, 167

rape, 32, 44, 120
Rapper, Irving, 94
Rapping, Elayne, 59–60
Rebecca, 27, 83, 85, 86, 94
Red Rock West, 14
Red Shoe Diaries (cable series): as escap-
    ism, 49–50; narrative structure of, 38,
    40–41, 44–47; popularity of, 38–39, 158;
    as romantic fantasy, 43–47, 52, 54; style
    of, 41–45, 124; and women's sexuality, 23,
    41–49
Red Shoe Diaries (film), 30, 38, 40
Richards, Amy, 62
Richards, Cybil, 58, 149, 154
Robbins, Lance, 15
Rogers, Rosemary, 32
Roiphe, Katie, 59, 62, 63
role-playing, 53–54, 71–73, 75, 134, 147–48
romance: awkwardness of, 54–55; as con-
    structed, 65–67; as dangerous, 13, 36, 50;
    elusiveness of, 121; in erotic thriller, 21,
    50–52, 169; and fantasy, 66–67; of first
    time, 114; as genre, 5, 17, 29; lack of, 99,
    101–3, 120, 150–51; outside marriage, 113
    (*see also* infidelity); and sex, 17–18, 28. *See
    also* gothic film
romance novels: and erotic thriller, 5, 20,
    27–29, 39, 41, 43, 68, 81; and romantic
    sexuality, 18, 32–35; and women's culture,
    4, 30
Rommelman, Nancy, 159, 162, 165–66, 168
Rosetti, Dick, 164
Rothstein, Elisa, 159–60, 163, 165–66
Royalle, Candida, 165, 168

sadomasochism, 53, 59
Schor, Naomi, 26
Schultz, Connie, 64
Scorned, 94
The Secret beyond the Door, 27, 83
Secret Games series, 37, 71
Sedan, Mike, 1, 2, 27, 71
Seidel, Kathleen Gilles, 30
separate spheres: blurring of, 38, 86, 103, 106,
    110; definition of, 79–80, 82–85; mainte-
    nance of, 127; male control of, 90–91; ten-
    sions of, 94, 96, 100, 114–16
Severance, Joan, 14, 41, 95, 123

sex: casual, 41, 55, 130; clinical, 118–19;
   dangerous, 4, 30, 35–36, 40; as power,
   62, 70; permissible, 15; surrogate, 110–11,
   114, 117–21, 134; and technology, 137–39,
   142, 146–48; uses of, 69–70, 79, 81, 101; as
   weapon, 48. *See also* sex scenes; sex wars
Sex and the City, 108, 163
sex scenes: as choreographed, 14–15, 52–53;
   compared to hard core, 23–24; features
   of, 23–25, 131; lesbian, 46, 53–54; and narrative, 34–37, 80, 104; and oral foreplay,
   34, 97; and problem of male nudity, 163–
   65; role of, in films, 85, 130, 148; romantic,
   17–18, 140; and sex acts as performance,
   73–74, 76, 117–19, 138–39; as supportive of
   traditional marriage, 41; in virtual reality,
   151, 155; voyeuristic, 86, 109, 117–18, 123–
   24, 138–39, 144–45; with woman aggressor, 97–98, 104–7; in women's films, 162
sex therapist thriller, 90, 110, 112–21
sexual agency, 77, 144
sexual competition, 35
sexual discourses, 111–12
sexual dissatisfaction, 35
sexual double standard, 49, 163–64
sexual dysfunctions, 35, 113, 117–18
sexual exploration, 64–66, 96
sexual frustration, 124–25. *See also* wives
sexual fulfillment: as dangerous, 81–82, 120,
   130–31, 144; elusiveness of, 121, 146–47;
   and love, 33; and men, 132; and self-de-
   struction, 125–26; through technology,
   74–76, 147, 153–55; through infidelity, 13,
   45–46, 84, 86, 90, 90–93, 129; and undermining of women's authority, 94, 128;
   without guilt, 57–58, 71; without love,
   87, 89
sexual harassment, 60, 95–96
sexual identity, 77
sexual instruction, 64–67, 77–78, 86–87, 90;
   via videos, 66–67, 71–73
Sexual Intent, 122, 124–25
sexuality, representations of: ambiguity of,
   14, 24, 49; changes of, 77, 134, 136, 161–65,
   168–69; in erotic thriller, 10–11, 17, 22–24,
   32, 85, 130, 148
sexual liberation, 39, 59
Sexual Malice, 27, 83, 85–89

sexual performance, 73–74, 76, 77
sexual politics, 39–40, 61–62, 77. *See also*
   feminism
Sexual Predator, 19, 31, 94
Sexual Response, 18, 83, 89–90, 128–29
sexual transgression, 44, 157
sexual virtue, 85
sex wars, 59, 107
Shalit, Ruth, 60
Shame, Shame, Shame, 38, 58, 124, 144
Shattuc, Jane, 65, 111–12
Showgirls, 15
Showtime, 39, 50, 157, 164, 168
Simon, Adam, 106
Singer, Mark, 102
slasher films, 89, 93
Sliver, 15
Smith, Murray, 94
Smooth Operator, 31
Snitow, Ann Barr, 29
soap operas, 18, 21
Sommers, Christina Hoff, 59
spectacle, sexual, 25, 36–37, 139
spectator: active, 68, 89; critique of, 139;
   expectations of, 137; female, 20–21, 25, 27,
   30, 35, 42–43, 49, 67, 102, 107; gendered,
   37–38, 45, 85, 98, 160–61, 179n21; and
   identification, 25, 31–33, 80, 87, 93, 98, 106,
   110, 161; in-the-know, 104–5; male, 22, 43;
   objective, 117–18; restricted, 95, 100–101,
   132, 166; self-reflective, 137–38; and vicarious pleasure, 27, 34, 86, 102, 108. *See also*
   voyeurism
Spellbound, 122
stalking, 125
Stern, Leslie, 32
Stevens, Andrew, 14, 25, 36, 90, 103, 137
St. George, Randall, 71, 143
Stone, Sharon, 70, 107
Story of O, 22, 26
Strange Days, 150
Stretch, Gary, 42, 52
stripping. *See also* exotic dancing
Striptease, 15, 75
subjectivity: faltering of, 88, 91, 152; female,
   80, 82, 85, 87, 93–94, 100, 106, 113; gendered, 151–52, 158–59; male, 126; sexual,
   139; and surveillance, 134–35, 144–45

subject/object: and conflict, 38, 41, 95, 97, 114; flexibility of, 136; gendered, 116–17; instability of, 101, 118–19, 123–24, 140; merger of, 134–35; and objectification, 132, 147–48; shifting of, 135, 162; subversion of, 160

surveillance: dangers of, 141–43; and gender relations, 141–42; as marital aid, 146–49; pleasures of, 139, 142, 144–45; technology of, 134–36, 140, 143–44; uses and abuses, 137–40, 156. *See also* surveillance thriller

surveillance thriller: defined, 136–37; female sexuality in, 143–46; internal tension of, 141–43, 156; voyeuristic nature of, 137–41

talk show thriller, 9, 110, 127–33

Teach Me, 57, 58, 67, 74, 154–55

technology: abuse of, 140–43, 156; gendered uses of, 154–56; limitations of, 149, 151, 153; and sex, 134–36, 142, 146–52, 155, 183n20; as therapeutic tool, 144–47

terrorism, domestic, 91

therapeutic thriller, 9–10, 34, 73, 109–113, 122. *See also* countertransference thriller; sex therapist thriller

Thurston, Carol, 33, 34

Tibaldi, Antonio, 1

Tourneur, Jacques, 101

Troche, Rose, 166

Tudor, Andrew, 16

Turner, Guinivere, 166

Tweed, Shannon: and costumes, 25; as erotic-thriller star, 14, 68, 137; photo of, 138; in role of endangered woman, 36, 96; in role of professor/stripper, 30–31; in role of therapist, 109, 113, 115, 125, 128; in role of unhappily married woman, 18, 90–91

twice-told tale, 34, 35, 97, 123

Two Moon Junction, 28, 38

Two Shades of Blue, 1, 83

Tyson, Richard, 42

uncanny, the, 91–92, 179n22

utopian eroticism: and end of family, 13, 108; in erotic thriller 29, 13, 44, 50, 53; and technology, 146, 153–55

Victoria's Secret, 42, 162

Vincent, Jan-Michael, 113, 148

Virtual Encounters, 58, 149, 154–55

Virtual Encounters 2, 149

virtual reality, 10, 74, 136, 149–55

virtual reality thriller, 149–56

Visions of Passion, 71, 143–44

Vixen! 26

Voerhoven, Paul, 16, 99

Voyeur Confessions, 58, 144–46

voyeurism: dangers of, 143–46; educational, 57–58, 73–74, 86–87; and gender relations, 10, 37, 42–43, 97–98; gendered, 5, 142–46, 148, 160, 162, 167; interactive, 137–39; legitimated, 149; pathological, 143, 145, 154; pleasures of, 27, 45–46, 67, 109, 116–18; and sex talk, 128; as therapeutic, 147–48; and video, 136–37, 140–46; and viewer, 123

Waldman, Diane, 84

Walker, Janet, 116, 122

Walker, Rebecca, 59, 62

Webster, Paula, 44

Westheimer, Ruth, 21, 119

White, Mimi, 119

Whitney, Ruth, 64

Whirry, Shannon, 14, 126, 146

Wild Orchid, 28, 38, 50

Wild Orchid 2, 23, 27–28, 38

Wilder, Billy, 101

Williams, Linda: on nature of pornography, 21–22, 23, 28; on porn and gender, 165; on porn as escapism, 13–14; on spectacle, 36

Winning, David, 122

wives: as sexually frustrated, 84–86, 92–93, 120, 128, 132, 137; traditional role of, 90–91, 107; as victims, 105

Wolf, Naomi, 62, 63, 64, 69, 70, 108, 159

women, as film audience, 80–81, 83–85, 157–58

women, professional: as authority figures, 109, 113, 117; authority of, undermined, 112–16, 122, 125–26, 129; conflicted nature of, 9, 84–87, 118–25, 128–29; as dull, 71; as endangered, 36, 85, 87–89; as erotic, 25, 30–31; as murderous, 105

women filmmakers of erotic thrillers: adherence to genre conventions, 157–58, 162–64, 168; and feminist aesthetic, 158–60, 168–69; and a feminist erotica, 165–68; problems of, 160–62, 164–65

Women of the Night, 38, 129–30
Women: Stories of Passion, 38, 124, 157–65, 168–69
women's autonomy: dangerous, 81–82, 89, 141; and the femme fatale, 94, 101; and sex, 49, 107–8; as sexually limited, 38, 41–42
women's magazines, 4, 58, 63–65, 70

Woodiwiss, Kathleen, 32
Wurtzel, Elizabeth, 63, 68–70
Wynorski, Jim, 103

Yosha, Yaki, 18

Zane, Billy, 42

NINA K. MARTIN teaches in the Department of Film Studies at Emory University. Her essays have appeared in the *Journal of Film and Video, Jump Cut,* and the edited collections *Pornography: Film and Culture* and *Virgin Territory: Sexual Innocence in Film.*

The University of Illinois Press
is a founding member of the
Association of American University Presses.

Composed in 10.5/13.5 Minion
with Meta display
by Type One, LLC
for the University of Illinois Press
Designed by Dennis Roberts
Manufactured by Sheridan Books, Inc.

University of Illinois Press
1325 South Oak Street
Champaign, IL 61820-6903
www.press.uillinois.edu